THE GLOBAL RISE
OF CHINA

China Today series

THE GLOBAL RISE
OF CHINA ———————————

Alvin Y. So and Yin-wah Chu

polity

First published in 2016 by Polity Press

Polity Press
65 Bridge Street
Cambridge CB2 1UR, UK

Polity Press
350 Main Street
Malden, MA 02148, USA

ISBN-13: 978-0-7456-6473-6
ISBN-13: 978-0-7456-6474-3 (pb)

A catalogue record for this book is available from the British Library.

Library of Congress Cataloging-in-Publication Data

So, Alvin Y., 1953-
    The global rise of China / Alvin Y. So, Yin-wah Chu.
        pages   cm
    Includes bibliographical references and index.
    ISBN 978-0-7456-6473-6 (hardback : alk. paper) – ISBN 978-0-7456-6474-3 (pbk. : alk. paper)   1. China–Economic policy–2000-   2. China–Foreign economic relations.   3. China–Foreign relations–1976-   I. Chu, Yin-wah.   II. Title.
    HC435.3.S587 2015
    337.51–dc23
                                                                                    2015011705

Typeset in 11.5 on 15 pt Adobe Jenson Pro
by Toppan Best-set Premedia Limited
Printed and bound in the UK by Clays Ltd, St Ives PLC

For further information on Polity, visit our website:
politybooks.com

This book is dedicated to our teachers, colleagues, friends, and students in Hong Kong

Contents

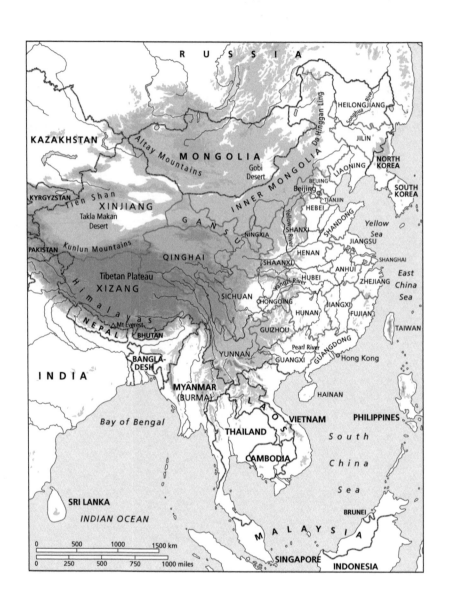

Chronology

1894–95	First Sino-Japanese War
1911	Fall of the Qing dynasty
1912	Republic of China established under Sun Yat-sen
1927	Split between Nationalists (KMT) and Communists (CCP); civil war begins
1934–5	CCP under Mao Zedong evades KMT in Long March
December 1937	Nanjing Massacre
1937–45	Second Sino-Japanese War
1945–9	Civil war between KMT and CCP resumes
October 1949	KMT retreats to Taiwan; Mao founds People's Republic of China (PRC)
1950–3	Korean War
1953–7	First Five-Year Plan; PRC adopts Soviet-style economic planning
1954	First constitution of the PRC and first meeting of the National People's Congress
1956–7	Hundred Flowers Movement, a brief period of open political debate
1957	Anti-Rightist Movement
1958–60	Great Leap Forward, an effort to transform China through rapid industrialization and collectivization

March 1959	Tibetan Uprising in Lhasa; Dalai Lama flees to India
1959–61	Three Hard Years, widespread famine with tens of millions of deaths
1960	Sino-Soviet split
1962	Sino-Indian War
October 1964	First PRC atomic bomb detonation
1966–76	Great Proletarian Cultural Revolution; Mao reasserts power
February 1972	President Richard Nixon visits China; "Shanghai Communiqué" pledges to normalize US–China relations
September 1976	Death of Mao Zedong
October 1976	Ultra-Leftist Gang of Four arrested and sentenced
December 1978	Deng Xiaoping assumes power; launches Four Modernizations and economic reforms
1978	One-child family planning policy introduced
1979	US and China establish formal diplomatic ties; Deng Xiaoping visits Washington Sino-Vietnamese War
1982	Census reports PRC population at more than one billion
December 1984	Margaret Thatcher co-signs Sino-British Joint Declaration agreeing to return Hong Kong to China in 1997
1989	Tiananmen Square protests culminate in June 4 military crackdown
1992	Deng Xiaoping's Southern Inspection Tour reenergizes economic reforms

1993–2002	Jiang Zemin, President of PRC, continues economic growth agenda
November 2001	World Trade Organization accepts China as member
2001–2	Hu Jintao, General-Secretary of CCP (and President of PRC from 2003)
2002–3	SARS outbreak concentrated in PRC and Hong Kong
2006	PRC supplants US as largest CO_2 emitter
August 2008	Summer Olympic Games in Beijing
2010	Shanghai World Exposition
2012	Xi Jinping appointed General-Secretary of the CCP (and President of PRC from 2013)

Preface

We still remember vividly our first trips to China. Alvin visited in the early 1970s when the country first opened its door to foreign visitors at the tail end of the Cultural Revolution. China was at that time a typical poor third world nation: the border city of Shenzhen had no building taller than four floors; restaurants closed at 8 p.m. The street light in the city was very dim and the stores closed very early, so there was not much city life after dark. Even when the stores were open, however, there was nothing for customers to buy except for some very simple necessities. A black-and-white TV, a refrigerator, or an electric fan was considered to be a luxury that few Chinese citizens could afford. No one owned a car, and everyone rode a bicycle or walked to work. Yin-wah's first visit was to her parents' remote native village situated at the northern part of Guangdong province in the early 1980s. Everywhere there were lush paddy fields and, blessed with a hydropower dam located at the upper reach of the village's river, villagers got a free electricity supply, allowing them to turn on their lights after dark, which was a rare sight in the region. People were optimistic; an entrepreneurial teenage boy took the initiative to contract out pieces of grassland to herd geese.

When Alvin visited China again a few years ago, he never stopped being impressed by the drastic transformations over the last thirty years. High-rise buildings are everywhere, as are modern facilities like high-speed railways, modern airports, four-lane freeways, five-star hotels, fancy shopping malls, and office complexes. The cities have suddenly come alive: restaurants and shopping malls are packed with people in the evening, new buildings are everywhere, and bicycles have almost disappeared. The village visited by Yin-wah some thirty years ago has changed drastically, too. Newly constructed three- or four-story houses are everywhere, replacing the rundown huts built over the generations. Motorbikes and occasionally cars are used in the place of bicycles. Almost all the paddy fields are deserted, as the young men and women have gone to nearby towns or remote cities to take up jobs as factory workers, cooks, waiters and waitresses, cleaners, hairdressers, peddlers, tradesmen, among others.

It is amazing how fast the old China has disappeared and how quickly the new China is emerging. The change intrigues us. We have always been interested in studying the historical processes, policies, and institutions that have transformed China from a poor third world country to a modern nation and allowed it to rise as a global power.

We would therefore like to thank Jonathan Skerrett, our editor at Polity, who encouraged us to write a book telling the story of the rise of global China. This is meant to be a textbook for students and it seeks to provide a comprehensive introduction to China's remarkable economic development over the past forty years. We consider the complicated rise of China historically, the understanding of which traverses narrow disciplinary boundaries. Hence, differing from most prevailing texts, we examine the topic not only from a social, economic, and political angle, but also from a historical and global perspective.

In striving for an inter-disciplinary perspective on the rise of global China, we are deeply indebted to many outstanding researchers who have laid the groundwork, provided the crucial materials, and developed numerous insightful analyses on this topic. In particular, we want to acknowledge the contributions of Giovanni Arrighi, Berch Berberoglu, Martin Hart-Landsberg, Huang Yashing, Hung Ho-fung, Victor Lippit, Christopher McNally, Barry Naughton, Victor Nee, Jean Oi, Jamie Peck, Mark Selden, Judith Shapiro, Susan Shirk, Andrew

Walder, Martin K. Whyte, David Zweig, and many others whom we have cited in our references section.

Finally, we want to note that this book project is truly a collaborative effort between the two of us. We devised the concept of "state neoliberalism" together. Each of us revised the other's first draft of a chapter a couple of times. Consequently, we both contributed equally to the conceptualization, drafting, and revision of this book.

Alvin Y. So
Yin-wah Chu

1 Introduction

Since the turn of this century, the mass media have been buzzing regularly about China's remarkable development (e.g. *China Daily* 2009; Pomfret 2009; Wines 2010a):

+ China is the largest exporter and second largest importer of goods in the world. As a result, there has been a dramatic change in the country's status in the global economy. In 1980, China barely registered on the global economic scale, commanding a mere 1 percent of global GDP. In 2010, it captured 9.1 percent of global GDP owing to increases in advanced technology, competitiveness, and the expansion of foreign direct investment flows (Lin 2011; Tabassum and Ahmed 2014).
+ China has surpassed the United States to become the world's largest automobile market – in units, if not in dollars. China has also superseded Germany as the biggest exporter of manufactured goods (Barboza 2010a).
+ In 2010, China – the world's fifth largest economy four years previously – overtook Japan as the second largest economy in the world. If China moves in the same rate as it has been growing over the past three decades, then it might overtake the US economy by 2020 (Tabassum and Ahmed 2014).
+ China had a US$265 billion trade surplus with the US and held US$1.4 trillion in the US Treasury in 2009. In the early 2000s, China's foreign reserves were nearly US$3 trillion – the largest in the world (Lin 2011).

Influenced by these promising economic indicators, both the mass media and policy circles have been using terms like "the rise of China" or "the China Model" to discuss China's rapid economic development. Since 2004, these two terms have been upgraded to "the Beijing Consensus," representing the alternative non-Western economic development model to the Western advanced countries' model of "the Washington Consensus," which is a US-led plan for reforming and developing the economics of small third world countries (Ramo 2004).

Since the mass media and policy studies reports have not spelled out systematically the nature of the China Model, we have taken the liberty of bringing together key arguments in the literature for a reconstruction of the distinctive pattern of China's development:

- *Rapid economic growth.* From 1979 to 1990, China's annual average growth rate was 9.0 percent. At the end of that period and even up to the early 2000s, many scholars still believed that China could *not* sustain that growth rate much longer owing to the lack of fundamental reforms. But the country's annual growth rate between 1990 and 2010 increased to 10.4 percent. On the global economic scene, China's growth over the last few decades has been unprecedented (Lin 2011). This has been a dramatic contrast with the depressing performance of other transitional economies in Eastern Europe and the former Soviet Union. In a short span of forty years, China's GDP rose 18.6 times (Kiely 2008, p. 355) and the country has been suddenly transformed from a poor, backward third world nation to a global economic powerhouse.
- *Export-led industrialization.* Since the turn of the century, China has become the factory and the workshop of the world. The country's exports grew from US$18.1 billion in 1978 to US$266 billion in 2001, reflecting an annual average growth rate of 12 percent. By 2001, manufacturing exports accounted for 90 percent of total exports (Nolan 2004, p. 9).

+ *Innovation and technological upgrading.* Despite the assumption that China is trapped in labor-intensive, low-tech, sweatshop export production, It has modernized its educational system, upgraded its science and research capabilities, and participated in high-tech production. From the 1990s on, foreign corporations began to transfer a significant amount of their research and development activity into China. Microsoft, Oracle, Motorola, Siemens, IBM, and Intel have all set up research laboratories in China because of its "growing importance and sophistication as a market for technology" and "its large reservoir of skilled but inexperienced scientists, and its consumers, still relatively poor but growing richer and eager for new technology" (Buckley 2004). In the first decade of the new century, China began to move up the value-added ladder of production and to compete with South Korea, Japan, Taiwan, and Singapore in spheres such as electronics and machine tools.

+ *Poverty reduction.* China managed to reduce the share of the population living on less than US$1 per day from 64 percent in 1981 to 16 percent by 2006; in effect lifting 400 million people out of absolute poverty (China CSR 2006). Thus, the China Model has worked more effectively than the IMF-designated Structural Adjustment Program in the Washington Consensus model for sub-Saharan Africa and the "shock therapy" for Russia (W. Zhang 2006).

+ *Independent and autonomous development.* According to Joshua Cooper Ramo (2004, pp. 3–4), China shows "how to fit into the international order in such a way that allows [developing countries to be] truly independent, to protect their way of life and political choices in a world with a single powerful center of gravity." As such, the Beijing Consensus can be interpreted as "a theory of self-determination, one that stresses using leverage to move big, hegemonic powers that may be tempted to tread on your toes" (Dirlik 2004, p.3).

In short, the major characteristics of the China Model are rapid economic growth, export-led industrialization, innovation and technological upgrading, poverty reduction, and independent and autonomous development.

Although China's remarkable economic development has been labeled "the China Model" and "the Beijing Consensus," there is simply no consensus concerning the major ingredients of the Chinese path of development since 1978. While the proponents of the China Model want to highlight its positive features, its critics debate the extent to which China is autonomous and whether it is able to achieve genuine technological upgrading. There are also serious disputes as to whether China has contributed to poverty reduction or to rising social inequality, rural bankruptcy, and social conflict on a scale hitherto unknown (Dirlik 2004; Hung 2009; J. Y. Lin 2011; Nolan 2004).

Although we agree with the critics that China is not without its developmental problems, they seem to have gone overboard by defining away the remarkable achievement of Chinese development over the past forty years. We argue that if researchers want to make any advance in understanding the remarkable development of China, they need to move beyond the ideological lens to capture the complexity and ambiguity of the country's development and to explain why this has worked while other development packages like neoliberalism and state socialism have failed.

In other words, why was it possible for China to achieve such remarkable economic growth over the past forty years? What explains China's successful transition from a backward socialist state in the 1970s to a global economic powerhouse in the 2010s?

EXPLANATIONS OF CHINA'S REMARKABLE ECONOMIC DEVELOPMENT

In the literature, there are three competing explanations of China's remarkable development, namely, the world-systems explanation, the neoliberal explanation, and the social explanation.

The World-Systems Explanation

Ho-fung Hung (2009) has contributed to this debate by spelling out the macro-historical context for the dazzling economic expansion of China. Hung, in particular, identifies the following three transformations of the capitalist world-system in the late twentieth century as the most important background factors for understanding the rise of China.

First, there was *a new international division of labor* in the 1970s. The Fordist–Keynesian regime of capital accumulation, which accounted for the more than two decades of postwar prosperity in most advanced capitalist countries, ran into deep crisis. Fordist corporations became ailing dinosaurs, simply too big and too bureaucratic to adapt to the increasingly volatile and competitive world economy. Fiscal deterioration of advanced capitalist states curtailed their capacity to continue the Keynesian strategy of stimulating the economy through ever-enlarging public expenditure (Harvey 1990).

Starting in the late 1970s, Western corporations shifted from a Fordist, vertically integrated mode of organization to a more flexible form of organization based on multi-layered subcontracting to cope with falling profits and to cut costs. This network of subcontracting soon transcended national borders when labor-intensive segments of production were outsourced to manufacturers in low-wage developing countries in the South. Replacing the old core–periphery division of labor based on the periphery's export of raw materials in exchange for manufactured products from the core, the new international division of labor turned part of the periphery into new manufacturing bases of the global system.

In the 1970s, the original East Asian tigers – South Korea, Taiwan, Hong Kong, and Singapore – became the prime destination of these shifting manufacturing activities. The scale and scope of this new international division of labor expanded dramatically in the 1980s and

1990s in the wake of the collapse of most import-substitution regimes in other parts of the developing world, in addition to the world trade liberalization that had been aggressively promoted by the United States since the Reagan administration. In the 1980s and 1990s, China became the most important destination of transnational relocation of manufacturing activities as it receives manufacturing relocation not just from the Western advanced countries but from the newly industrializing countries (like South Korea) as well.

Second, concurrent with the advent of the new international division of labor was the *erosion of the legitimate leadership of the United States* in the capitalist world economy and *the decline of the Cold War*. When economic competition among the United States, Europe, and Japan intensified in the 1970s amidst protracted economic woes, the struggle for export markets spiraled into trade wars, and the ideological homogeneity within this triple alliance against the Soviet bloc began to unravel. The intra-core rivalry escalated in the 1980s, when the common enemy that had bound the Western core powers together – the Eastern communist world – weakened dramatically. When it became all too clear that the socialist bloc no longer constituted a threat to the capitalist core, the socialist states (including China) were welcomed back to reintegrate with the capitalist world economy because the Western capitalist states could benefit immensely from the socialist states' cheap labor, abundant raw materials, and potential market and investment opportunities.

Third, there was *the implosion of most working-class-based, state-power-oriented social movements* that had once effectively constrained the class power of capital across the capitalist world-system. In the 1980s, when the Reagan government and the Thatcher government moved in concert to dismantle the Keynesian welfare state, to revise state protection of stable employment, and to promote free trade globally, they met considerable initial resistance from organized labor and the social movement sector in general at home and abroad. But when

Thatcher later famously declared that "there is no alternative," she seemed to realize the dissipation of resistance to her neoliberal onslaught. The labor movement and the so-called "New Left" were too tamed to resist neoliberal reforms. In the 1990s, under the banner of the neoliberal globalization project, capital was freed from the past constraints of the Fordist–Keynesian regime of capital accumulation, and the class power of capital vis-à-vis labor was substantially elevated by the energetic neoliberal states in the name of the free market; outsourcing, deindustrialization, and casualization of work swept through major cities in advanced capitalist states. Developing countries, too, opened their gates voluntarily or involuntarily to the influx of transnational capital. Export-processing zones populated by unregulated despotic regimes of factory production proliferated throughout the developing world (Harvey 2005).

In short, Ho-fung Hung contends that the triple transformations of the capitalist world-system in the late twentieth century – the rise of the new international division of labor, the decline of US hegemony and the Cold War order, and the general retreat of antisystemic movements – made the rapid economic expansion of China possible.

Delineating the macro-historical forces in the late twentieth century certainly helps us to understand the important underlying background which possibly explains the rise of China. However, as Hung (2009, p. 13) himself points out, "possibility differs from inevitability, and it still cannot fully explain the rise of China." That's why we need to bring in the other two explanations.

The Neoliberal Explanation

The second explanation may be characterized as neoliberal in that pertinent scholars emphasize the dynamism of the market and commensurate institutions wherein the role of the state is confined to the maintenance of law and order.

In *Capitalism with Chinese Characteristics: Entrepreneurship and the State*, Yasheng Huang (2008) argues that in order to understand the China story, researchers need to recognize the existence of two Chinas – the entrepreneurial, market-driven rural China vis-à-vis the state-led urban China. Unlike many countries, the most dynamic, risk-taking, and talented entrepreneurs in China reside in the country-side. These rural entrepreneurs created China's true miracle growth in the 1980s, first by dramatically improving agricultural yields and then by starting many small-scale businesses in food processing and construction materials. The direction of economic policy in that decade was progressively liberal, primarily in the rural areas of the country. Access to finance by the private sector improved rapidly and rural entrepreneurship was vibrant. The result was rapid as well as broad-based growth.

However, in the 1990s, urban China triumphed and the Chinese state reversed many of the productive rural experiments of the previous decade. While this reversal does not show up in the GDP numbers, it is apparent in the welfare implications of growth. Since the early 1990s, household income has lagged behind economic growth and the labor share of GDP has fallen.

Yasheng Huang concludes that when and where rural China had the upper hand, Chinese capitalism was entrepreneurial, politically independent, and vibrantly competitive in its conduct and virtuous in its effect. When and where urban China had the upper hand, Chinese capitalism tended toward political dependency on the state and was corrupt. In short, Yasheng Huang argues that China suc-ceeded when and where private entrepreneurship could emerge from the bottom-up; it stagnated when and where private entrepreneurship was suppressed.

Yasheng Huang's neoliberal explanation is further elaborated in Victor Nee and Sonja Opper's *Capitalism from Below: Markets and Institutional Change in China* (2012). Using the lens of institutional economics, Nee and Opper have offered a micro-analytic perspective that focuses single-mindedly on endogenous grassroots processes of institution-building, as bottom-up entrepreneurs build networks, develop trust, and create informal enforcement mechanisms in the context of relentless competition in product and labor markets. These in turn alter the choice and incentives for the government, creating pressures for the design of supporting regulations and laws.

Similar to Yasheng Huang, Nee and Opper also perceive the entrepreneurs as the dominant agent and the motive force of China's developmental miracle. But going beyond Yasheng Huang, they have traced the historical origins and development of a thriving private business sector in the 1980s.

In particular, they examine how the entrepreneurs started with their technically illegal firms by borrowing capital from their friends and relatives, and recruiting unskilled and skilled labor on informal markets. Developing in close-knit communities in rural China, the entrepreneurs created dense social networks. Repeated transactions in local communities led to emergent business norms that stabilized expectations about trustworthy behavior and yielded confidence in contracts. Furthermore, entrepreneurs in nominally competing lines of enterprises often find it in their interest to band together to ensure export opportunities and supplies of inputs at lower cost.

At the same time, early success bred imitation and attracted a flood of new entrants into markets, which intensified competition and spurred innovation and improvement in quality. Norms of cooperation fostered strategic alliances among firms and the exchange of information. Specialty industrial clusters grew up in localities, and private enterprises built independent supply and distributional networks and cooperated to enjoy economies of scale and competitive advantages. These alliances and networks further served as conduits for the flow of information across markets, yielding access to novel ideas and technical innovation from the global economy.

Nee and Opper's book shows that all of the above activities grew without the benefit of clear legal regulations or effective contract law, and the reality of a growing private sector in turn created pressures for the government to clarify regulations and establish legal protections, albeit with partial success. Thus, their volume may provide a clue to the puzzle: how a thriving private economy could establish itself without secure private property rights and a credible commitment on the part of the communist party-state not to expropriate assets or engage in arbitrary and confiscatory taxation.

This neoliberal explanation contributes to our understanding by identifying the entrepreneurs and the market forces in rural China in the 1980s as the historical agents to jumpstart China's remarkable economic development. However, this explanation needs to be supplemented by the social explanation in order to understand why the Chinese were so eager to turn themselves into entrepreneurs and why they were so good at it.

The Social Explanation

Martin King Whyte (1995) points out that families and kinship patterns at the base of society have played a positive role in China's recent economic surge. These grassroots social patterns help explain why China has been much more successful than the countries of Eastern Europe and the former Soviet Union in making the transition from a centrally planned economy.

In explaining why the Chinese family is an engine of development, Whyte (1996) stresses that loyalty to the family is a very strong source of motivation and performance. For the sake of the family, young Chinese study diligently, pursue advanced education, and strive to maximize their qualifications. Once in a job, they are willing to work very hard and put in extremely long hours, again more for family than for personal benefits. They are willing to accept lower pay than those who are not members of the family would, take pay cuts if needed to allow the family business to succeed, or even work for room and board alone.

Family loyalties and entrepreneurial aspirations also lie behind the high rates of saving that are characteristics of Chinese families. The formation of family sentiments additionally makes it possible to deploy the energies of underutilized family members, such as grandparents and young children, to help the firm to succeed. Family members are likely to stay with the firm even when better-paying opportunities arise elsewhere, contributing to continuity in firm management.

The use of family roles to organize management also provides a cultural basis for enterprise authority, reducing conflict with the boss and inhibiting strikes and other disruptive behavior. Family loyalty, moreover, helps maintain secrecy about firm operations and plans, making it easier to protect proprietary information. In addition, it provides powerful incentives for the heads of family firms as well as for family member employees. The obligation to provide for an entire family, for multiple heirs, and for a family or lineage estate creates a powerful source of entrepreneurial drive.

In short, Chinese families are an extraordinary source of economic dynamism. However, Whyte (1996) argues that this developmental potential of the family cannot be fully realized unless a number of contingencies are present, including relatively secure property and contractual rights, open channels to upward mobility, government policies that foster entrepreneurial familism, and a world economy that creates niches that are suited to Chinese family-run firms.

In socialist China during the Mao era (1949–76), these contingencies were by and large absent, as public ownership, hostility toward mobility aspirations, and an economic strategy based mainly on capital-intensive firms and autarky were the orders of the day. However, in the reform era since 1978, conditions more favorable toward entrepreneurial familism have been instituted, and arguably the unleashed entrepreneurial behavior of Chinese families is at least part of the story behind the county's dramatically improved economic performance.

Critical Evaluation of the Three Explanations

The literature has offered three interesting explanations for China's developmental miracle. The world-systems explanation highlights the macro transformations of the capitalist world-system that made the Chinese developmental miracle possible; the neoliberal explanation emphasizes the important role of small rural entrepreneurs and the liberal market institution; while the social explanation underlines Chinese family as the source of economic dynamism in post-1978 China.

Obviously, all the above three factors – the world-systems, entrepreneurship, and the Chinese family – have played some role in propelling China to becoming an economic powerhouse. Maybe it is true that China's developmental miracle, as Whyte (1996, p. 21) remarks, is "over-determined," with the relative contribution of any particular factor hard to disentangle from the rest. However, one common weakness that is shared by the above three explanations is that they fail to capture the historical specificity of China's development in the late twentieth century.

For example, although Chinese family is important, this factor is common in all Chinese societies in mainland China, Taiwan, and Hong Kong throughout the entire twentieth century. Thus, this family explanation needs to specify the historical context and the socio-political setting in China during the 1980s and 1990s through which the Chinese family operated before it could unleash its entrepreneurial potential. In other words, it needs to explain why the entrepreneurial potential of the family was unleashed only in rural China during the post-socialist transition in the 1980s but not in other periods.

Similarly, the neoliberal explanation treats China like another developing country that is on its way to capitalist development. It assumes that so long as there are favorable market institutions, entrepreneurship will flourish and this entrepreneurship will propel the country to rapid economic development. As Andrew G. Walder (2014, p. 44) aptly observes, China was no ordinary developing country. Even as many robust entrepreneurs emerged in rural China in the 1980s, the nascent private sector existed side by side with the dominant state sector of corporate giants, many of which are now among the largest in the world, and their share of employment and output appears to have stabilized at around 25–30 percent. More capital-intensive, their share of total assets is much higher than their share of employment. They are fully under government control; their top management is part of the civil service system and is frequently transferred between the party-state and business posts.

These state firms are given preferential treatment in obtaining loans on favorable terms from state banks, and they receive regulatory protection, hidden subsidies, and tax breaks. They frequently enjoy monopolistic or oligopolistic positions in the domestic economy, and they do not compete with firms in the sectors examined by Nee and Opper. Such state firms are in civil aviation, telecommunications, shipbuilding, overseas shipping, banking, mining, energy production, and a range of other strategic industries where entry barriers are still almost prohibitive. This dominance of state-led strategic industries is a novel Chinese creation, and the communist party-state defends this dominance of the state sector in the Chinese economy as the foundation for national strength and its continued rule.

As such, even though we agree with the neoliberal and social explanation that entrepreneurship, market institutions, and the family are crucial factors for China's remarkable economic development, we argue that researchers need to bring the communist party-state and the political setting back in before we can better understand the socio-political context which serves to constrain or unleash business entrepreneurship in Chinese society.

TOWARD A STATE-CENTERED EXPLANATION

In advancing a state-centered explanation of China's development, it is necessary to make a few preambles. First, as the above has suggested, we recognize the importance of the world economy and its dynamics as well as local socio-economic institutions in the making of China's miraculous development. Not only have changes in the world economy generated opportunities for China, the country has from the beginning sought foreign investments, engaged in the export of manufactured products, and inserted itself progressively into global production and knowledge networks. The deep engagement with the capitalist world economy has generated imperatives that infuse the Chinese state's policies on land, labor, and civil society with elements of exploitation and suppression. At the same time, the present study also recognizes the importance of private entrepreneurship as well as social institutions like the family and social networks that make it flourish. Overseas Chinese connections from Hong Kong and elsewhere as well as homegrown ones within the country have been well documented (e.g. Hsing 1998; Smart and Smart 1991; Wank 1996). Hence, in advancing our state-centered argument, which we call "*state neoliberalism*," we do not claim to put forth a comprehensive account of China's development, much less trace the contours of a Chinese variety of capitalism, as some authors have attempted (cf. McNally 2012). Instead, we seek to delineate the critical roles played by the Chinese state in the country's global rise and the tension-ridden strategies underlying the country's trajectory of development.

Specifically, we argue that the communist party-state has played an instrumental role in guiding and facilitating the country's post-socialist development. However, apart from instituting policies that are in many ways similar to a developmental state, a large dose of its policies involve deregulation, marketization, privatization, and the reduction of welfare support – policies that some observers call neoliberalism. This being the case, we propose the rather contradictory concept of "state neoliberalism" to describe China's trajectory of post-socialist development and to distinguish it from the East Asian developmental states, from the neoliberal state as practiced in Western capitalist societies, and from the post-socialist state in Eastern Europe. The following will start with an examination of the metamorphosis of the communist party-state, the substance of state neoliberalism, and its distinctions from the developmental state as well as neoliberalism that emerged in Western and Eastern European societies.

The Metamorphosis of the Communist Party-State

Whyte (2009) points out that China was particularly ill prepared to become a positive model of a successful developmental state. Before it experienced economic take-off, the country was known for its recent history of persistent and even monumental mismanagement of the economy (Naughton 1991). The Chinese state in 1978 was led by lifelong communist apparatchiks who presided over a bureaucracy largely composed of poorly educated but politically loyal and obedient officials whose career success did not depend substantially on economic expertise or performance. In other words, the Chinese communist party-state was hardly the highly trained technocracy that was widely given credit for the success of other East Asian economies (Onis 1991; So 2013). It is necessary to examine how the Chinese communist party-state could overcome its bureaucratic inefficiency and "successfully direct the transformation from an increasingly inefficient centrally planned economy to a vibrant market economy" (Whyte 2009, p. 372; see also Oi 1992).[1]

According to Whyte (2009), part of the explanation is that China had models close at hand in East Asia of developmental states that successfully guided market-oriented development, models that could be studied and adapted to the Chinese context. By the 1980s, the planned socialist model was recognized as a dead end, but China could turn to its East Asian neighbors for models of how to organize a high-growth, market-oriented economy with a potential for rapidly improving the living standards of the population. The borrowing is usually thought of primarily in terms of China's shift from capital-intensive autarkic development to labor-intensive export-led industrialization. However, an equally important adaptation concerns China's strategy of reforming its economic institutions without changing its political system (especially the one-party authoritarian government).

A most fundamental change that allowed China to model itself on its East Asian neighbors was the overhaul of the communist party-state, which involved a rapid and thorough transformation in personnel recruitment, promotion, and incentive practices at all levels of the party and the state bureaucracy. In the 1980s, younger and better-educated people were recruited to replace the poorly educated but politically loyal officials at all levels. The party-state implemented, for the first time, a mandatory retirement system for officials, clearing the way for younger officials to rise. The communist party-state was rapidly transformed from a *"virtuocracy"* (Shirk 1984) to a *meritocracy*, with even the top party leadership now composed mainly of college-educated technocrats, particularly alumni of China's prestigious Tsinghua University (C. Li 1994).

China also repudiated the late Mao-era prohibition on material incentive and adopted a quantitative system for assessing and rewarding local officials, using *economic development success as the primary indicator for determining compensation*. Those leaders of localities or enterprises that performed well economically were given sizeable monetary rewards in recognition of this success (Oi 1992). That explains why local officials are so eager to initiate new development projects under their jurisdiction; such projects not only bring revenue and jobs to their region, but they themselves would also get handsome merit increases and career advancement in the Chinese bureaucracy.

Another important component of the reforms of the state administrative system was the double decentralization: *administrative decentralization* and *fiscal decentralization*. From the 1980s, large numbers of formally centrally administered state enterprises were transferred to provincial and lower levels of administration (building on the decentralization waves of the Mao era). In addition, subordinate governments entered contractual agreements with higher levels specifying the amount of revenue the lower level had to turn over to the next higher level. Remaining and additional budgeted revenue and any new extrabudgetary funds generated by the lower levels did not have to be remitted to higher levels, as had been the case before, but could be used locally to stimulate economic development, supply public goods, and fulfill other purposes.

Similar arrangements were adopted for production enterprises in their relations with their supervising levels of government. Furthermore, enterprise responsibilities for pensions and other welfare benefits for their employees and retirees began to be taken over by pooled funds supervised by local governments in a move designed to allow enterprises to concentrate on their core economic activities.

As a consequence of these policy changes, Whyte (2009) points out, local government and enterprises were provided with a relatively secure set of administrative and fiscal arrangements that enabled them to concentrate on pursuing new market opportunities and developing their economies with the assurance that, if they were successful, most of the increased revenue could be used locally to generate more of the same, not to mention financial rewards for those in charge.

Firms and local governments also knew that if they lost money they would no longer be bailed out by higher levels, thus *forcing them to face market competition* in a structure imposing relatively hard budget constraints. Localities and enterprises that were relatively slow to pursue new market opportunities could readily observe how they were falling behind the prosperity of their neighbors, and the resulting envy stimulated increased effort to copy the successful market-oriented policies and institutions of the front-runners. The combination of financial rewards for local officials for success in economic development and increased public revenues generated by local firms provided powerful incentives to quickly adopt practices suited to operating in the market environment. Thus, Whyte (2009, p. 381) concludes that "the hectic market competition among local firms and governments unleashed by these changes was a fundamental source of China's new economic dynamism." Making a related point, Gabriella Montinola and her colleagues (1995) suggested that policies of administrative and fiscal decentralization constitute what they called "federalism, Chinese style." They generated not only economic dynamism but also political protection from intervention by the central government, which rendered the economic reform durable (cf. H. Cai and Treisman 2006; Shirk 1993).

State Neoliberalism

There are three unique ways in which the communist party-state has shaped China's post-socialist development, and we coin the rather contradictory term "*state neoliberalism*" in order to capture its distinctive characteristics.

First of all, a large dose of the Chinese state's development strategy involved what might be called neoliberalization. Apart from the cutback on welfare commitments (housing, medical, retirement, and other benefits) and systematic oversights of the violations of labor laws and commensurate regulations, the Chinese state also undertook to decollectivize agricultural production, deregulate the commodity and labor markets, and privatize numerous state enterprises. It is in part the coexistence of the strategic role played by the Chinese state to guide and propel the country's development, on the one hand, and the irony that part of the effort involves rampant neoliberalization, on the other hand, that the term "state neoliberalism" seeks to capture.

Second, the Chinese state continued to declare its adherence to socialism even as it adopted a neoliberal path of national development. It is this persistent hold of the socialist ideology which infused China's brand of post-socialist transformation with tensions and contradictions more acute than in the other East Asian developmental states. For one thing, the adherence to socialism had favored a course of gradual reform, which contributed to the incomplete dispossession/ proletarianization of peasant workers, and the prolonged dependence of capitalists on the state. For another, the exploited and suppressed peasants and workers could condemn their sufferings (which were induced by neoliberal practices) by appealing to the party-state's avowed socialist ideology. Similarly, state elites, who found their material and cultural interests undergoing assaults under neoliberalism, also could seize the opportunities of social dislocations and disruptions by saying that the neoliberal reforms had gone too far.

Similar to other East Asian developmental states, the Chinese party-state introduced some welfare programs at a later stage in order to contain the worst repercussions of neoliberal practices it orchestrated and attenuate the worst abuses of the workers, peasants, and other disadvantaged groups. In the Chinese case, however, this often played out with a bifurcation between a benign central state and malign local ones. Apart from introducing policies like the Labor Contract Law, the central state also responded every now and then to social protests by issuing censures to reprimand the local states for their oversights of labor rights, environmental degradation, or peasant suffering. At the same time that these practices deflected social discontents, they also shielded the communist party-state from demands for political change. The term "state neoliberalism," then, is also used to capture the Chinese state's upholding of socialist ideology while introducing neoliberalization, which manifested in the emergence of acute tensions and contradictions in the country.

Third, while China's economy grew progressively, its institutional transformations were intermittent and marked by apparent policy reversals whereby state-oriented and market-oriented policies took turns to predominate. For instance, just as neoliberal policies were halted in response to massive structural dislocations and social conflict in the late 1980s, they were quickly reinstated and even intensified in the mid-1990s, calling for the privatization of state enterprises on a grand scale. Rather than depicting an attained condition, then, "state neoliberalism" captures an ongoing process of policy ebbs and flows between market-oriented and state-oriented policies.

To further elaborate on the uniqueness of China's state neoliberalism, the following will contrast China with the developmental state and neoliberalism as practiced in Western and Eastern European societies.

China and the Developmental State

The above analysis of the metamorphosis of the communist party-state and policies it has pursued since 1978 suggests that it has taken on substantial characteristics of a developmental state. The latter, as pointed out by Peter B. Evans (1995, p. 12), is one that not only presides over industrial transformation but also plays a role in making it happen, or, in the words of Chalmers A. Johnson (1995, p. 67), "establishes as its principle of legitimacy its ability to promote and sustain development." The developmental state set economic growth as its highest priority, despite the fact that this goal can only be attained at the expense of other important goals, such as social equality, democracy, and environmental sustainability.

However, despite its strong commitment to economic growth, the Chinese state differs from the East Asian developmental states in important ways. First of all, the local states played a much bigger role in China's development, thanks to its policies of administrative and fiscal decentralization introduced to revamp the communist party-state (Howell 2006; Oi 1995; Whyte 2009).

In addition, instead of subjecting the market to state guidance, China's socialist legacy rendered it necessary for the communist party-state first to reinvent the market before liberating it. Thus, the party-state had to nurture the market institution in the late 1980s because many rural capitalists still were afraid of the anti-market, anti-capitalist policy of the Cultural Revolution.

Also, although the party-state was eager to groom national champions or at least to preserve the strategic sectors (which was not unlike its East Asian neighbors), China's socialist legacy had led it to rely on the state enterprises rather than work with the private sector, as in the case of the catalyst states of Japan and South Korea. Hence, after more than thirty years of capitalist development, China's state sector is still much larger than those of its East Asian neighbors.

Furthermore, state-led development in China was also fraught with hesitations and reversals of both economic and social policies, which was seldom the case with the East Asian developmental states. Such hesitations and reversals, as suggested earlier, were symptoms of the acute contradictions experienced by a communist party-state that sought to facilitate capitalist development. The coping strategy, which took the form of a bifurcation between the benign central state and malign local ones, was also unique to China's decentralized development strategy.

Given all the above, we consider it appropriate to coin the term "state neoliberalism" to capture the distinctive characteristics of China's state-led post-socialist development. In addition, the term highlights the importance of the party-state's bid for survival as an inherent aspect of China's development.

Neoliberalism: East and West

If a large dose of China's post-socialist development involved the introduction of neoliberalism, the historical process whereby neoliberalism was introduced also set China apart from both the capitalist countries of the West and former-socialist ones in Central and Eastern Europe.

Neoliberalism was a new class project that emerged in the 1970s in the Western capitalist societies. Before the late 1970s, capitalism in the West took the form of what David Harvey (2005) called *"embedded liberalism."* In order to resolve the problems generated by unbridled marketization that culminated in the 1930s depression, the state had to take a more active role in managing the market to provide full employment as well as to promote the economy. In embedded liberalism, the state takes on more and more roles (like providing more welfare and social services, strengthening workers' trade unions, imposing more regulations on the market, and imposing higher taxes on the capitalist class). Thus, capital was induced to compromise and to form a new social contract with the working class; and it was also embedded in a web of social and political constraints and in a new regulatory environment that restricted its "greedy" profit-making behavior. After World War II, a variety of social democratic, liberal democratic, and dirigiste states emerged in Western Europe and the United States that exemplified this trend of embedded liberalism.

According to Harvey (2005), *"neoliberalism"* is a new class project through which the capitalist class fights back against the high taxes and the strict regulations of the state as well as the "rigidities" imposed by the state and the trade unions on production relations. On the one hand, neoliberalism aims to liberalize the market so that members of the capitalist class can have more freedom to hire and fire their workers, and to expand their trading and investment within the state boundary or beyond into global space. On the other hand, neoliberalism aims to downsize the state, so that its role is confined to the setting up and preservation of the institution for market liberalism. Hence, in the late 1970s, neoliberalism was accompanied by deregulation, privatization, and the marketization of social services. Indeed, Harvey (2005, p. 7) uses the term "neoliberal state" to refer to "a state apparatus whose fundamental mission was to facilitate conditions for profitable capital accumulation on the part of both domestic and foreign capital."

In the advanced capitalist societies of the West, neoliberalism emerged in a historical setting wherein both the state and the capitalist class were fully institutionalized and were the two most powerful players in their societies. Neoliberalism was a new project prompted by members of the capitalist class who wanted to revamp the unfettered market when confronted by a crisis of capital accumulation in the 1970s. As "neoliberalism" replaces "embedded liberalism," state–market relations shift from a situation of state domination to one of market domination.

When China embarked on reform and opened up in the 1980s and 1990s, it was during the high tide of neoliberalism in the West. The World Bank, the International Monetary Fund, and other advisors to the developing countries also preached the superiority of the market mechanism. The Washington Consensus, which emerged in 1989 as a series of advice given to the crisis-ridden Latin American and Eastern European countries, emphasized precisely the need to cut back state spending and maintain fiscal policy discipline, privatize state enterprises, and open up the economy to foreign trade and foreign direct investment, among others. In their haste to address problems of structural dislocations in their countries, Poland, Yugoslavia, Czechoslovakia, Bulgaria, Romania, Hungary, and later Russia even adopted the so-called "big bang" approach to scrap their socialist establishments and institute neoliberal capitalism.

Like other developing countries in the capitalist world economy, China found the impulse to carry out neoliberal market reforms almost irresistible in the 1980s and 1990s. The above has already suggested that the Chinese state introduced neoliberal practices not unlike those practiced in the Western capitalist societies and the Washington Consensus taken up by the Eastern European countries as counseled by the World Bank and the IMF.

However, the historical context within which neoliberalism emerged in China was totally different from that in the West. China was a state socialist society where property was owned predominantly by the state and the collectives. In addition, in the early 1970s it had just gone through the devastating Cultural Revolution, the primary aim of which was to suppress market relations and destroy the capitalist class. Before the initiation of the 1978 reform, market institutions were rudimentary and a capitalist class was nonexistent. Given the strong anti-capitalist sentiment in the aftermath of the Cultural Revolution and the practical absence of the private sector, the communist party-state in China rather than the capitalist class had to take the driver's seat to propel the neoliberalism project forward. The communist party-state generated room for the rise of market relations and the emergence of a capitalist class, and for a long time played instrumental roles in the imposition of blatant neoliberal practices. The term "state neoliberalism," therefore, also serves to contrast China's unique experience of introducing neoliberalism with that of the West.

Chinese state neoliberalism also differs from the neoliberal market reforms that took place in post-socialist Eastern Europe, in the following ways. In the first place, market reforms like "shock therapy" and mass privatization undertaken in Eastern Europe had the *goals* of dismantling communism and stripping communists of power and privileges. However, in China, neoliberal market reforms were intended to allow the communist party-state to survive as an instrument of economic development (Walder 1996).

Furthermore, the *speed of market reforms* was also different. Unlike the "big bang" and "shock therapy" approaches practiced in Eastern Europe, which called for the dismantling of the centrally planned economy and the building up of neoliberal market institutions as quickly as possible, the neoliberal market reforms in China have been a gradual, adaptive process without a clear blueprint. John McMillan and Barry Naughton (1992) remark that China's market reforms proceeded by trial and error, with frequent mid-course corrections and reversals of policy. In other words, the Chinese economic reforms were not a completed project settled in the first stage, but an ongoing process with many adjustments, whether two steps forward and one step backward, or one step forward and two steps backward. In China, there was no rapid leap to free prices, currency convertibility, or cutting of state subsidies; nor was there massive privatization and the quick selling off of state enterprises.

Similar to the Western embedded liberalism that emerged out of the 1930s depression, Chinese state neoliberalism emerged and was consolidated during socio-political crises (like the 1989 Tiananmen crisis and the 2008 global economic crisis). It also is aimed at managing the problems of the unfettered market, and the Chinese communist party-state has taken an active role in re-regulating the market, cutting down its role, and expanding the state sector.

However, Chinese state neoliberalism is different from Western embedded liberalism because it emerged out of a different historical setting. China's state neoliberalism emerged out of a state socialist economy and China had a strong communist party-state, whereas Western embedded liberalism emerged out of a liberal capitalist economy. In Western embedded liberalism, the market is embedded in a liberal, democratic state wherein the civil society and social movements are quite active. In Chinese state neoliberalism, the market is embedded in a communist, authoritarian state with a highly suppressed civil society and social movements.

THE CONTENT OF THE BOOK

This book has a total of nine chapters, which include this introductory chapter, a concluding one, and seven other chapters divided into two parts. Having spelt out our state-centered framework in this introductory chapter, the three chapters in the first part will trace the making of the Chinese developmental miracle as it went through three historical turning points. Specifically, chapter 2 will examine the socialist foundation of China's development and the critical transition in 1978 to a post-socialist economy. Chapter 3 will examine the substance of neoliberal market reforms introduced in 1978, the interlude of state neoliberalism that emerged after the 1989 Tiananmen Incident, the deepening of neoliberal market reforms in the second half of the 1990s, and once again the consolidation of state neoliberalism in the early twenty-first century. In turn, chapter 4 will examine the further consolidation of state neoliberalism in the first two decades of the twenty-first century, with special emphasis on events that occurred after the 2008 global economic crisis.

The second part examines how the Chinese party-state has handled the various developmental challenges that have emerged when it pursues state neoliberalism. Chapter 5 will examine the challenges of catching up, especially how China can upgrade technologically and move up the value chain. Chapter 6 will examine the challenges of staying in power, focusing on how the party-state has prolonged its survival by successfully managing the emergent social conflicts from workers, peasants, and citizens in Chinese society. Chapter 7 will examine the challenges of sustainability, especially how China resolves the pressing problem of environmental destruction and resource depletion. Chapter 8 will examine the challenges of global rivalry, focusing on how China handles the growing tensions and disputes in Asia and in the global economy.

Finally, chapter 9 will serve as the concluding chapter to summarize the major arguments in this book. It will also discuss the prospects for the rise of China and the implications of it becoming the center of the global economy in the twenty-first century.

PART I

THE CHINESE DEVELOPMENT MIRACLE —————

<table>
<tr><td>2</td><td>Socialist Foundation and the Critical Transition to State Neoliberalism</td><td>———</td></tr>
</table>

After the Communist Revolution in 1949, the Chinese Communist Party (CCP) under the leadership of Mao Zedong took control over China when it defeated the Nationalist Party (Guomindang or Kuomintang) in the civil war.[1] For almost thirty years, the communist party-state pursued revolutionary socialist programs in the form we have called "state socialism" as a strategy to achieve the twin goals of economic development and social equality. Then, in 1978, the party-state shifted gears, suddenly dropped its socialist aspirations, and adopted the "reform and opening up" policy, which unleashed a whole series of changes that launched China gradually but unmistakably on the path of "state neoliberalism." In this chapter, we attempt to answer three research questions:

+ What were the distinctive features of China's state socialism between 1949 and 1978?
+ Had the Maoist socialist experiment been a total disaster or, alternatively, had it laid a solid foundation for the remarkable economic growth in post-socialist China since 1978?
+ What factors had prompted China to embark on the critical transition to state neoliberalism in 1978?

CHARACTERISTICS OF STATE SOCIALISM IN CHINA

Suppose you could travel through time to Maoist China in the mid-1970s, and you told the Chinese that their country would become an economic powerhouse of the capitalist world economy in the next thirty years. No Chinese would take your words seriously because they knew that China had experienced very serious developmental problems during the socialist period (since 1949), and this painful socialist legacy should prevent the country from making any progress in economic development.

First of all, when the Chinese Communist Party took power in 1949, China was a much devastated country owing to rounds of foreign encroachments that often escalated into wars, infighting among warlords and violent civil wars between the communists and the nationalists, and serious structural deficiency and dislocations such as the inadequacy of arable land, a shortage of investment capital, and technological stagnation. Raging hyperinflation in the last years of the Republic government's rule in the late 1940s also drove the Chinese economy into disarray.

In 1952, a year when China was deemed to have recovered from the worst of war devastation, its gross domestic product (GDP) amounted to 67,900 million yuan (Chinability 2014). With a population of about 588 million,[2] per capita income amounted to 116 yuan, making it one of the poorest countries in the world. As with most other poor developing economies, China was dominated by agriculture, with the primary sector contributing 50.5 percent, the secondary sector 20.9 percent, and the tertiary sector 28.6 percent to its GDP (Hitotsubashi University Team n.d.). In 1950, life expectancy at birth was around 36 and no more than 25 percent of the population attained primary education (Selden 1993).

Furthermore, China faced the problem of forced withdrawal from the world economy. Before the Chinese communist state could barely consolidate its power in the early 1950s, the US quickly mobilized warships to patrol the Taiwan Strait and supported the defeated Nationalist Party in Taiwan, sent soldiers to fight Chinese troops in Korea, imposed an economic embargo on mainland Chinese products, and waged ideological attacks on Chinese "communist totalitarianism" in the mass media. Until 1971, the country was also barred from assuming its place in the United Nations.

Indeed, in order to contain the spread of communism from China (and the Soviet Union), the United States was said to have gone so far as to pardon Japan immediately after the Pacific War, and helped to construct a "Greater East Asian Co-prosperity Circle," which allowed Japan to unite and lead South Korea, Taiwan, the Philippines, Malaysia, Singapore, and Indonesia in building a bulwark against communism (Cumings 1987).

Intense hostility from the US during this Cold War era served to preclude certain development options for socialist China. Cut off from contacts with capitalist states, the Chinese communist state could not possibly pursue either export-oriented industrialization (owing to the closure of Western markets) or import-substitution (owing to the economic embargo) in the global economy. The embargo imposed by the United States and other Western countries also denied China access to foreign inflow of capital and technology. The threat of property seizure and restrictions on the remission of profit among foreign enterprises also led to their departure from China, whether on the eve of the communist takeover or a little later (Siu-lin Wong 1988).

Under these circumstances, China had no recourse but to pursue a more or less autarkic path of socialist development. There was one exception. With the signing of the 1950 Sino-Soviet Treaty of Friendship and Cooperation, China was covered by the Soviet nuclear umbrella, granted military support, and given economic, technical, and planning assistance (Selden and Lippit 1982, p. 6). Thus, the Chinese state was forced to lean toward the Soviet bloc and miss the golden opportunity of achieving ascent during the postwar economic boom in the capitalist world economy. Furthermore, the Cold War had created a resource strain on the Chinese economy. From 1952 to 1977, defense spending on average accounted for 5.5 percent of China's GDP (Y. Lin 2003).

It has been suggested that China did not pursue just one single brand of socialist policies (Selden 1993, pp. 7–9). On the one hand, there were revolutionary socialist policies that gave emphasis to class struggle, mass mobilization, state-centered accumulation, collective and communal production, egalitarian distribution, as well as elimination of the market and household economy. These prevailed during the periods of land reform in 1947–8, the collectivization drive of 1955–6, the Great Leap Forward between 1958 and 1960, and the Dazhai movement of the Cultural Revolution decade from 1966 to 1976.

On the other hand, the party-state also sought a more moderate, broad-based coalition of social forces, striving to balance the market and plan, state and household interests, as well as tolerating the peasants' heterodox cultural, religious, and economic values during the early 1950s and early 1960s. While agreeing with Mark Selden that there were considerable policy oscillations between revolutionary socialism and its moderate retreat, we contend that economic pursuits in the first twenty-nine years (1949–78) of China could still be identified as "state socialism," which has the following distinctive features.

Land Reform and Collectivization

In order to eliminate the exploitation that stemmed from unequal land ownership, generate economies of scale in land cultivation, and obtain the rural surplus necessary for national accumulation, land reform and collectivization were implemented in the country. The approach to land reform was moderate, for in attending to the poor peasants' demand for land, the party-state made sure that it would restrict the scale of both redistribution and retribution so as not to antagonize the middle peasants or even the rich peasants (Selden 1982, p. 47; Selden and Lippit 1982, pp. 6–7). The reform was completed by 1952 and, according to Victor D. Lippit (1974, p. 95), it redistributed 44 percent of the

arable land in the countryside from the landlords to the poor and land-
less peasants.

Similarly, collectivization was to proceed slowly. While mutual-aid
teams were formed early on, advanced collectivization would await the
commensurate growth in mechanization, which required in turn the
development of industries. By 1955, however, leaders of the party-state
became impatient. The First Five-Year Plan (1953–7), drafted under
the tutelage of the Soviet Union, gave special emphasis to the development of heavy industries. With China unable to obtain investment
capital elsewhere owing to its forced withdrawal from the capitalist
world economy, the only option was to expropriate the agricultural
surplus, which party leaders believed could be given a boost by collectivization. Instead of relying on voluntary participation, Mao argued
in 1955 that, in order to check the polarization of the peasantry, large-
scale cooperation had to be carried forward at full speed (Selden 1982,
p. 60). Collectivization stepped up after July 1955 and, by 1958, the
formation of rural communes was complete (Selden 1982, p. 55).

Rural social relations were completely transformed by this wholesale
collectivization. If the 1949 "land to the tillers" program was geared to
the creation of independent commodity producers by giving land to
the poor peasants, forcible collectivization abolished the private ownership of land. In the words of Selden (1982, pp. 69–70),

> In less than a year the entire countryside passed from a mixed system
> of private ownership of land and the means of production with varying
> degrees of small-scale mutual aid and elementary forms of cooperation,
> to large-scale collectivization and communes; from production organ-
> ized in most cases on a scale ranging from single households to a few
> dozen households, to one embracing an entire village or even a town-
> ship and typically involving several hundred families.

Through the levy of agricultural tax and compulsory sales of food
grains at very low prices to the state, agricultural surplus was siphoned

off from the countryside to the cities in order to promote heavy industrialization.[3] Collectivization, moreover, assured the success of this expropriation of rural surplus. Proceeds of the grain sales were then distributed to the peasants.

Whereas both land and labor inputs were recompensed in the elementary cooperatives, only labor input was rewarded in the advanced cooperatives and communes according to a rather complex work-point system. Aside from monetary compensation, peasants were also provided with basic education, rural healthcare, and access to rural infrastructures. It has to be emphasized that, just as socialist egalitarianism was the guiding principle, it had not been easy in practice to devise work-point systems that adequately balanced motivation for individuals and fulfillment of collective goals. This was particularly the case as the size of the collectives expanded beyond the boundary of a traditional village (F. Cai et al. 2008; Oi 1989; Shue 1980, pp. 313–17).

Nationalization and State-Owned Enterprises

Among other measures undertaken by the communist party-state to end labor exploitation and promote rapid industrial development was the nationalization of private enterprises. In the late 1940s under the New Democracy policy, the communist party only wanted to "confiscate monopoly capital," but it claimed to "protect the industry and commerce of the national bourgeoisie" (Selden and Lippit 1982, p. 7). Indeed, starting with businesses already nationalized by the Nationalist Party, the communist party-state proceeded to confiscate foreign capital and comprador bureaucratic capital, after which the state took a commanding position in banking, trade, and transportation (Reiitsu 1982, p. 239).

However, in the 1950s, small and medium-size private enterprises were also nationalized with compensation and small workshops (numbering 2.2 million by 1953) were physically combined into cooperatives or small state enterprises. The large number of handicraftsmen,

7.6 million in number by 1954, were either recruited into the new enterprises or grouped by trade into cooperatives (Walder 1986, p. 32). By 1956, the process of nationalization was complete and, in the words of Lippit (1982, p. 139), "leaving no possibility of capitalist restoration." In that year, the number of relatively large modern state enterprises increased to some 50,000 from just under 3,000 in 1949 (Walder 1986, p. 33).

Having nationalized all the private enterprises and transforming them into relatively large-scale enterprises, the party-state proceeded to pour resources into them and, in particular, the heavy industries. The First Five-Year Plan (1953–7), which defined the basic framework of China's planned economy and was set up under Soviet tutelage, poured half of China's total industrial investment (amounting to some 25 billion yuan) into the 156 Soviet-aided projects, most of which were large-scale and capital-intensive (Fairbank 1986, p. 286). The Soviet Union provided loans of about 60 million yuan a year,[4] supplied 10,000 specialists to the country, and offered training for 28,000 Chinese specialists sent to various Soviet institutes. Soviet support played an important role until 1960, when escalating tensions between the two countries (owing to their disagreement on the direction of China's development after the Great Leap Forward) led to the abrupt departures of Soviet scientists and engineers in that year.

The emphasis on large-scale and heavy industries, however, continued in the 1960s and the 1970s. As of 1980, there were around 1,000 very large state enterprises with over 5,000 employees employing 12–14 million workers, accounting for between one-third and a half of the total value of industrial fixed assets, and producing one-fifth to one-third of gross value of industrial output (GVIO). At about the same time, there existed some 580,000 small and medium-size collective enterprises (62 percent of all industrial enterprises) at the local level, employing an average of 17 workers per plant and producing just 3.4 percent of GVIO (Nolan and Ash 1995, pp. 993–4).

These state and collective enterprises did not get their workers through open recruitment (because there was no free labor market under state socialism), but mostly via matching provided by the Bureau of Labor and Personnel or other, lower-level government agencies. In state socialism, Chinese workers labored and lived in work units (*danwei*); these units not only paid them a decent wage, but also provided them with all sorts of benefits, like housing, healthcare, childcare, education, and a pension. Such benefits were given at levels differentiated according to the occupation, industry, region, ownership (state versus collective), administration level (central versus local), and type of workplace (size, technological level) (F. Cai et al. 2008; Whyte and Parish 1984).

As analyzed masterfully by Andrew G. Walder (1986), state-sector workers were the most privileged, distinguished above all by their high pay, high degree of job security (they never got fired!), and special access to valuable commodities and services in a society of scarcity. Nonetheless, owing to China's fast rate of population growth, the need to control unbridled urban expansion, the generosity of the benefits given to state-sector workers, and the difficulty of the state enterprises (mostly in heavy industries) in generating such jobs speedily, the communist party-state introduced a stringent household registration system (*hukou*) in 1955 to control rural–urban migration, and assigned much lower levels of compensation and benefits to temporary jobs or jobs with the smaller-scale collective enterprises (see also Whyte and Parish 1984). In 1981, about 42 percent of the total industrial workforce were hired as permanent state employees[5] (Walder 1986, p. 41).

The Communist Party-State

Having won the civil war and attained national unification, the Chinese Communist Party went on to establish state machinery that allowed it to promote its socialist aspiration, economic development, and other national goals. A number of factors worked to its advantage. Among these was the leadership that the party provided both in the people's wars that defeated Japanese imperialism in China and in the civil war that triumphed over the US-backed Nationalist Party. These victories put an end to a century of national humiliation and massive sufferings, thus allowing the communist party to gain legitimacy and so provide moral-political leadership for the Chinese people.

Another factor working to the party's advantage was that more than two decades of guerrilla warfare and the management of regional bases had given it considerable administrative expertise, which it could utilize in the formidable task of national reconstruction (Selden and Lippit 1982). Indeed, immediately after 1949, the same soldiers who had freed the various areas of the country were relied upon to provide local leadership. In time, when the communist party had gathered all political and economic forces not deemed hostile to the revolution, it proceeded to create a powerful state bureaucracy that commanded a high degree of autonomy and had the capacity to carry out its twin goals of socialist equality and rapid development (Tomba 2010a).

The higher levels of the Chinese state overlapped considerably with the Chinese Communist Party despite their formal organizational distinction. It is because of this complicated interlocking between state officials and communist party members (one person usually wears two hats) that we use the term *"party-state"* to characterize the Chinese state after the 1949 Communist Revolution.

The extent of power concentration in the party varied with the leader's credentials and personal charisma. Mao Zedong's power was indeed unparalleled in much of the period after 1949, which allowed him to sidestep some institutional constraints, abandon extant policies, and back his reputation on radical ones. The speed-up of collectivization and the launch of the Cultural Revolution were cases in point. Furthermore, Mao's idea of "permanent revolution" was incorporated into the party's statutes of 1969, 1973, and 1977, which confined the recruitment of party members to workers, poor and fairly poor peasants, as well as soldiers. Caught up in this torrent, the party-state also gave priority to ideological purity rather than professionalism in the assessment of state administrators.[6]

In addition, the communist party-state was distinguished by its strong capacity to penetrate society and the economy. For the first time in Chinese history, the party-state was able to exert political control vertically from the center all the way down to the village, the family, and the individual. Notably, the party sponsored social organizations like labor unions, peasant associations, and youth leagues, while incapacitating or banning independent groups. The agricultural production teams in the collectives and communes, and the urban work units in state enterprises, through their control over the dissemination of valued goods and services, also played an important role in social control and mobilization (Walder 1986; Whyte and Parish 1984). At the same time, the party-state vastly expanded its traditional functions to encompass not only tax collection and maintenance of social order, but also new functions such as education, healthcare, marriage, culture, economic growth, and socialist development. We have already seen that, through the land reform and collectivization, the communist party-state assured its control over agricultural production and gained access to its surplus. Similarly, nationalization of business enterprises enabled the party-state to direct the economy as it saw fit. In all the social and economic domains, state planning replaced the market, collective goals overshadowed individual interests, and special attention was given to egalitarianism and national security under state socialism during the Maoist era.

For example, in the domains of education and scientific research, which had direct implications for China's economic development, the concerns with egalitarianism were unmistakable. From the start, elementary and junior middle education was provided for all eligible youngsters for moderate tuition fees. This early strategy, while successful in generating more or less universal primary education, could not address the problems of school dropout among children of poorer peasants, variations in school quality, and the reliance on academic results as a sorting mechanism. By the 1960s, it became clear that children with worker, peasant, and peddler origins tended to get fewer years of education from schools of poorer quality. By contrast, as the entrance into "key-point" schools was determined as much by academic examinations as by recommendations, these elite schools admitted mainly children of the new administrative cadres and those of older professionals and intellectuals (Whyte and Parish 1984, p. 46).

Policies were adopted to reverse this tendency toward growing inequality in the education system, which was considered highly undesirable by the radical leaders of the Cultural Revolution era. Academic excellence was abandoned as a sorting criterion. To use the resource to support a larger student population, work periods during school increased and the length of pre-college education was reduced from twelve to nine or ten years (Whyte and Parish 1984, p. 50). From the start of the Cultural Revolution, admissions of undergraduates were stopped for six years and graduate students for twelve years. Peasant and working-class students were admitted to "attend, manage, and reform universities" and, in 1971, a plan was proposed to consolidate, close, and reconstruct 106 of the 471 institutions of higher education (Hannum et al. 2008, p. 216).

The new revolutionary policies attained most of their objectives to promote egalitarianism. Advantages wielded by children of the cadres, former capitalists, and professionals dissipated. With "special schools closed, and exams watered down, worker, peasant, and other 'good class' children simply passed through the school system for their allotted number of years" (Whyte and Parish 1984, p. 50). Unfortunately, this attempt to narrow education to "a common denominator" had denied talented youths the opportunity to acquire sophisticated skills and advanced knowledge, while the abolition of technical and vocational schools deprived the country of skilled technical workers. In 1978, China's adult literacy rate had reached 66 percent, whereas 93 percent and 51 percent of people in the appropriate age groups were enrolled in primary schools and secondary schools, respectively. While these developments had brought China closer to being a middle-income country, no more than 1 percent of people between 20 and 24 years of age were enrolled in institutes of higher education, which ranked China among the worst of the low-income economies (Nolan and Ash 1995).

STATE SOCIALISM: POLICY FAILURES, ECONOMIC GROWTH, AND THE CRITICAL TRANSITION

It would not be easy to assess the overall impacts of China's experiment with state socialism. For one thing, there is a lack of reliable statistics, which is inevitable given China's geographical spans and other deficiencies that undermined accurate record-keeping. For another, the Cold War period was a time fraught with ideological contention. Just as left-oriented scholars had lavished the country's socialist experiment with fervent support, neoliberal scholars were never shy of stinging criticisms. It would therefore be difficult to sift through all the conflicting information and arguments to arrive at an objective position to assess the state socialist period.

Policy Failures: The Great Leap Forward and the Cultural Revolution

In the literature, it is often reported that the communist party-state endured rounds of policy-induced failures in the first three decades of its emergence. The Great Leap Forward (1958–61) and the Great Proletarian Cultural Revolution (1966–76) were the most notable among them.

Impatient with China's pace of industrialization, Mao Zedong proposed in November 1957 that the country would overtake Britain in industrial production within fifteen years. To achieve this goal, agricultural production teams were organized hastily into large-scale communes and peasants were mobilized to undertake non-agricultural tasks such as mining, ore-transportation, and iron-smelting in so-called "backyard furnaces" (Kung and Lin 2003; Peng 1987). It is reported that some 3 million tons of the steel produced in these backyard furnaces was of such poor quality that half of it was considered a total waste. The crops that were due to be harvested in the autumn of 1958 were left to rot in the fields as the communes devoted themselves to steel manufacturing. The level of grain production actually declined for three consecutive years. Owing to the poor harvest and the urban-biased grain procurement policy, between 16.5 million and as many as 30 million people died in the three-year period[7] (Kung and Lin 2003).

In turn, efforts to promote egalitarianism and concern with the reemergence of an elite social class had led Mao Zedong to declare in late 1965 that socialist revolution in China was not yet complete. Responding to Mao's call to become Red Guards, some tens of millions of young students from all over the country congregated in Beijing the following year and undertook to "destroy the Four Olds" (old ideas, culture, customs, and habits). Throughout 1967 and into 1968, they were encouraged to oust state officials and take over many parts of the CCP establishment. The ensuing chaos led Mao to demobilize the Red Guards in mid-1968 and declare officially in April 1969 the conclusion of the Cultural Revolution. However, it was not until eight years later, when Mao died in 1976, that the ultra-leftist Red Guard faction (i.e. the "Gang of Four") was finally expelled from positions of power (Fairbank 1986, p. 317). Today, the Chinese authority labels the Cultural Revolution "ten cataclysmic years" that caused "millions of deaths and left some 100 million people scarred victims" (Pye 1986, p. 597).

The Socialist Legacy

In sum, it is often argued in the literature that the socialist experiment under Mao was a disaster. The Great Leap Forward in the late 1950s led to famine and the deaths of tens of millions of Chinese. The ten years of the Cultural Revolution turned Chinese society upside down and induced massive political anarchy. In this scenario, China's march to modernization began only in 1978, after the rise of Deng Xiaoping, a pragmatist who paid little attention to Mao's revolutionary ideology. Deng became the hero of Chinese modernization, whereas Mao was held responsible for the economic backwardness and political turmoil in the first thirty years of communist rule.

What is missing in the above account, however, is the important way in which the historical heritage of the Maoist state socialist era has contributed to China's present development miracle (Bramall 1993). Despite its many shortcomings, the Maoist legacy has provided China with a strong Leninist party-state that has a high degree of legitimacy, autonomy, and capacity. The party-state was able to build a strong organizational framework capable of mobilizing popular energies for large-scale infrastructural projects. In turn, the rural infrastructure and related local institutions were instrumental for carrying out the post-1978 economic reforms.

Specifically, it was during the Maoist era, the Great Leap Forward in particular, that the state mobilized millions of peasants to construct and improve dams, reservoirs, drainage networks, and irrigation systems. It was also during the socialist experiment that rural industries and enterprises were set up in the communes, local officials accumulated managerial experience and human capital through running the commune and brigade enterprises, and local governments were asked to promote development in the community. The Maoist commune model and its decentralization policy provided the medium to tap local resources, to train local leaders, and to arouse local initiatives. Without all these infrastructural and institutional foundations built in the Maoist era, it is doubtful whether agricultural productivity could have increased so rapidly in the early 1980s, whether rural entrepreneurs could have emerged so quickly from the local official stratum, whether local village and township enterprises could have played the leading role in China's industrialization since 1978, and whether the local forces could have played such an important role in the country's remarkable economic development.

Economic Growth and Structural Transformation

Researchers should detect the positive legacy of the socialist experiment if they care to look beyond the lens of Cold War ideology. For example, despite the above policy failures in the Great Leap Forward and the Cultural Revolution, China did achieve rapid economic growth and significant structural transformation over the three decades' socialist experiment.

China's GDP grew annually at an average rate of 7 percent between 1952 and 1978, and at 5 percent between 1960 and 1981, which compared most favorably with the 1 percent achieved by all the "low-income countries excluding China and India" (Chinability 2014; see also Nolan and Ash 1995, p. 981). Between 1952 and 1976, industry grew at about 11 percent per year, whereas grain output grew at about 2.4 percent per year, which outpaced population growth of slightly over 2 percent by a narrow margin (Lippit 1982, p. 141).

In addition, China had experienced significant structural transformation over the state socialist era. As a result of the heavy industrialization program of the party-state, China's *industry* occupied an elevated position and contributed 47 percent to the country's GDP, whereas agriculture and services contributed 31 percent and 22 percent, respectively. China had significantly industrialized on the eve of the transition to state neoliberalism (Nolan and Ash 1995, p. 983).

In view of the positive legacy of the state socialist era, researchers should raise a different question, namely, why did the communist party-state fail to go further, propel China to economic takeoff, and attain remarkable economic growth?

We argue that although the communist party-state had the capacity to mobilize resources and to pursue its developmental goals, *socialist ideology* and Cold War hostility together limited its chance of attaining remarkable economic development. The communist party-state was inclined to attack "capitalist roaders" who deviated from official socialist policy, and this ideological rigidity was reinforced during the 1950s and 1960s by the Cold War, whose line of conflict was drawn between capitalism and communism. Part and parcel of the Cold War tension was the United States' stringent effort to contain Chinese communism from spreading to other places. Before the era of neoliberal globalization in the 1980s, China was forced to withdraw from the capitalist world economy owing to this strong hostility from the US and the anti-communist front.

Indeed, China's growth in industry and agriculture during the socialist era was made possible by its own heavy capital investment and massive labor input, respectively. While China could rely on its own resources to pursue this investment-driven growth for a short while, its continuation over an extended period required the influx of capital, the injection of new technology, and the expansion of domestic and global markets, all of which were lacking owing to China's withdrawal from the capitalist world economy during the Cold War years.

Short of these inputs, China encountered much difficulty disentangling itself from constraints and structural dislocations that were inherent in the strategies of development it pursued. They were, namely, the problem of low productivity, an urban-industrial bias, and the stagnation (if not decline) of the real income of workers and peasants.

First, both agriculture and industry suffered from the problem of low productivity. Drawing upon official statistics, Peter Nolan and

Robert F. Ash (1995, p. 982) found that the incremental output–capital ratio was halved between the First and the Fourth Five-Year Plans. Referring more specifically to agricultural labor productivity, Lippit (1982, p. 141) also found that, measured on a labor-day basis, it had fallen by between 15 and 36 percent between 1957 and 1975. In the view of many economists, low productivity could be attributed to the rigidity of the planned economy and the lack of appropriate incentives.[8] For one, many of the small-scale enterprises were inefficient because they had often been required to produce capital goods (Nolan and Ash 1995, p. 982). For another, owing to the urge among the large and very large enterprises to hoard resources and their tendency to produce all spare parts and machinery requirement in-shop, they often produced small-batch output at below-optimal scale. Above all, despite the grave wastages and inefficiency of these enterprises, managers and workers could hold onto their jobs without penalty (K. Chen et al. 1988). Agriculture experienced similar constraints. Having exhausted the economies of scale gained during the initial phase of collectivization, inefficiency set in as the peasants found their efforts and inputs poorly reflected in the work-point system (Shue 1980).

China's second constraint was its urban-industrial bias. With the country's effort to promote heavy industry, it gleaned an agricultural surplus and injected no more than 8 to 13 percent of the government's investment from 1960 to 1978 into agriculture (UNFAO 1999, p. 129). To prevent the unbridled sprawl of urban slums, the *hukou* system was introduced to lock the peasants in the villages. The resultant underdevelopment of the agricultural sector and deficiency in raw material production were said to have backfired and circumscribed China's industrial growth. In turn, labor power, which was locked into the rural area by the *hukou* system, had been left underutilized.

Third, China's general public and especially the peasants had suffered stagnation if not decline in their real income and consumption as the communist party-state expropriated agricultural surplus for investment (Z. Hu and Khan 1997). Lippit, drawing upon information released after the conclusion of the Cultural Revolution, described the situation as follows:

> In 1957, per capita income from collective labor in the countryside was 57 yuan, half in cash and half in kind. It fell sharply during the Great Leap Forward, recovered up to 1965, and thereafter rose to 65 yuan in 1977. Thus over a twenty-year period, real income rose by 8 yuan, equivalent to US$5.2. ... Since we know that over the same interval the collective labor effort per person increased sharply, the real income per hour worked actually fell. (Lippit 1982, p. 129; see also Selden 1993, p. 22)

As for the urban industrial workers, the pattern of frequent wage increases that occurred during the years of the First Five-Year Plan was broken for two decades after 1957.

To conclude, three decades of state socialism had indeed provided China with a solid economic foundation. Its rate of economic growth during the era of state socialism, as we have seen, far exceeded most developing countries. However, having reached a moderate level of development, China's economy had run into a distinct barrier, namely, *low productivity despite massive capital and labor input.* The problem with the Chinese socialist economy, as Lippit (1982, pp. 142–4) suggested, was that it "vanquishes flexibility, timeliness and, perhaps most important, the initiative and ingenuity of the cadres and workers responsible for production." It also failed to tap the capitalist world economy for capital, market, and technology.

The question becomes: how could China overcome this structural barrier to promote rapid economic development after 1978?

THE CRITICAL TRANSITION IN 1978

The year 1978 marked the historical turning point when China started the so-called "reform and opening up" policy to reintegrate itself back into the capitalist world economy, thus initiating the critical transition from state socialism to a post-socialist economy.

This critical transition was ratified and launched at the Third Plenary Session of the Eleventh Central Committee of the Chinese Communist Party in December 1978. Since then, China has experimented with various policies that have gradually, sometimes hesitantly, yet nonetheless unambiguously, led it toward what we call "state neoliberalism." Why did China initiate the critical transition in 1978? And what made this possible?

The Fading of the Cold War and Neoliberal Globalization

If the Cold War and the forced withdrawal from the world economy prevented China from pursuing either export-oriented industrialization or import substitution, the fading of the Cold War since the 1970s provided the precondition for the country to reenter the world economy to pursue its developmental objectives.

The late 1970s was a period of declining American hegemony. Economically, the US faced the problems of inflation, low productivity, and recession. Its products were under strong competition from Japanese and German manufacturers in the world market. Politically, the US was still plagued by its defeat in Vietnam and its failed attempt to fend off global Soviet expansionism. At this historical conjuncture, the US welcomed China back to the world economy, as exemplified by Henry Kissinger's historic visit to Beijing in 1971, China's displacement of Taiwan to become a member of the United Nations in the same year, and the establishment of the diplomatic relationship between the US and China in 1979. China was seen by the US as a potential new regional power to counterbalance Soviet military expansion and Japanese economic expansion in East Asia. Moreover, the vast Chinese market, cheap Chinese labor, and abundant Chinese raw materials and minerals could considerably increase the competitive power of American industry in the world market.

In addition, the United States and other developed economies ran into increasing difficulties in the early 1970s as the rigidity of Fordism began to take effect (Harvey 1990). The rising strength of labor unions heightened the cost of production and decreased the competitiveness of these economies, whereas the increase in welfare expenditure threatened these countries with budget deficits. To tackle their problems, these economies adopted the neoliberal globalization project, including global sourcing and global marketing, international subcontracting, and the relocation of their industries to the less developed economies.

East Asian Industrial Relocation

In addition, the Chinese party-state was impressed with the economic success of its East Asian neighbors. With US support in the 1950s and the 1960s, Japan, South Korea, Taiwan, and Hong Kong had become highly industrialized and their people enjoyed a much higher living standard than that in China. Thus, the Chinese communist party-state was motivated to follow the path of its successful East Asian neighbors to engage in export-oriented industrialization.

Furthermore, as Hong Kong, Taiwan, and South Korea were upgraded to the status of newly industrialized economies (NIEs) in the late 1970s, they gradually lost their geopolitical privileges with the US. They, too, had to face trade restrictions (tariffs, quotas, and pressure to raise their exchange rates). Owing to their economic success, the East Asian NIEs also experienced labor shortages, increasing labor disputes, escalating land prices, and the emergence of environmental protests – all of which served to raise the costs of production. As a result, the East Asian NIEs felt the need to promote an industrial relocation in the 1980s so as to secure a stable supply of cheap, docile labor and other resources.

Industrial relocation of the NIEs presented an excellent opportunity for the Chinese state to promote developmental objectives. From the Chinese perspective, China could be a favorable site for the NIEs' relocation because it has abundant cheap labor, land, and other resources. China is also quite close to Hong Kong, Taiwan, and South Korea, and they share a common Confucian cultural heritage. Therefore, China initiated an open-door policy to set up four special economic zones (SEZs) in 1979, opened fourteen coastal cities and Hainan Island in 1984 and three delta areas in 1985 for foreign investment, and pursued a coastal developmental strategy to enhance export industrialization in 1988 (So 2001).

Growing Societal Dissatisfaction: Stagnant Income and Political Alienation

As the previous section has shown, the level of income in both the rural and urban areas had stagnated for two decades, and per capita consumption of food grains and edible oil in 1978 was actually lower than that of 1957 (Selden 1993, p. 21). Walder (1982, p. 222) relates how most workers experienced the Cultural Revolution "as little more than (1) discontinuation of regular wage increases, (2) cancellation of bonuses tied to work performance, and (3) intensification of political study, campaigns, and criticism sessions." In view of the peasants' sacrifice for urban industrialization, they were unlikely to be any more enthusiastic than the workers. In fact, they had every reason to be skeptical about the constant policy changes and lost faith in the ability of the party-state to improve their livelihood after thirty years of socialist experiment.

In addition, there was the problem of political alienation. A long period of political struggle during the Cultural Revolution had alienated the general population, making them highly cynical about the slogans of class struggle and absolute egalitarianism. It seems ironic that in just a few years, the revolutionary fervor and intense ideological struggles of the Cultural Revolution were replaced by widespread disillusionment and political alienation.

The Undercurrent against Ultra-Leftism

According to Tang Tsou and his colleagues (1982, pp. 277–8), a certain ideological undercurrent emerged alongside the ascendency of ultra-leftist policy in the Great Leap Forward and the Cultural Revolution. The political forces in this countercurrent consisted of

> almost all of the leaders and cadres at every level who had been disgraced, persecuted, or pushed aside during the Cultural Revolution and during the purge of anti-Party elements after the Lushan Conference of 1959; all intellectuals, scientists, technical personnel, educators, and other professionals who had suffered from one kind of denunciation or another since 1957; and those moderate leaders who had reluctantly gone along with the ultra-leftist policies of Mao....

Backed by the growing societal dissatisfaction over stagnant income and political alienation, these leaders and cadres came to believe that a change of direction from ultra-leftist policies was necessary. If two decades of experiment with radical egalitarianism and never-ending social mobilization had only led to economic stagnation and popular dissatisfaction, it was about time to try alternative strategies, in particular, those that paid greater attention to individual interests and sought to unleash the forces of production. Only in so doing could the party hold on to its leadership position.

Triggering Events

Even if the fading of the Cold War, the industrial relocation of the NIEs, growing societal dissatisfaction, and the undercurrent against ultra-leftist policies presented the precondition and incentive for communist party-state leaders to drop state socialist programs, it still required several triggering events to overcome the inertia of the communist status quo.

Yimin Lin (2003) points out that the critical event that set in motion the efforts to reform the economic system was the passing of the old generation of revolutionary leaders. The death of Mao in 1976 was followed by the rise of a new coalition of political leaders who were leaning toward or receptive to some form of economic institutional change. Most of them were victims of the Cultural Revolution. Their return was accompanied by a national rehabilitation of lower-level party-state functionaries. Most of these functionaries had prior experience in formulating and implementing economic policies.

Yimin Lin (2003) further explains that the shift in policy focus from socialist egalitarianism to economic development and the reshuffling of local leaders opened the way for bottom-up institutional innovation. In provinces like Anhui, pro-reform leaders tolerated and even encouraged certain attempts made by grassroots officials. This significantly changed the political risk perceived by the rank-and-file of the local state apparatus. Subsequently, when severe national disasters hit between 1977 and 1979, some local officials resorted to various forms of family production and justified their rule-breaking on the ground of coping with these emergencies.

The good results of family farming in turn provided a ground of justification for the arrangement to be introduced to other provinces, which later led to decollectivization and the institutionalization of the household responsibility system in the countryside. The great success of the economic reforms in the agricultural sector – as shown by the crop output growth from 2.5 percent between 1954 and 1978 to 5.9 percent between 1978 and 1984 – further empowered the Chinese state to pursue various developmental strategies (Zweig 1989).

The Slippery Path of Economic Reforms

Selden (1993) remarks that the *initial* phases of reform in 1978 and the early 1980s were not without historical antecedents. In fact, they were quite similar in spirit to those undertaken by the party in the 1930s when it fought the anti-Japanese war and in the early 1950s when collectivization was initiated. These policies aimed to gain the allegiance of a wide segment of the population, and they were endorsed as much by Mao Zedong as by the more moderate leaders of the party. Particular policies pursued in the late 1970s had also previously been given trial runs. For example, the policies of greater enterprise autonomy and flexible pricing in mid-1979 were not too different from those put forth in September 1956 (Solinger 1993, pp. 14–15; see also Fewsmith 2008).

Indeed, up until the early 1990s, the reforms were still pretty moderate. The changes were confined merely to the development of a commodity economy around the planned one. In the beginning, no attempt was made to privatize or bankrupt the state and collective enterprises. At the same time, massive restrictions were imposed on personal entrepreneurship and private enterprises, while foreign investors were confined to special economic zones set up in the southern parts of the country. Save for the "Gang of Four," there was no attempt to purge ultra-leftist elements within the party. Similarly, with the state enterprises and the state sector intact, state managers and the privileged state-sector workers suffered no massive layoffs.

The gradual approach to market reform and its coexistence with socialist practices also suggest that Deng Xiaoping was not entirely putting up a façade when he characterized his approach as "crossing the river by groping the stones" and his reform policy as "market socialism." In his understanding and that of his followers, the incorporation of market mechanisms into a collective-ownership system was by no means a betrayal of socialist principles. In fact, Deng had introduced this kind of policy before in the era of state socialism, especially right after the failure of the Great Leap Forward in 1958. Martin Hart-Landsberg and Paul Burkett (2005) argue that the increasing drift of the Chinese economy onto a slippery path in the direction of state neoliberalism was not something the party-state leaders had foreseen in the very beginning of the critical transition in 1978.

In sum, it was the interplay between several global, political, and historical factors that explained China's critical transition to a post-socialist economy in 1978. The fading of the Cold War, the rise of the neoliberal globalization project, and the industrial relocation of the NIEs had provided the global precondition for the critical transition. Growing societal dissatisfaction over income stagnation and political alienation made the Chinese population more receptive to try a path of development other than state socialism; and the emergence of a certain undercurrent against ultra-Leftism served to mobilize the support of middle-class professionals and former disgraced state officials against the Maoists and the Red Guards. Finally, historical factors – including the triggering events and the slippery path of reforms – came into play. The passing of Mao and other senior revolutionary leaders in the mid-1970s helped to clear the way for the reforms. Even though the reforms were initially very moderate and were not too different from the previous polices, they would soon drive China onto a slippery path with no return, quickly transforming it from a poor, backward economy to a global economic powerhouse in the twenty-first century – a topic we are going to explore in the next few chapters.

State Neoliberalism: The Political Economy of China's Rise

3

The "reform and opening up" policy initiated in 1978 is identified by the Chinese authorities as marking the critical transition from "state socialism" to "market socialism." There is no question that 1978 did mark an important turning point, not least the start of astounding annual growth rates of nearly 10 percent for some three decades. However, as this chapter will show, the so-called "transition" was permeated with hesitations, crises, and policy reversals. Taking a long-term perspective, most of the policies initiated during the 1980s and 1990s involved deregulation, marketization, and privatization, which set China on a course of reform that assumes many characteristics of neoliberal capitalism. However, the communist party-state continued to occupy the driver's seat in the country's economic development and upheld socialism as its guiding ideology. Over time, as human devastation set in as a result of the neoliberal reforms, social conflicts involving workers and peasants surged, while disgruntled state elites also took the opportunity of intermittent crises to criticize the reforms. The notion "state neoliberalism" is coined to capture the dual tendency of an avowed socialist state that led national development along the path of neoliberal capitalism, with the acute contradictions that this entailed, and the resultant policy hesitations and reversals. While state neoliberalism refers to an ongoing process rather than an attained condition, the terms "neoliberalization" and "emergence/consolidation of state neoliberalism" will be used in the following to characterize, respectively, the relative prevalence of market-led and state-led policies at particular phases of development.

In the following sections, we shall examine the series of policy transitions after 1978 that propelled China increasingly toward state neoliberalism. The first section will examine the policies introduced immediately after 1978, highlighting above all the trend toward neoliberalization in the 1980s. The second section will analyze the emerging contradictions and their culmination in the 1989 Tiananmen tragedy as well as the stop-gap measures adopted between 1989 and 1992. These measures made possible the strengthening of state power and indicated the historical emergence of state neoliberalism in the three-year interim. However, when the communist party-state regained political control and restored social order, it quickly started another wave of neoliberalism in the second half of the 1990s. The third section will examine policy changes after 1992, analyzing the deepening of neoliberalism, especially the stringent effort to dismantle the state sector. The final section then presents an overview of the social contradictions and conflicts that ensued as well as the policy responses introduced after 2003. It will argue that growing social conflict, coupled with the once-a-decade leadership transition, led to the consolidation of state neoliberalism between 2003 and 2012.

THE 1978 TRANSITION AND THE TREND TOWARD NEOLIBERALIZATION (1978–89)

As pointed out in the previous chapter, the 1978 policy change was to a large extent a state-initiated reform from above. Since the 1978 transition was not a revolution, the communist party-state was not weakened by the process. Instead, it continued to be very strong and had the capacity to carry out all sorts of developmental policies.

The first phase of reform was introduced formally through the issuance of policy statements at the Plenary Sessions of the Chinese Communist Party in December 1978 and in October 1984. Although the cumulative outcomes of these policies were marketization, proletarianization, and privatization, there had been no attempt to reform basic economic institutions. Policy changes in 1978 were confined to the development of a commodity economy alongside the planned one. They were geared toward the enhancing of productivity, exploring export promotion, introducing foreign investment, and learning advanced scientific knowledge, as well as changing production relations through the decentralization of management and remuneration of workers according to their work (ZZDYY 2002, pp. 26–8). The reform was pursued cautiously: most of the changes started with the rural sector and were trialed in remote provinces before being introduced to Beijing or Shanghai. Quite unlike the cases of the former Soviet Union and Eastern Europe, which undertook a course of "shock therapy," reform in China was marked by gradualism (Sachs and Woo 1994, 2000). The following pages will look at these changes analytically.

Decollectivization

One of the first reforms to take place was the decollectivization of agricultural production. Before the reform, peasants were organized into production teams, brigades, and, after 1958, communes. They undertook production tasks collectively, sold their grain and other agricultural products to the state, shared the income based on a highly egalitarian work-point system, and were given access to basic education, rural healthcare, and other infrastructures provided by the collectives. Because of the low procurement prices and other factors, including China's rapid population growth, peasants' consumption levels remained stagnant over a prolonged period.

In the late 1970s, villages threatened by low agricultural productivity were said to have taken initiatives to abandon the commune system and experiment with what had come to be known as the *"household responsibility system."* This bottom-up viewpoint was disputed by other scholars, who pointed to the importance of state coercion instead[1] (Bernstein 1999; A. Chan et al. 1992; J. Y. Lin 1988; Z. Xu 2013). Regardless, decollectivization was considered to be complete nation-wide by 1983 (F. Cai et al. 2008). In this new system, land continued to be owned collectively by the village, but households were given the option of contracting out plots of land to cultivate crops of their choice, sell the surplus in the market, and be responsible for their own gains and losses.

At the same time, commune and brigade enterprises were trans-formed into *township and village enterprises* (TVEs).[2] Even as the TVEs faced harder budget constraints than the state-owned enter-prises (SOEs), they were also less regulated. To the surprise of state officials and other observers, the TVEs thrived, became a locus of entrepreneurship, and generated ample competitive pressure for the SOEs. Indeed, the number of TVEs increased sharply from 1.5 million in 1978 to 12 million in 1985 (Yasheng Huang 2010, p. 5). Further-more, even though the TVEs were owned collectively at the beginning, private TVEs soon emerged. Citing the Ministry of Agriculture data, Yasheng Huang (2010, p. 6) contended that some 10.5 million of the 12 million TVEs in 1985 were actually private (cf. Naughton 1994; Nee 1992; Walder 1995, p. 966).

In highlighting the fabulous success of the (private) TVEs, it must be emphasized that the communist party-state during this period placed tremendous restrictions on personal entrepreneurship and private enterprises. Until 1984, in order to prevent exploitation, rural entrepreneurs were not encouraged to hire more than seven employees (L. Zhou and Xie 2008, p. 12; ZZDYY 2002, p. 35). Personal entre-preneurship (*geti jinying*) in cities and townships was permitted slightly later in 1979, mainly to ease the pressure of unemployment among youths returning from the countryside. Hence, even though private enterprises (*siying qiye*) employing eight workers or more were thought to have emerged as early as 1983, their legal status was affirmed only after the April 1988 constitutional reform. Many of these personal entrepreneurs and private enterprises (or alliance enterprises) were counted as private TVEs, the dramatic growth of which during the 1980s has just been noted.

The TVEs absorbed a large number of surplus rural laborers and served as the precursor of flexible labor practices. According to one source, the level of TVE employment grew phenomenally from 28 million in 1978 to 70 million in 1985 and 123 million by 1993 (F. Cai et al. 2008). Yasheng Huang (2010, p. 7) calculated that, in 1985, collective TVEs employed 41.5 million people as compared with 4.75 million in private-run TVEs and 23.5 million in household businesses.

Reforms of State and Collective Enterprises

The reform of state and collective enterprises was another goal spelt out in the December 1978 policy transition (ZZDYY 2002, pp. 26–8). However, the reform was very moderate during this period. It was confined initially to the decentralization of management; some forms of profit-sharing between the state, management, and workers; permission to sell surplus products at higher prices; clearer delineation of responsibilities among the manager, enterprise, and the state; as well as permission for employees to invest in the shares of their firms (ZZDYY 2002, p. 186). These policies had to be tested out in Sichuan before being introduced to Beijing, Tianjin, and Shanghai; the more drastic measures of privatization, bankruptcy, and merger were out of the question at this stage.

Proletarianization of the Peasantry

Going hand in hand with decollectivization and the reform of state enterprises were proletarianization of the peasantry and the emergence of an urban labor market. For the peasants, the loss of collective social rights in the countryside meant that they had to face burdensome user charges for schools, medical care, and the like. Apart from working for the TVEs, they were also enticed by the expansion in non-state employment opportunities to migrate into the cities. Owing to the rigidity of the *hukou* system, these peasant workers were initially not authorized to migrate and had no right of urban residency. Only in 1985 were procedures introduced to allow the peasants to register, with permits and later identity cards, as temporary urban residents. Even then, their rights as citizens were limited and precarious. It is not easy to estimate the number of peasant-workers in the 1980s. To give a rough indication, some 44 million people were found to reside in 1995 within urban areas using temporary residential permits (K. W. Chan 2003). Given their dubious legal status, the "floating population" was subjected to exploitation on a grand scale, and formed an immense labor reserve that placed tremendous downward pressure on the wages of urban workers (Pun 1999).

Emergence of an Urban Labor Market

Before the 1978 reform, urban workers and prospective employers were matched by the Bureau of Labor and Personnel, with individual workers and managers of the enterprises having very little say in the process. The work units (*danwei*) paid the workers subsistence wages and provided them with housing, healthcare, childcare, pensions, and related benefits (F. Cai et al. 2008; Walder 1986). After the "contract labor" system was introduced in the mid-1980s, the share of contract workers in total employment increased from 4 percent in 1985 to 39 percent in 1995 (F. Cai et al. 2008).

Up to the late 1990s, the communist party-state still exercised tight control over the dismissal of workers and the municipal governments still continued to place new graduates in government or state-sector jobs. Nonetheless, the neoliberal practice introduced in the mid-1980s had facilitated the rise of flexible labor practices, made possible the hiring and firing of workers on the basis of productivity and efficiency, and gradually put an end to lifelong employment and the job security guaranteed in the era of state socialism.

The emergence of private enterprises after the mid-1980s also led to the expansion of private sector employment, which indirectly contributed to the rise of an urban labor market. According to official statistics, the share of state-owned enterprises in urban employment dropped from 78 percent in 1978 to 70 percent in 1989, indicating a moderate but unmistakable turn in the tide (F. Cai et al. 2008).

Reentry into the Capitalist World Economy

A centerpiece of the 1978 reform was to reengage with the capitalist world economy. To this end, policies were devised to decentralize import/export decisions to local government, replace administrative restrictions on international trade with tariffs and quotas, loosen up the control over foreign exchange, and, above all, set up four special economic zones in Shenzhen, Zhuhai, Xiamen, and Shantou in 1979, and opened up fourteen coastal cities for foreign investment in 1986. This effort has been lauded as a massive success. China's total export doubled between 1978 and 1989, raising the country's rank in world export from thirty-second to thirteenth during the same period. Foreign direct investment (FDI) also increased from practically non-existent before 1979 to a cumulative value of US$34.5 billion in 1992. In this early period, Hong Kong played a particularly strategic role. The island's share of FDI was above 50 percent for practically all the years between 1984 and 1990, with Japan and the United States as the next most important contributors, supplying around 10 percent each (Wei 1995, p. 75). The emphasis on export and the opening up of China to foreign direct investment, among other things, exposed

Chinese enterprises and workers to the imperatives of the capitalist world economy.

Once again, it has to be stressed that the policies were pursued with caution and restraint. Trade remained very much monitored and regulated by state agencies, whereas overseas investors initially worked in collaboration with local partners and within a handful of carefully selected special economic zones that were located in the southern part of the country and far removed from the national center (ZZDYY 2002, p. 93).

The Communist Party-State and Gradualism

All the above changes were initiated (or sanctioned) and orchestrated by the communist party-state. As mentioned in the previous chapter, the Chinese Communist Party set up modern bureaucratic machinery when it took power in 1949. Ministries and departments responsible for economic planning, production, tax collection, labor deployment, education, welfare, family affairs, and social order were established in a way that placed all aspects of socio-economic life in a modern society under the purview of the state. The party-state also came to oversee all aspects of socio-political lives, regulating if not monopolizing the organization of labor, women, youth, religious believers, academic and professional bodies, as well as other civil society organizations and political associations.

A distinguishing feature of China's approach to economic transition was gradualism, which contrasted sharply with the former Soviet Union and Eastern Europe, which, as we have noted, adopted "shock therapy" or wholesale political and economic reform (Sachs and Woo 1994, 2000). As the above has shown, the state sector remained intact even as a market economy and neoliberal practices emerged around it. There was also no attempt on the part of the CCP leaders to initiate political reform.

The Chinese communist party-state, which pursued economic reform with a view to strengthening its rule, was understandably wary about undercutting the state sector, discharging state managers *en masse*, or introducing political reform. Above all else, China did not need to pursue radical economic or political reform. The country benefited from the high level of decentralization that occurred during the Cultural Revolution, which inadvertently formed the political counterweight for reform (Walder 1994, 1995). TVEs, mentioned above, which emerged through the conversion of commune and brigade establishments, were considered by observers to be non-state yet non-private enterprises that had prospered and generated much market competition. The success of these firms soon led the state enterprises to demand the same flexibility in management (Goldstein 1995). By the same token, provincial politicians and local officials emerged as the reformist counterweight to the conservative center, and enabled Deng Xiaoping to "push his reform program through the bureaucratic decision-making process and avoid the risks of changing the political rules of the game"[3] (Shirk 1993, p. 14; cf. H. Cai and Treisman 2006; Konai 1986; Montinola et al. 1995).

Policies of decollectivization and foreign investment examined above demonstrated quite clearly that there were ample incentives for cadres at the provincial level to pursue the reforms. Fiscal reform, which will be examined here, was another pertinent case in point. For thirty years since 1949, much of the country's tax revenue came from state-owned enterprises. Most important, even as local governments participated in the generation of tax revenue, they had no discretionary spending rights. In general, while the central government was responsible for national defense, economic development, and the administration of national institutions, sub-national governments were to deliver day-to-day public administration and social services such as education, healthcare, and social security, with deficits to be covered by the "intergovernmental transfer system" (Shen et al. 2012, pp. 4–5). The pre-reform fiscal system therefore provided few incentives for local governments and enterprises to raise their revenues.

To redress this issue, several rounds of fiscal reform were initiated, namely, the 1980 "contract responsibility system," the 1985 "modified contract responsibility system," and the 1988 "fiscal contracting system." With these, local governments were authorized to collect taxes, although various revenue-sharing schemes were negotiated and put into place to address the issue of fiscal deficits that emerged as a result of the localities' differential capabilities in revenue generation (Shen et al. 2012, pp. 6–7). The fiscal decentralization policy allowed the local states to become independent fiscal entities with unprecedented rights to use the revenue they retained (Oi 1992; S. Wang 1997). The fiscal reform made it feasible and generated incentives for local governments to encourage (or at least not obstruct) entrepreneurial activities. The room opened up for inter-local competition also generated unprecedented levels of economic dynamism (Whyte 2009).

THE TIANANMEN CRACKDOWN AND THE EMERGENCE OF STATE NEOLIBERALISM (1989–92)

As pointed out above, leaders of the party-state introduced economic reforms gradually without making direct changes to the state sector. Despite the cautious approach, a decade-long neoliberal reform project set in and, intertwined with the preexisting socialist institutions, caused considerable social dislocations in the Chinese economy and social conflict in Chinese society. By the mid-1980s, food production slowed down. Inflation surged by 18.5 percent between 1987 and 1988 as a result of the oversupply of credit and overdevelopment of industries (ZZDYY 2002, p. 232). The "double-track" pricing system generated scope for profiteering and corruption among the cadres and cadre-capitalists (ZZDYY 2002, p. 220). Workers showed signs of discontent as neoliberal reforms began to exert tighter control over work schedules and raised work quotas. A government source estimated that 70 percent of enterprises got rich through profiteering and speculation, while another source revealed that the private sector had evaded from 70 to 80 percent of its taxes (So and Hua 1992). Mounting dissatisfaction coupled with examples from Eastern Europe led to requests for social and political reform.

In 1989, these economic problems and social grievances triggered a robust democracy movement that led to a confrontation between protesters and the party-state in Beijing's central Tiananmen Square. The Tiananmen Incident was the first major challenge to the Chinese communist party-state during the post-socialist era. It led to the bloody suppression of the protesters and serious political division within the party-state between the so-called "reformist" faction (which was pro-neoliberal reform) and the "conservative" faction (which was skeptical of such reform). What then happened after the Tiananmen crackdown?

First of all, in the next few years, economic construction ceased to be the party-state's core mission. Instead, a number of stop-gap measures were introduced to tackle the socio-economic problems induced by the first decade of economic reform. On the one hand, the CCP took steps to evaluate the conduct of party members and to strengthen ideological education within the party and its auxiliary organizations. It passed a number of resolutions between 1989 and 1990 to address the problem of corruption and other abuses of authority among the cadres and their children. Efforts were also made to open more channels of communication with the people (ZZDYY 2002, pp. 250–63). On the other hand, the party proceeded to tackle China's structural dislocation problems, addressing the issues of the "dual-track" pricing system, "triangular loans," inflation, and the over-rapid expansion of light industries before the basic infrastructure was ready, among others (ZZDYY 2002, pp. 273–7). Economic reforms, together with the trend of neoliberalization, were halted.

Second, in contrast to the image of a weakened state in much of the neoliberal literature, the communist party-state considerably strengthened its managerial and fiscal capacity during the aftermath of the Tiananmen Incident. A new *"cadre responsibility system"* was instituted in the early 1990s by the central party-state to strengthen its control over the evaluation and monitoring of local leaders. County party secretaries and township heads signed performance contracts, pledged to attain certain targets laid down by higher levels, and were held personally responsible for attaining those targets. There were different contracts for different fields, such as industrial development, agricultural development, tax collection, family planning, and social order. The communist party-state had the capacity to be selective, that is, to implement its priority policies, to control the appointment of its key local leaders, and to target strategically important areas. Thus, Maria Edin (2003, p. 36) argues that "state capacity, defined here as the capacity to control and monitor lower-level agents, has increased in China, and that the Chinese Communist Party is capable of greater institutional adaptability than it is usually given credit for" (see also Whiting 2001; Zhu 2003).

Third, the state *strengthened its fiscal capacity*. Despite the alleged success of the earlier round of tax reform in the 1980s in providing incentives for economic reform among local governments, it weakened the central state's extractive capacity. The latter was unable to control local governments' extra-budgetary funds and experienced so drastic a decline in tax revenue that it was considered to have lost effective control over China's economic life[4] (Oi 1992). In 1994, a more thorough fiscal reform took place. Among other things, it simplified the tax structure, unified the tax burden on taxpayers, and devised a set of rules – the *tax assignment system*[5] *(fenshuizhi)* – to guide the system of central–local revenue- and expenditure-sharing. Significantly, "taxes that can be used in the pursuit of maintaining national objectives are assigned as central tax; taxes considered more relevant to economic development are assigned as share tax; whereas taxes more suitable for collection and administration by local governments are deemed local taxes" (Shen et al. 2012, pp. 13–14). In turn, the central government is responsible for nationwide services such as national defense, foreign affairs, and macroeconomic control, whereas sub-national governments are responsible for delivering most public goods and services as well as the development of the local economy. Together with the establishment in 1994–5 of the National Tax Services (NTS) in all provinces to collect central-fixed and shared taxes, the fiscal reform helped to curb fiscal decline and provided sufficient resources to the central government (Shen et al. 2012, p. 11).

The 1994 fiscal reform was a great success. The unified tax system forbade local governments from giving tax exemptions, thus halting the fall in the ratio of revenue to GDP. Formation of the NTS, collection of value-added tax (VAT), and the tax assignment system also made it possible for the central government's share of total revenue to jump from 22 percent in 1993 to 56 percent in 1994, and for it to stay above 50 percent until 2005. In turn, the central and sub-national governments' share in total expenditure were 1125.55 billion yuan and 3,527.30 billion yuan, or 24 percent and 76 percent, respectively, in 2005 (Shen et al. 2012, p. 16). Given the hierarchical assignment of responsibility, the county and township governments were particularly burdened (see also Loo and Chow 2006). As pointed out by Yongnian Zheng (2004, pp. 118–19), the tax assignment system shifted fiscal power from the provinces to the center, so "now, it is the provinces that rely on the central government for revenue."

Fourth, in contrast to the neoliberal doctrine's call for less intervention, the Chinese state intervened more in the economy once it recentralized and enhanced its administrative and fiscal capacity in the aftermath of the Tiananmen Incident. It engaged in debt-financed investments in mega-projects to transform physical infrastructures. Astonishing rates of urbanization (no fewer than forty-two cities expanded beyond the 1 million population mark after 1992) also required huge investments of fixed capital. New subway systems and highways were built in major cities, and 8,500 miles of new railroad were proposed to link the interior to the economically dynamic coastal zone. China also tried to build an interstate highway system more extensive than America's in just fifteen years, while practically every large city was building or had just completed a big new airport. These mega-projects had the potential to absorb surpluses of capital and labor for several years to come (Harvey 2005, p. 132). It was these massive debt-financing infrastructural and fixed-capital formation projects that made the Chinese state depart from the neoliberal orthodoxy and act like a Keynesian state.

Fifth, the party-state also made concerted efforts to enhance the country's technological capability. On May 6, 1995, the State Council promulgated the "Decisions on Speeding Up Progress in Science and Technology," which announced the policy of "advancing the nation with science and education" (*kejiao xingguo*). Among other matters, it advocated the use of science and technology to increase productivity and achieve economic and social development, and in turn the use of economic reform as a platform to revitalize scientific research (ZZDYY 2002, pp. 393–402). To facilitate such development, the Science Committee made a number of long- and short-term plans: whereas the central state injected 2.5 billion yuan over the five-year period of 1998–2002, universities, research centers, and private enterprises were asked to increase their levels of collaboration.

The above new policies seem to indicate that there emerged a new path of "state neoliberalism" in China in the aftermath of the Tiananmen crackdown between 1989 and 1992. In this period, we observed a halt (or a reversal) of the neoliberal policies of the 1980s. This period also observed the centrality of the state in the development process, with the communist party-state recentralized and rebuilt after the Tiananmen Incident, making it more capable, more resourceful, and more interventionist. Finally, as neoliberal practices tend to intensify social contradictions and conflict in society, state neoliberalism is aimed to soften the rising social conflict in order to enhance the legitimacy of the communist party-state and to prolong its survival in the post-socialist era.

However, since the communist party-state saw the above state neoliberal policies merely as a stop-gap measure to deal with the 1989 democracy protests, it was inclined to drop the most interventionist practices after the democracy protest had died down, its power was restored, and its survival was no longer at stake.

A number of factors have underlain the return of neoliberal "reform and opening up" policies in the wake of the Tiananmen Incident. In the first place, although the leaders of the conservative faction attributed the social disorders leading up to the Tiananmen protests to the policies of neoliberal reform, a return to the planned economy seemed unpopular. A decade of reform facilitated rapid economic growth and led to the rise of living standards among the Chinese population, which contrasted sharply with the first thirty years of socialist experiment. Even as the reform may have hurt the interest of state enterprise managers, it benefited a vast number of local state officials, private entrepreneurs, and professionals. On the other hand, the harm of neoliberal reforms was still not so obvious in the 1990s. This perhaps explained the enthusiastic response given to Deng Xiaoping's 1991 and 1992 speeches to local party leaders in the provinces. Hence, if a return to the planned economy was politically a lost cause, deepening the neoliberal reform could possibly gain the support of the majority of the people.

In the second place, intertwined with the contestation between divergent economic interests and political values was the problem of legitimacy. As Xue Liang Ding (1994) argued, the Tiananmen crackdown pushed popular disillusionment with communist ideology to the limit and undermined the party's legitimacy to rule. Deepening reform and greater prosperity appeared to be the only alternative. In this connection, it was perhaps not accidental that Deng's commitment to reform was hardened by the failure of the 1991 Soviet coup. Although an unswerving adherence to socialist planned economy might delay the collapse of the Soviet Union, it could not prevent it. A reform that promised economic betterment for the public without compromising the party's political domination was then chosen as the way forward.

THE DEEPENING OF NEOLIBERALISM (1993–2003)

Having reconsolidated its institutional capacity and resolved on the future direction, the communist party-state proceeded to deepen neoliberal reform. In fact, neoliberalism did not just come back to China for a decade between 1993 and 2003, but it did so with a vengeance. The party-state under the leadership of President Jiang Zemin issued several policy proposals, which in general fortified a more comprehensive course toward neoliberalism. The sections below will examine the deepening of neoliberalism in the period, focusing on the following four policy changes which were particularly remarkable.

Privatization and Corporatization

The state-owned enterprises, which were subjected to very mild reforms in the 1980s, become the target of reorganization in the 1990s. The decision to turn the SOEs into "modern enterprises" was declared at the Fourteenth Party Congress held in October 1992 and a few measures were introduced to this end. Among them, the 1994 policy of *"seizing the large and letting go of the small"* (*zhuada fangxiao*) was most significant. While encouraging the largest SOEs to expand into inter-regional, inter-industrial conglomerates that excel in production, technology, trade, and, in some cases, to get them listed on the stock market, the policy also made it possible to privatize or even bankrupt the smaller, less efficient, and loss-making ones. The process was slow at the beginning, yet large and unsustainable losses incurred by the SOEs during the 1997 financial crisis threatened the solvency of the banking system, which led the Chinese state to initiate aggressive restructuring. The number of industrial SOEs dropped sharply from about 85,000 in 1994 to about 47,000 in 2001 (Fewsmith 2008; R. Yang and Zhang 2003; Jefferson and Su 2006).

Of equal importance was the adoption in 1993 of a system of corporate law that sought to introduce a more sophisticated structure of corporate governance and property rights. Depending on the extent of state ownership, the law required that a board of directors and a CEO be appointed, in some cases to be supplemented by a board of supervisors and a general meeting of the shareholders (Aivazian et al. 2005). The new governance structure was expected to give incentives to the management for the pursuit of profit and to make them accountable for their business decisions. With privatization, corporatization, and the introduction of the shareholding system, the SOEs could no longer depend on the state for funding, but had to operate independently in the market in the search for profit.

To complete the restructuring of the SOEs, changes in labor regulations were also introduced by the Ministry of Labor to allow the listed SOEs to set their own wages by taking into account skill and productivity in addition to occupation and rank. Most important, the SOEs were given permission to lay off redundant workers and, in some cases, government subsidies were provided to reduce workers' resistance. According to Fang Cai and his colleagues (2008), "the number of state sector workers fell from a peak of 113 million in 1995 to 88 million in 1998 and 64 million in 2004," which means the state enterprises laid off 49 million workers in nine years. As another indication, the share of SOEs in urban employment dropped drastically from 70.2 percent in 1989 to 28.9 percent in 2002, and further to 18.4 percent in 2012 (F. Cai et al. 2008; National Bureau of Statistics 2014b).

Farewell to Welfare and Hello to the Commodification
of Human Services

If reforms introduced in the 1980s greatly retrenched human services such as healthcare, housing, education, and pensions, the SOE and labor market reform introduced in the 1990s rendered the cutbacks almost complete. This was because SOE privatization required not only the permission to lay off workers, but also the portability of social benefits. To prepare for this, insurance at the municipal and provincial levels was pooled together in the 1990s and, beginning in 1994, public housing was sold to the current occupants at highly subsidized prices. New SOE employees were asked to find accommodation in the emerging private housing market, whereas workers in general had to pay a part of the costs for services and social insurance, such as pensions, medical care, and the newly created unemployment insurance, higher education, and many personal services (Guan 2000).

Joining the World Trade Organization

This particular phase of reform also saw the opening up of many more cities in China to investment by overseas Chinese and foreigners. To facilitate international trade, the Chinese state reduced import tariffs, abandoned its long-standing policy of artificially overvaluing the renminbi, eliminated the double-track exchange rates system, and introduced a market-based exchange rate regime.

The trends of marketization and opening up to foreign investors intensified as China became a member of the World Trade Organization on December 11, 2001. The process led to a further dismantling of trade barriers, the removal of subsidies, an assault on the state sector, the savaging of the countryside, and a near unquestioning orientation toward the export market strategy (Petras 2006). More specifically, it involved a sharp reduction in the tariffs for agricultural produce and the opening up of the services sector of telecommunications, banking, and insurance to foreign investors. Over time, the production of an increasing number of products and services, whether for export or local consumption, was subjected to the imperatives of the capitalist world economy.

There were a few other institutional reforms, including commodity price management and the banking system, the details of which cannot be reported here. However, as in the above, neoliberalism deepened at the same time that state power was reconsolidated. Hence, just as efforts were made to differentiate commercial-oriented financial institutions from policy-oriented ones, a central bank was set up. The latter allowed the party-state to use "economic tools" such as the control of the money supply and the interest rate, in addition to administrative measures, to maintain macroeconomic stability (ZZDYY 2002, p. 315).

The Recruitment of Capitalists into the Communist Party

In 2000, Jiang Zemin articulated the viewpoint that the party was able to attain public support because it had always represented the future direction for China's progressive culture, the fundamental interests of China's people, and, above all, the developmental needs of China's progressive social productive forces at different stages of development. This idea, which came to be known as the "Three Representatives" (*sange dai biao*), was formalized in the speech delivered by Jiang at the eightieth anniversary meeting of the Chinese Communist Party held on July 1, 2001. He emphasized that China was still at an early stage of socialist development and it was in its interest to broaden its social base. Consequently, when the party adopted a revised constitution in 2002, it stated that in addition to workers, peasants, soldiers, and intellectuals, progressive elements from other social strata aged 18 or above who identified with the party could apply to become its members.

For the first time in history, then, private entrepreneurs could become members of the Chinese Communist Party (Xinhua News 2002). Although communist theoreticians might not have been impressed by Jiang's viewpoint, the constitutional change generated an official channel for the party to co-opt exceptional members of the nascent social classes and formally allowed it to provide leadership for all segments of the population. It also legitimized the presence of private entrepreneurs in "socialist" China and gave these individuals a sense of security they lacked before. These new capitalist party-members also would provide the social basis to support the drive to neoliberalization in the future.

Taken together, these measures reveal that, instead of a return to the planned economy, the party-state in China decided to deepen its neo-liberal reform in the aftermath of the Tiananmen crackdown. Ruthless capitalist principles were applied to hitherto protected institutions, such as the state-owned enterprises, SOE employees, and the financial institutions. Inefficient state enterprises were sold off or bankrupted, while workers were laid off on a massive scale. A wide range of social benefits were also retrenched. Even capitalists were invited to join the communist party-state. However, the deepening of neoliberalism was not accompanied by the weakening of the state. The newly introduced "cadre responsibility system" and the "tax assignment system" allowed the communist party-state to reconsolidate its power and enhance its administrative-cum-fiscal capacity. The institutional reforms also released the party-state from some of its burdens, generated new policy tools, and rendered it more nimble and more capable of making strategic interventions.

We want to point out that administrative and fiscal reforms introduced after 1992 intensified, if not triggered, what Alvin So (2007a) called *the bifurcation of the Chinese state* into the benign central state and malign local ones. The 1978 reform allowed the local state apparatus to acquire "greater managerial power over public enterprises, more flexibility in local budgetary processes, increased freedom to approve foreign investment and to engage in international trade, and expanded jurisdiction over resource distribution and taxation" (So 2007a, p. 564). With the 1994 tax reform and the bankruptcy of numerous TVEs after the 1980s, many township and village governments were almost always in debt. The "cadre responsibility system," while introduced with good intentions, had the inopportune effect of awarding cadres who had no scruples about the means deployed in achieving governmental goals (J. F. Lin et al. 2006, cited in So 2007a; Shukai Zhao 2004). Hence, at the same time that local governments sought to cope with their fiscal deficits with mechanisms such as "deferring wages, borrowing from the budgets of various local government bureaux, or cutting expenditure on social development" (So 2007a, p. 566), others even resorted to the collection of extra (non-approved) tax, arbitrary fees, and land expropriation. Thus, whether by design or accident, the deepening of neoliberalism in China led inadvertently to the emergence of local predatory states, the repercussions of which were increasingly felt in the country (Y. Cai 2005; Oi and Zhao 2007; So 2007b).

GROWING SOCIAL CONFLICT AND THE CONSOLIDATION OF STATE NEOLIBERALISM (2003–12)

Neoliberal practices, introduced to China in 1978, were deepened in the second half of the 1990s. Although China's economic performance continued to be impeccable, growing on average around 10 percent between 1992 and 2003, it was attained at the cost of deep social divisions and growing social conflicts. Indeed, the repercussions of neoliberal practices could be detected as early as the late 1980s. With the deepening of neoliberalism after 1992, the divisions and conflicts also became more intense, and the party-state leaders found it necessary to provide more concerted responses lest they lose control over the country. The following section will examine the emergence of social differentiation in the form of social classes, the rise of social protests, and then the policies pursued by the state leaders to regain their moral-political leadership.

Income Inequality and Class Differentiation

During the era of state socialism from the 1950s to the 1970s, China was considered a model of achieving equality under socialism and became one of the most egalitarian societies in the world. However, when China started to abandon its socialist planned economy in urban areas in the early 1980s, its level of equality plummeted and it became one of the world's most unequal countries (F. Wang 2008).

In tandem with the rise in income inequality was the sharpening of class differentiation. In a 1999 study of four cities with different levels of development, Xueyi Lu (2002) and his colleagues found that economic reform had led to fundamental changes in the class structure. The share of production workers and business service workers increased to 22.6 percent and 12 percent, respectively, thus reducing the share of agricultural workers to 44 percent from the height of 70 percent in 1978. This drastic structural transformation led to the emergence of professional technical personnel (5.1 percent), owners of private enterprises (0.6 percent), and personal entrepreneurs (4.2 percent).[6] With their superior command of knowledge and capital, these nascent social actors could be expected to be more aggressive in advancing their social, economic, and political interests.

While Lu and his colleagues found in 1995 that most people considered their livelihood to have improved since 1978, 15–24 percent of those surveyed in 2001 found their living standards to have deteriorated since 1995 (Lu 2002, p. 38; see also S. Wang et al. 2002). The disgruntled were mostly from the lower social classes, including personal entrepreneurs, production workers, service workers, and peasants. More recently, the 2005 China General Social Survey found that most people considered it necessary to impose higher taxes on the rich, and felt that the government should do much more to help the poor (Wu 2009).

Dissent and Social Protests

The decade after 1992 was characterized by the surge of social protests, individual and collective, institutionalized or otherwise. The number of "letters and visits" (*xinfang*) and collective petitions (*jiti shangfang*), two institutionalized mechanisms of voicing dissent, reached 10.2 million by 2000, or an increase of 115 percent over 1995 (C.-k. Lee 2007, p. 231). Just as important, the number of "mass incidents" increased from some 8,700 cases in 1993 to about 60,000 in 2003, with the number of participants increasing from 730,000 to 3.07 million, respectively (Sun 2011). Speaking in relation to the year 2004, the Minister of Public Security noted that there were some 74,000 cases of "mass disturbances" (*quntixing tefa shijian*) with more than 3.8 million people involved.[7]

Labor disputes and peasant land rights were the most prevalent causes of petitions and mass disturbances, though there were many other points of contention. Protests in relation to land rights were reported as early as 1993, and a few of the disputes involved tens of thousands of participants and some protests went on for months (Thornton 2004, cited in So 2007a; Chu Y.-w. 2007). At the same time, the number of labor dispute arbitrations increased from 19,098 in 1994 to 154,621 in 2001 (C.-k. Lee 2007). With the emergence of various grassroots efforts to build new labor institutions under the rubric of service, education, and health, workers had become more conscious of their rights and knowledgeable of the strategies of protest open to them. Finally, although the middle-class professionals and private entrepreneurs were numerically small and their positions were politically precarious, they showed signs of coalescing into forms of organizations that portended the growth of the civil society (B. He 2003; Howell and Pearce 2001).

How did the communist party-state tackle the challenges of rising income inequality, class differentiation, and social protests that emerged in the course of China's neoliberal deepening?

The Consolidation of State Neoliberalism

To contain the disruptive impacts of neoliberal practices, enable the continued expansion of capitalism in China, and preserve the party-state's moral-political leadership, the party center promoted itself as the defender of national interests and redresser of the most outrageous inequalities by initiating the "socialist countryside" and the "labor contract law" as a means to develop a "harmonious society."

In 2002, President Jiang Zemin, who served as China's top leader for more than thirteen years, retired. President Jiang was inclined to pursue economic growth at all costs and presided over the deepening of neoliberal reforms, including corporatization and privatization, commodification of human services, accession to the WTO, and introduction of "The Three Representatives" policy to recruit capitalists into the communist party.

Jiang's regime was succeeded by that of President Hu Jintao and Premier Wen Jiabao in 2003. Responding to China's escalating social resistance and class conflicts, and perhaps reflecting a change of ideological orientation in the Chinese state, the new regime began to institute "state neoliberalism." While market reforms would continue, the state would also play a more active role in moderating the negative impacts of marketization. Instead of one-sided emphasis on GDP growth, the new leadership proposed that the country should aim at "comprehensive, coordinated, sustainable development, and promote comprehensive economic, social, and human development" (Fewsmith 2008, p. 252; see also Kahn 2006). More specifically, the new leadership shifted its priorities to emphasize *environmental sustainability* and *social development*.

In 2006, the Hu/Wen regime promoted the policies of "building a new socialist countryside" and a "harmonious society" (Saich 2007). These policies advocated a transfer of resources from the state to strengthen the fiscal foundation of the countryside. In this connection, the party-state *abolished the agricultural tax* so as to relieve the peasantry's burden; it also increased its rural expenditure by 15 percent (to US$15 billion) to bankroll guaranteed minimum living allowances for farmers, and an 87 percent hike (to US$4 billion) for the healthcare budget (Melinda Liu 2007). These policies indicate a massive infusion of funding from the state for the peasants and rural areas. In addition, there has been a *de-commodification of human services*. As part of a national campaign to eliminate school fees in the countryside for the first nine years of education, rural residents were exempted from paying primary school tuition fees as well as many miscellaneous charges levied by the schools. The state also increased its subsidies for rural health cooperatives that would become available in 80 percent of the rural counties. This marked major progress, for rural residents had originally had to pay market rates at the villages' private clinics; most peasants did not have medical insurance and spent more than 80 percent of their cash on healthcare (Melinda Liu 2007).

The new policy also aimed at *reducing social inequality*, especially the widening gap between the countryside and the city. Thus, pensions were no longer given solely to people enjoying the privileged status of registered urban residents, but made available to everyone. Likewise, the party-state promoted the spread of the Minimum Living Standard Assistance for the rural population, which opened for the first time the real possibility of instituting a social safety net that would cover the entire population, urban or rural (*Economist* 2006; Hussain 2005).

At the same time, the working conditions were so appalling and employer–employee relationships so abusive that the central government decided to introduce a new "Labor Contract Law." As one example of the abusive relationships, wages that remained unpaid to peasant-workers up to 2003 amounted to a total of 100 billion yuan. The Labor Contract Law was legislated in June 2007 and was to take effect by January 1, 2008 (State Council 2007). Among other things, the Law made provision for negotiations between employers, workers, and/or their representatives on such matters as remunerations, working hours, holidays, occupational safety, training, and labor discipline. There were also other provisions that, if implemented, could benefit the workers tremendously.

We argue that the above new polices indicate the consolidation of state neoliberalism between 2003 and 2012. Unlike the emergent phase of state neoliberalism right after the Tiananmen Incident, this consolidation phase lasted longer (ten years), was more clearly articulated through the concepts of "balanced development, a new socialist countryside and harmonious society," and had more policy impacts (e.g. the abolition of agricultural tax) than the stop-gap measures between 1989 and 1992. As we will discuss in the next chapter, the policies of state neoliberalism would get further consolidated when China faced the challenge of the 2008 global economic crisis.

As policies of reparation, there were obvious limits to Hu's initiatives for a harmonious society. In the first place, those policies were introduced in the context of escalating dissatisfactions and inflammatory social conditions. They were by no means attempts to facilitate a fundamental alteration of state–society relationships.

Second and related, despite better social welfare and enhanced "rights" for workers and peasants, these were handed out without any intention of enfranchising these subterranean social actors. The policies were to be implemented through government agencies and measures were taken to prevent the emergence of autonomous labor and peasant organizations. At the same time, Hu Jintao and Wen Jiabao were presented as enlightened leaders, or indeed patriarchs, who in their genuine care for the poor and benighted people had gone out of their way to help them. It was perhaps not accidental that they addressed themselves as "Hu Yeye" (Grandpapa Hu) or "Wen Yeye" (Grandpapa Wen) when coming face to face with the nation's young people.

In the third place, although Hu Jintao demonstrated his concern with distributive justice and talked about the need to develop socialist democracy, the rule of law, and improve the governing capability of the party, his inclination was far from liberal in the Western sense. In responding to the problems of corruption and the alleged inability of the central government to control sub-provincial officials, he actually called for the strengthening of party discipline as a means to better control the government bureaucracy. Measures included "democratic recommendation, democratic assessment, multi-candidate examination, public announcement before appointment, and open selection and competition for post," or in other words "inner-Party democracy" (Fewsmith 2008, p. 256). This, according to Joseph Fewsmith, actually reversed the liberal reforms since the 1980s, which had sought to separate the government from the party.

Finally, and most importantly, the policies failed to address the country's key contradiction. As argued above, policies introduced after 1978 and those in the aftermath of the Tiananmen crackdown encouraged the nascent capitalists and local-level state managers to undertake profit-making activities, whereas the "tax assignment system" and "cadre responsibility system" effectively forced the local cadres into embracing neoliberalism, however ruthless it was (So 2007a; cf. S. Wang et al. 2002). The central state could continue to hold the moral high ground, maintain its authority, and condemn local state managers and nascent capitalists for the exploitation of workers, plundering of the environment, and corrupt behavior. However, so long as the neoliberal policies and the central–local relationship remain unchanged, all the initiatives to promote a "harmonious society" could do no more than to contain the worst damage or tackle the surface symptoms of neoliberalism.

CONCLUSION

This chapter has reviewed China's experiment with neoliberal capitalism between 1979 and 2012. In the course of doing so, we have suggested that the communist party-state orchestrated neoliberalization as a means of attaining national development and holding onto political leadership. Unlike the former Soviet Union or Eastern Europe, the country did not adopt "shock therapy" but pursued piecemeal changes interrupted by intervals of policy reversals.

Specifically, while the first stage of reform introduced in 1979 launched decollectivization, proletarianization, and commensurate changes, it left the state sector more or less intact. Despite this restraint, however, neoliberal practices generated enough conflicts and contradictions to lead to a showdown in the 1989 Tiananmen Incident.

After that, the party-state called a brief retreat from neoliberal development in 1989–92. During those few years, economic development ceased to be a foremost concern and policies indicating the emergence of state neoliberalism were introduced. However, robust economic growth during 1978–89, rising living standards among the Chinese population, and the strong support from local officials, especially those in the southern provinces, made it possible for neoliberal reform to return with a vengeance.

After 1992, there was a deepening of neoliberalism once the party-state had recentralized, regained its administrative and fiscal capacity, and reassumed an active role in the economy. Hence, at the same time that we observed the provision of state support to the big state enter-prises in the strategic sector, the injection of massive state funding for technology research and education, and the tireless state effort at mac-roeconomic stabilization by non-administrative means, we also observed the bankruptcy and the privatization of many small and inef-ficient state enterprises in the non-strategic sector and the opening of many economic sectors to foreign firms.

Finally, even though China did not experience any more political crises (like the Tiananmen Incident), hardship brought about by the decade-long intensification of neoliberalism did culminate in petitions, protests, demonstrations, and civil unrest. In 2003, during the leader-ship transition, the party-state changed its course again, launched the politics of a harmonious society, strived for balanced development, and introduced more policies for social protection in ways comparable to Polanyi's "double movement."[8]

The above process of state-led development exemplifies what we call "state neoliberalism." As examined in detail in the introductory chapter, the term signifies the centrality of the Chinese state in directing the country's post-1978 development, its continued appeal to the socialist ideology, its instrumental roles in imposing blatant neoliberal practices, the resultant surge of acute social contradictions, and the tendency for policy hesitation and reversals.

In addition, the above provides hints as to why China pursued gradualist economic reform rather than adopted "shock therapy" as in the case of the former Soviet Union and the Eastern European coun-tries. Specifically, decentralization introduced during the Cultural Revolution had already provided China with a political counterweight to the state center, which was conservative and inclined to resist eco-nomic reform. So long as local governments embraced economic reform, it was unnecessary to initiate political reforms. Furthermore, unlike the Eastern European countries eager to part with their socialist pasts, the Chinese Communist Party undertook neoliberalization so as to stay in power, and it understandably proceeded gradually and confined reform to the economic arena.

Finally, the above discussion points to the policies of a harmonious society as measures to address the worst abuses of neoliberalism. However, so long as the general public was not "enfranchised," it was doubtful if the new Labor Contract Law, the new policies of the "social-ist countryside," and even the timid party reform to curb corruption could take effect (see Pun 2008). The inherent contradictions in state neoliberalism, we contend, will still set China on a politically fluctuat-ing course in the years to come.

The Global Economic Crisis and the Deepening of State Neoliberalism

THE GLOBAL ECONOMIC CRISIS

In 2008, the subprime mortgage crisis in the United States grew into the deepest economic crisis since the 1930s Great Depression. The crisis was not simply confined to the financial sector, but has spread to the larger global economy. The 2008 crisis not only marked the end of the golden era of unbridled free-market economics in the United States, but also could serve as the turning point of the capitalist world economy.

At the onset of the global financial crisis in 2008, there was speculation whether China might seize upon it as an opportunity to rise up to become a dominant player in the capitalist world economy (Hung 2009). However, since the country's economic growth is mostly export-driven, it faced very serious economic problems, and social protests triggered by the crisis. Indeed, at its onset in fall 2008, China's exports slowed drastically, declining by more than 20 percent from the previous year (Barboza 2009). Nouriel Roubini (2008) reported that China might be on its way to a hard landing, as the macro data from China all pointed toward a sharp deceleration of economic growth, drastically reduced spending on consumer durables, declining home sales, and an acute fall in construction activities. As a result, unemployment became a growing concern in urban areas in late 2008. China needed a growth rate of at least 5 percent to absorb about 24 million people joining the labor force each year. The sharp decline of export trade left millions without work and set off a wave of social instability.

In the light of the above gloomy data, researchers began to speculate whether China was heading toward a crisis. Eamon Javers (2009) argued that the Chinese economic miracle was nothing but a paper dragon. The Chinese had dangerously overheated their economy, building malls, luxury stores, and infrastructure for which there was almost no demand, and the entire system was teetering toward collapse. Ho-fung Hung doubted that China could challenge the United States after the crisis. He argued that the crisis had deepened China's market and financial dependence on the United States and that China would remain "America's head servant" in the near future (Hung 2009, p. 5). Because China was so dependent on foreign technology, production, and markets, Martin Hart-Landsberg (2010, p. 28) similarly contended that the crisis had, at best, had minor effects on current Chinese economic strategies and could not possibly lead to the rise of China as a global economic power.

In contrast to the above interpretations, Alvin So (2012) claimed that China emerged strengthened from the 2008 global economic crisis. The crisis provided not only a golden opportunity for China to strengthen its state neoliberalism model, but also a chance to expand its power in the inter-state system. It also increased the probability that China would rise as a global power and signaled a shift of the center of global capital accumulation from the West to the East in the twenty-first century.

This chapter will first discuss how China took advantage of the 2008 global economic crisis, leading to the deepening of state neoliberalism, including the expansion of the state sector, the strengthening of state capacity, and the realignment of social forces in society. Although state neoliberalism jumpstarted the Chinese economy in the short term (2008–12), it also produced many unintended structural problems. Consequently, when the global economic crisis continued into the 2010s, there were calls, after the decade-long leadership transition (to President Xi Jinping and Premier Li Keqiang), to launch another wave of neoliberalism, including more market liberalization and market competition, in order to resolve the problem of the decelerating economic growth rate.

CHINA'S RESPONSE TO THE CRISIS IN 2008

State neoliberalism enabled China to respond quickly to the crisis. Beijing announced a massive stimulus program in early November 2008 – only seven weeks after the Lehman Brothers collapse. China's stimulus package was budgeted at 4 trillion yuan (US$586 billion), which was equivalent to 13.3 percent of China's 2008 GDP. It is one of the largest economic stimulus packages (both in spending levels and as a percentage of GDP) that has been announced by the world's major economies to date. The package included the following key items (Morrison 2009, p. 6):

+ public transport infrastructure (37.5 percent), including railways, highways, airports, and ports;
+ the rebuilding of areas hit by disasters (25 percent), including areas hit by an earthquake in Sichuan Province in May 2008;
+ affordable public housing (10 percent);
+ rural infrastructure (9.3 percent), including irrigation, drinking water, electricity, and transport;
+ technological innovation (9.3 percent), including research development and structural change;
+ healthcare and education (3.8 percent); and
+ environmental projects (5.3 percent).

China's stimulus program was aimed both to promote capital accumulation and to soften the acute social contradictions that have emerged in Chinese society over the past few decades.

In order to promote capital accumulation, the state targeted ten strategic industries (i.e. those deemed by the state to be vital to China's economic growth) to enhance their long-term competitiveness. Those industries included autos, steel, shipbuilding, textiles, machinery, electronics and information, non-ferrous metals, and logistics. State support policies for the ten industries included tax cuts and incentives (such as tax rebates), industry subsidies and subsidies to consumers to purchase certain products (such as consumer goods and autos), fiscal support, directives to banks to provide financing, direct funds to support technology upgrading and the development of domestic brands, government procurement policies, and funding to help firms invest overseas (Morrison 2009, p. 7).

In addition, the stimulus program was aimed at softening the acute contradictions that had emerged as a result of rapid development over the past three decades, such as the rising gap between city and countryside, and the growing inequalities and conflict among different sectors of Chinese society.

Thus, on April 7, 2009, the state announced plans to spend an additional US$124 billion over the next three years to create a universal healthcare system. The health plan would attempt to extend basic coverage to most of the population by 2011, and would invest in public hospitals and training for village and community doctors. A number of efforts were made to boost rural incomes and spending levels and to narrow the gap in living standards between rural and urban citizens. For example, since February 2009, an estimated 900 million Chinese rural residents have been eligible to receive a 13 percent rebate for purchase of home appliances (Morrison 2009, p. 7).

In short, the stimulus programs sought to encourage consumer spending as a means to bolster the domestic economy. To attain the latter goal, the party-state also sought to improve collective consumption and social insurance, contending that, unless the social safety net and social insurance were expanded, Chinese consumers would be more inclined to save than to spend, and the enlarged domestic market would not be able to offset the slack in the export market caused by the global economic crisis of 2008–9.

In retrospect, China's stimulus package has worked very well. Whereas the United States, Japan, and the "big four" European countries of Germany, France, Britain, and Italy suffered a contraction of up to 4 percent in their economies in 2009, China still managed to attain a GDP growth rate of 9 percent in that year (Hiro 2010). By 2010, newspapers consistently reported that China's economy was roaring ahead:

* *New York Times:* "China surged past the United States to become the world's largest automobile market – in units, if not in dollars, figures" (Wines 2010a).
* *USA Today:* "China is on track to overtake Japan as the second-largest economy behind the USA this year, cementing its status as one of the world's most formidable superpowers" (K. Chu 2010).
* *New York Times:* "China is also on track to make nearly half of the world's wind turbines this year … and the country passed the United States last year as the world's largest wind turbine market" (Bradsher 2010a)

What has been the impact of the stimulus program on China? How has it affected the country's economy, polity, and society? This chapter argues that the stimulus program has made a significant impact on China, leading to the deepening of state neoliberalism, the strengthening of state capacity, and the realignment of social forces in society.

THE DEEPENING OF STATE NEOLIBERALISM

"Guo Jin, Min Tui"

There was a huge expansion of the state sector at the expense of the private sector, aptly expressed in the catchphrase "*guo jin, min tui*" or "the state advances, the private sector retreats." During 2008–9, investment by state-controlled companies skyrocketed, driven by hundreds of billions of yuan of government spending and state bank lending to combat the global financial crisis.

There are no comprehensive statistics to catalog the expansion of the state's influence on the economy, so the shift is partly inferred from such coarse measures as the share of financing in the economy provided by state banks (which sharply rose during the financial crisis); the number of private firms (one) versus state-owned enterprises (ninety-nine) in the 100 largest publicly listed Chinese companies; or the growing political and financial influence of China's state-owned giants – 129 huge conglomerates that answer directly to the central government, and thousands of smaller ones run by the provinces and cities (Wines 2010b).

While no public breakdown exists, most experts say the vast bulk of the 4 trillion yuan (US$586 billion) stimulus package that China pumped out for new highways, railways, and other big projects went to state-owned companies. Some of the largest state companies used the flood of money to strengthen their dominance in their current market or to enter new ones. Michael Wines (2010b) reports that "some of the upstream state-owned enterprises are now expanding downstream, organizing themselves as vertical units. They are just operating on a much larger scale."

At the local level, Wines (2010b) further reports that the government set up 8,000 state-owned investment companies in 2009 alone to channel government money into business and industrial ventures. A publicized case is the Zhejiang Geely Holding Group, a Chinese automaker which made worldwide headlines in March 2010 when it agreed to buy Sweden's Volvo marque from Ford. Much of the $1.5 billion purchase price came not from Geely's relatively modest profits, but from local governments in northeast China and the Shanghai area.

When China's state-run companies were on the march, there were news stories that neoliberal privatization of the state companies had been blocked. In August 2009, for example, when thousands of workers came out in protests in Linzhou, Henan Province, the provincial government quickly halted the privatization of a state-owned steel mill (Bradsher 2009a).

Upgrading and Relocating

The global economic crisis deepened the fear that the low-cost manufacturing industry that helped propel China's rapid economic growth was becoming obsolete because of the rising cost of production. Government efforts to improve conditions in the interior provinces through the stimulus program have lifted growth in those regions and persuaded many young workers to find jobs closer to home, leading to labor shortages in the coastal provinces. Because of labor shortages, the growing intensity of labor unrest, and government efforts to raise the minimum wage as a means to improve migrant workers' livelihood, pay rates in the Pearl River Delta nearly doubled between 2005 and 2010 (Barboza 2010c).

As a result, manufacturing costs have risen rapidly in China in response to nagging labor shortages and worker demands for higher wages to help offset soaring food and property prices. Those pressures were evident in mid-2010, when a series of big labor strikes in southern China disrupted several Japanese auto factories and resulted in hefty pay raises. There was also the looming prospect that China's currency, the renminbi, would strengthen against other world currencies in the near future, which would make goods produced in China even more expensive to export, and further erode what manufacturers said were already thin profit margins.

Subsequently, in seeking lower costs, manufacturers responded by relocating to poor inland regions of China where wages were as much as 30 percent lower than in the coastal provinces. *China Daily* (2010) reported that rising labor costs triggered industrial relocation from coastal areas to interior provinces: for example, global computer manufacturer Hewlett Packard (HP) and Foxconn International Holdings (a manufacturer of electronic products) planned to jointly invest US$3 billion to build a manufacturing plant for laptops in Chongqing in southwestern China.

In addition to relocation, companies also felt the need to upgrade and to revamp their labor-intensive industries so as to embark on a higher level of development that was encouraged by the government's stimulus program. For instance, the TAL group, which operated an immense garment-making plant, was expanding into supply-chain management for J. C. Penny, one of its big shirt-buyers. Through an extensive computerized system, TAL could stock and restock shirt shelves in all 1,100 of Penney's retail stores in the United States, as demand warranted (Barboza 2010c).

In order to provide technicians, scientists, researchers, and a highly skilled workforce to upgrade China's industries, *China Daily* (2010) reported that the Chinese state issued a Medium and Long-Term Talent Development Plan (2010–20) which aimed at increasing the share of citizens with a higher education background in the workforce from 9.2 percent in 2008 to 20 percent by 2020.

Developing Green Industry

During the global economic crisis, China had stepped up its effort to become a dominant player in green energy, including wind, solar, and geothermal power. Of the US$31.6 billion from the stimulus program allocated to green industries, 51 percent went to solar firms, while the remaining 49 percent went to a diverse cross-section of the economy – materials science, agriculture, water and waste management, energy efficiency, and energy storage (Goswami 2010).

Keith Bradsher (2009b) reported that "Chinese governments at the national, provincial, and even local level have been competing with one another to offer solar companies even more generous subsidies, including free land, and cash for research and development. State-owned banks were flooding the solar industry with loans at considerably lower interest rates than were available in Europe or the United States." For example, Suntech, based in Wuxi, was on track in 2009 to pass Q-Cells of Germany to become the world's second largest supplier of photovoltaic cells. In order to reduce shipping costs and to bypass WTO rules, Suntech planned to go overseas and build a solar panel assembly plant in the United States.

As a result, China has become the world's leading producer of wind turbines and solar panels, and has already begun exporting its technology to the United States (Klare 2010). In the area of green energy, China is rapidly catching up with the advanced capitalist states in the West.

Since China quickly restored its remarkable growth rate in 2009 and 2010, it was widely believed at the time that the state neoliberalism model served the country well, and that growth of 9–10 percent a year would continue for the next decade or longer (Pettis 2013).

CONSOLIDATING THE POWER OF THE COMMUNIST PARTY-STATE

Facing a sharp economic downturn and growing social unrest, the Chinese communist party-state had abundant reasons to move further away from neoliberal capitalism toward state neoliberalism. The advantages of a developmental state, as Prime Minister Wen Jiabo explained in a March 2010 address, "enable [China] to make decisions efficiently, organize effectively, and concentrate resources to accomplish large undertakings" (Wines 2010b).

China's state neoliberalism was well equipped to deal with the global economic crisis during 2008–9 because it had gained considerable experience with designing and implementing stimulus projects a decade earlier during the 1997–8 Asian financial crisis. Harushiko Kuroda, President of the Asian Development Bank, explained that present-day China was more resilient to external shocks than it was a decade before when the Asian crisis hit the region. After years of prudent economic policy making, the country had achieved commendable fiscal consolidation and a strong external position (Kuroda 2009).

In addition, after ten years of intensive financial reform, Chinese banks were in relatively good shape and had ample liquidity to help fund the government-mandated lending. Unlike the United States (the largest debtor nation in the world), China had substantial reserves of foreign currency, sovereign investments, and domestic savings, enabling it to fund its deficits and stimulus spending without requiring external sources of capital. With US$2.2 trillion in reserves, China had a very strong fiscal position (T. Friedman 2009). The Chinese party-state could spend its way out of the global economic crisis for as long as it wished (Y. Yu 2009).

The communist party-state's legitimacy was not undermined by the growing protests during the economic downturn because most of the protests in the countryside and in the city were directed against local governments, not against the central party-state (So 2007a, 2007b). However, in order to prepare for potential social unrest during the global economic crisis, the central state took no chances and further strengthened its repressive apparatus. In late 2008, Hu Jintao, the leader of the Chinese Communist Party, called on the armed forces and police to pull out all the stops to uphold social stability by putting down disturbances and assorted conspiracies spearheaded by anti-China forces. Willy Lam (2009) labeled the above policies as "The Great Leap Backward" because they signaled a sharp U-turn from the more liberal policies of the late 1990s.

The Chinese party-state further consolidated its power when it successfully hosted the Olympic Games in Beijing in summer 2008 and actively participated at "G2" Summits in the inter-state arena.

REALIGNMENT OF SOCIAL FORCES

From the late 1970s onward, China pursued a neoliberal policy to promote export-led industrialization. The state actively promoted decollectivization, proletarianization, marketization, privatization, and corporatization, and opened up its coastal areas for foreign investment. Although these neoliberal policies had led to very rapid economic growth, they had also induced numerous social protests and political movements in the 1980s and 1990s. Despite all this social resistance, Ho-fung Hung (2009, p. 24) argues that the state refused to reorient its neoliberal policy because it was captured by a powerful "elitist faction" which consisted of "officials and entrepreneurs from the coastal provinces."

However, this chapter argues that at the turn of the twenty-first century, under the new Hu/Wen leadership, China adopted a more refined state neoliberal model, moving toward a more balanced development between economic growth and social development. The state would play an increasingly active role in moderating the negative impacts of marketization; instead of focusing narrowly on GDP growth, it included "the people and environment" in its development plan (So 2010b, p. 142). How, then, has the global economic crisis affected the social forces behind China's state neoliberalism?

Intensifying the Conflict between the State and the Transnationals

Both Hung (2009) and Hart-Landsberg (2010) contended that China would be more dependent on the transnationals after the global economic crisis, that is, it might remain as "America's head servant" because of its trade, export, and financial dependence on the United States. This chapter, however, points to a different path of Chinese development during the crisis.

To start with, the global economic crisis has led to a growing conflict between the Chinese state and the global capitalist class. In August 2009, the Chinese government arrested and prosecuted several executives of a foreign mining giant, the Anglo-Australian Rio Tinto, as spies for stealing state secrets. Although the spy charges were later dropped, the Rio Tinto executives still faced lesser charges of bribery and theft of trade secrets. These espionage threats stirred broad unease among the transnational companies operating in China, which feared they could face persecution and closed-door trials for engaging in what much of the business world would regard as bare-knuckle business tactics. As James Feinerman, an expert on Chinese law, commented, "China had undergone 'a real pushback' in the last five years on some fronts, reasserting political dogma in some areas where commercial norms and the rule of law had begun to have more sway" (Wines 2009).

In early 2010, Google threatened to shut down its search engine in China on grounds that the Chinese state had maintained tight control over its sites. However, Barboza (2010d) reported that Google had to leave China because Google, like other American Internet companies, including Yahoo and eBay, failed to gain significant traction in the domestic market and was out-competed by Chinese companies like Baidu, Tencent, and Alibaba.

By late 2010, foreign businesses in China were voicing frustration over the country's heavily regulated market – a bureaucratic maze many transnational capitalists say is designed deliberately to hamstring non-Chinese players to the advantage of their local competitors (Ford 2010). The European Union Chamber of Commerce in China also issued a position paper listing hundreds of market-access problems of foreign companies across a range of industries.

The transnationals' concerns have been heightened in recent years by a series of regulatory changes in China that appeared directly intended to shut out foreigners. For example, a proposal known as "Indigenous Innovation Accreditation" caused alarm among foreign high-tech companies because it set up a complicated licensing system that required companies to register their intellectual property rights (IPR) in China before registering elsewhere in order to qualify (C. Jiang 2010).

Foreign companies also complained loudly that they were being shut out of much of the lucrative government procurement sector. For example, not one of the twenty-five valuable contracts awarded to companies under the Chinese government's 4 trillion yuan (US$586 billion) stimulus program went to a foreign-owned company (C. Jiang 2010).

Adopting a Stronger Pro-worker and Pro-peasant Stand

If the global economic crisis induced the state to take more aggressive steps to protect Chinese industries from the transnationals, the crisis also motivated the state to take a stronger stand to protect Chinese workers from exploitation in the export sector. The new labor contract law took effect in 2008 despite strenuous resistance from the transnational business community, including the American Chamber of Commerce in Shanghai, the US–China Business Council, and the European Union Chamber of Commerce in China (So 2010a).

When a series of wildcat strikes broke out against Honda and Toyota in several cities in south and central China in the summer of 2010, the state allowed the Chinese mass media to cover the strikes in detail. The tacit approval of coverage of the strikes seems to reflect a genuine desire of the Chinese state to see higher wages for workers so as to increase domestic consumption during the global economic crisis. The above speculation is confirmed by the fact that soon after the strike wave in the summer of 2010, various local governments in Shenzhen, Nanhai, and Beijing quickly announced that they would raise the minimum wage by 10–20 percent in the following months (*Insurgent Notes* 2010).

Furthermore, Premier Wen Jiabao bluntly warned Japan in August 2010 during a high-level Japan–China meeting that "its companies operating in China should raise pay for the workers." Wen told the Japanese officials that behind the labor unrest was the relatively low level of pay at some foreign companies (Browne and Shirouzu 2010).

In addition, the decline of exports at the onset of the global economic crisis in fall 2008 also induced the state to engineer a rural prosperity policy as part of its effort to shift the driver of economic growth from export-led industrialization to domestic consumption.

The economic stimulus program included many allocations aimed at promoting collective consumption and social protection in rural areas so as to reduce social inequalities and narrow the gap between city and countryside. For example, as mentioned earlier, US$124 billion was allocated to a healthcare plan which would extend basic coverage, invest in public hospitals, and provide training for village and community doctors; US$59 billion was allocated to improve rural infrastructure such as drinking water, electricity, and transport; another US$59 billion was allocated to affordable public housing targeted to rural areas; and hundreds of millions of rural residents were offered hefty rebates for the purchase of home appliances. These massive allocations to the peasants, aside from pushing up domestic consumption, should also reduce social grievances in the countryside, arrest rural decline, and prevent the rural areas from becoming centers of protests as in the 1980s and the 1990s (So 2007a).

Adopting a More Pro-state Sector Stand

In the high tide of neoliberalism in the late 1990s, pundits predicted that China's state sector would gradually disappear because it was highly inefficient and state enterprises were losing money. On the other hand, China's private sector was expanding very rapidly because private enterprises were said to be highly efficient and profitable.

During the 2008 global economic crisis, however, there was a major expansion of the state sector at the expense of the private sector in China. The bulk of the Chinese stimulus program funds went into the state sector, that is, into the state banks and the state enterprises. The state also strengthened environmental regulations and tightened the tax loopholes on private business, leading to an avalanche of complaints from private enterprises in the export sector. For example, many Hong Kong companies said they had to close down their factories in the Pearl River Delta because of the worsening business environment due to new regulations and taxation.

DEEPENING OF THE GLOBAL ECONOMIC CRISIS AND SIGNS OF DISTRESS IN CHINA

As the world entered the fourth year of the continuing global capitalist crisis that began with the September 2008 financial meltdown on Wall Street, Berch Berberoglu (2012) remarked that the prospects for a rapid recovery of the economies of the United States and Europe appeared to be dim.

In mid-2013, even though the United States was growing at "encouraging rates," the Organization for Economic Cooperation and Development (OECD) reported that a sustainable recovery was not yet firmly established and important tasks remained, among them the seventeen-nation eurozone's continuing vulnerability to renewed financial, banking, and sovereign debt crises. Unemployment, currently at high levels across the developed world, could become entrenched. The OECD warned that as long-term joblessness become structural unemployment, high-level unemployment could remain even as the recovery took hold (Jolly 2013).

Furthermore, the global capitalist crisis had spread from the developed countries to the so-called "emerging markets," including the BRICS (Brazil, Russia, India, China, and South Africa). Paul Krugman

(2013) observed in mid-2013 that "India's rupee and Brazil's real are plunging, along with Indonesia's rupiah, the South African rand, the Turkish lira, and more."

If the continuing global capitalist crisis has led to a downward trend in the other BRICS, has it had the same impact on China? Has China experienced the same decelerating path as the other BRICS?

It seems that when the global economic crisis deepened, the Chinese economy began to show signs of distress in 2012 and 2013. The country's remarkable economic growth was propelled by throwing tons of resources into its economy – mountains of cash to build factories, roads and bridges, apartment towers and shopping malls, and to push millions of peasant migrants into making iPads, mobile phones, blue jeans, shoes, and cars. Under the imperative of developmentalism, the party-state often directed the cash into massive infrastructure projects or targeted industries. Nevertheless, this investment-driven growth engine is clearly not sustainable and cannot continue indefinitely. By 2013, researchers began to worry about whether China's robust growth model had reached its limit and outlived its usefulness (Pei 2013; Schuman 2013).

Facing declining demands in the global recession, China suddenly realized that its manufacturing industries had *massive excess capacity*. Excess capacity is plaguing major manufacturing industries – including in steel, cement, automobiles, solar panels, and wind turbines – and destroying profitability in sector after sector (Pei 2013). Take the case of green industry. In a mad-cap quest to dominate green energy, China's banks pumped billions into solar-panel manufacturing, creating hundreds of factories and vaulting China into the world's largest producer. Now the solar sector has become the victim of its own success: Chinese companies are failing, symbolized by the bankruptcy of market leader Suntech Power in 2013.

Chinese steel companies, too, continue to invest in new capacity even though debt is rising and losses are mounting. Each steel mill is backed by local officials eager to create jobs but dismissive of the larger costs. New investment projects prop up GDP to make China look good in development indicators, but only at the expense of the health of the overall economy. Inefficient, heavily subsidized state-owned enterprises gobble up credit while more nimble private firms starve.

When urban housing prices rose at around 10 percent monthly in early 2010, analysts warned of the formation of a *residential property bubble*, which could lead to serious political consequences. There was massive overcapacity in housing, with one Chinese electric company reporting 60 million units connected and not using any electricity, so presumably empty. Adding another 20 to 30 million units under construction, China's excess capacity could house the entire US population (Wasserstrom 2010a).

Much of China's recovery had been fueled by aggressive lending and soaring property prices. Lending by state-run banks was one of China's most aggressive forms of stimulus in 2009, but analysts constantly warned that banks could face risk from overbuilding, overcapacity, and non-performing loans (Barboza 2010b).

Indeed, the massive 4 trillion yuan (US$586 billion) stimulus package not only has left a legacy of murky accounting, off-balance-sheet transactions, and dodgy lending, it has also ended up as non-performing loans of the state enterprises and the mounting debts of local governments.

Minxin Pei (2013) reported that the biggest short-term risk for China was *financial over-leveraging*. Thanks to its decade-long credit boom, the Chinese economy as a whole was far more leveraged (indebted) than any of the major emerging market economies. Net domestic credit as a share of GDP was close to 140 percent in China, compared to 90 percent in Brazil and 75 percent in India. To make the matter worse, most of the debt was owed by state-owned enterprises, real estate developers, and local governments that were known for making risky, hasty decisions on their investments.

Bad loans hidden in Chinese banks vary, owing to the opacity of the Chinese financial system. The most conservative estimates suggest that they are around 10 to 15 percent of China's GDP. If this is true, the Chinese banking system is technically insolvent.

The risks have been heightened by the emergence of "shadow banking" – mysterious, unconventional sources of lending often kept off the bank's balance sheets – which George Soros recently warned could be as risky as the toxic subprime mortgage securities that tanked Wall Street.

Thus, in 2012, the Chinese economy began to show the following signs of distress: massive excessive capacity, a residential property bubble, financial over-leveraging, non-performing loans, the rapid rise of debt, and financial instability. China's GDP growth rate also has fallen to an annual pace of about 7.5 percent, down from a peak of more than 14 percent in 2007, before the global capitalist crisis (Lowrey 2013).

In mid-2013, it was reported that the Chinese economy had lost much of its previous vigor. Exports fell 3.1 percent from a year earlier, and imports declined 0.7 percent (Wassener 2013). Both figures were far below the expectations of analysts, who had projected a 4 percent rise in exports and 8 percent climb in imports, leading to a loss of confidence in the outlook for China's economic growth rate (Schuman 2013).

Since these signs of economic distress and falling growth rate happened at the same time as the once-a-decade leadership transition was taking place in the communist party (with incoming President Xi Jinping and Premier Li Keqiang replacing the outgoing President Hu Jintao and Premier Wen Jiabao), this distressing state of the economy led the new leaders to rethink whether they should adopt new policies to face the challenge of the global capitalist crisis (Summers 2013).

DEPARTURE FROM THE STATE
NEOLIBERALISM MODEL

Since taking office in mid-March 2012, Premier Li Keqiang and his state council have taken a different policy path from his predecessor. Yiping Huang (2013) labels Li's economic policy framework as "*Likonomics*," which has the following features.

The first feature is that Li *no longer insists that China needs to have a double-digit growth rate* to sustain its economy. It seems that the days of 10 percent annual growth rate are over in China. Growth potential is now projected around 6–7 percent. The minimum growth rate has also shifted downward. It is predicted that China's growth rate will probably fall to just 3 percent for this decade. In other words, China no longer sees economic growth as its highest priority in development or seeks to pursue the goal of a high growth rate at any cost (Parker 2013).

The second feature is *no more stimulus packages* to jumpstart the Chinese economy. Premier Li said, "We can no longer afford to continue with the old model of ... high investment" (K. Li 2013). He believes that relying on state-led investment for economic growth is not only difficult to sustain but also creates new problems and risks. The 4 trillion yuan (US$586) stimulus package in 2008 is said to be causing overcapacity in certain areas of infrastructure, significant fiscal risks due to reckless local government borrowing, asset bubbles, and the threat of bad debt following the huge credit expansion.

The third feature is *deleveraging*. The state bank move to curtail the credit bubble in the interbank market underlines Li's desire to deleverage and reduce future financial risks. Li wants to strengthen market discipline as a preparatory step toward interest rate and capital account liberalization. This implies that deleveraging is likely to continue and some of the smaller and weaker financial institutions may fail in the near future.

The state is holding off the loosening of credit for a reason: it is trying to restructure the economy, curb excesses in shadow banking and property sectors, engineer a shift from investment-driven growth to consumption-driven growth, and weed out the weaker banks and enterprises (Gough and Barboza 2013). The credit squeeze is getting the banks to adopt more cautious lending practices and Beijing is prepared to tolerate a degree of pain in its pursuit of financial overhaul.

The fourth feature is *structural reforms*. Current policy discussion indicates reforms in the areas of financial liberalization, the fiscal system, land use, administrative controls, monopolies, and the household registration system – many of which could be formally approved by the state over the next few years.

Li wants to open important sectors of the economy (finance, energy, railways, and telecommunication) to private businesses and market forces; foreign investors will be given more opportunities to invest in finance, logistics, healthcare, and other sectors. At the Davos Forum in Dalian in 2013, Li said that he "will continue to support the Doha round of World Trade Organization talks, work for the signing of bilateral free trade agreements, upgrade the China–Asean Free Trade Area, establish a Shanghai free trade zone, and provide a level playing field and a better legal environment for foreign investors" (K. Li 2013).

In addition, Li also wants to reduce the state's role in the market and allow more competition among businesses. In the Davos Forum, Li said "he will continue to streamline government and delegate power, press ahead with structural changes and grow economic sectors under diverse ownership. Government will leave to the market and society what they can do well while concentrating on those matters within its purview" (K. Li 2013; see also the report on the Davos Forum in Zakaria 2013).

Since 2012, Chinese state policies have surged again toward market liberalization and opening up the state sector to foreign investment. China also has taken a less active role in economic intervention, as shown by the no-stimulus and deleveraging policies. As such, is the country moving again back toward the direction of neoliberalism?

IS CHINA MOVING BACK TOWARD NEOLIBERALISM?

Since Likonomics just started in mid-2012, it is too early to tell whether its pro-market policies will become institutionalized and China will move toward the neoliberalism model. What is certain, however, is the Chinese path of development from 1978 to the present has been cyclical – usually taking two steps forward and one step backward, or one step forward and two steps backward – and it has never moved in a straight line. Thus, the final product is usually the uneasy and unstable combination of contradictory elements, a hybrid which defies any conventional labeling.

As such, the pro-market policies in Likonomics should not be taken as the triumph of neoliberal forces in China. Instead, it is more appropriate to treat the new policies as a balancing act by the Chinese state. Market forces were brought back in China during the global capitalist crisis in order to facilitate the party to stay in power.

In China's state neoliberalism, the party-state is further strengthened, not weakened, through the control over state officials, over domestic market forces, over foreign transnationals, and over the rising "middle class."

First of all, in order to strengthen the state, incoming President Xi Jinping quickly kicked off the Mass Line Education campaign in 2013, which is intended in part to purge the party of formalism, bureaucratism, hedonism, and extravagance. The mass line campaign is aimed to enforce party authority that goes beyond the party's periodic calls for discipline.

Second, President Xi launched a campaign on the ideological front. On the one hand, Xi's "mass line" campaign signaled a shift to a more leftist stance to defend the legacy of Mao Zedong, which included a publicized visit to a historic site where Mao undertook one of his own attempts to remake the Chinese Communist Party in the 1950s. Xi also said Mao Zedong's era of revolutionary socialism should not be dismissed as a failure. On the other hand, Xi has vehemently denounced Western constitutional democracy as an attempt to negate the party's leadership and a tool of Western subversion to weaken the communist state. The new leaders, therefore, have no intention of carrying out any bourgeois democratic reforms, despite the fact that they had opted for the introduction of more market forces into the Chinese economy (Buckley 2013).

Third, President Xi has called for the purification of state officials. State cadres should adhere to the "mass line" and develop close ties with the people. They should be critical and self-critical in the spirit of rectifying their work styles. The mass line campaigns should focus on self-purification, self-perfection, self-renewal, and self-progression. The party should adopt more comprehensive criteria for assessing the performance of its officials. In promoting officials, the party should consider integrity as a priority and then capability; and the *party should never judge a cadre simply by the growth of GDP*. In this respect, Xi has silently discarded the imperative of developmentalism, whose most important principle was to promote economic growth at whatever cost.

Fourth, although foreign corporations hope that under Likonomics market liberalization will give them more opportunities to do business in the excluded state sectors, they are bound to be disappointed. In mid-2013, a landmark ruling in the Supreme People's Court in China ruled that contracts used by non-Chinese citizens to gain access to sectors of the Chinese economy that are protected from foreign investment were invalid (Sue-lin Wong 2013).

In the past, sectors the Chinese government considers sensitive, like finance, media, technology, the Internet, and education, have long been off-limits to foreign investment. To get around this, some of the biggest companies in China, founded by Chinese people, including the Internet giants Baidu, Alibaba, Tencent, and Sina, have created variable-interest entities, or VIEs, that give overseas investors *de facto* control over companies technically owned by their Chinese partners. VIEs account for differing proportions of these companies' income and assets, ranging from several percent to as much as 100 percent.

Problems arise if the Chinese partners decide they do not want to follow the VIE contracts any longer because, for example, they already have the money and know-how they were seeking. When that happens, the foreign party most likely has no legal recourse once the above landmark ruling passed in mid-2013 and they remain excluded from the strategic sectors.

Fifth, a strong state also means that it can go after the transnationals if the Chinese government finds their business practices problematic. The *New York Times* reported that foreigners are relatively helpless when their foreign business owners are embroiled in legal disputes in China. For example, in mid-2013, Chinese officials investigated the Swiss food packaging giant Tetra Pak for abusing its market dominance in China. Tetra Pak is suspected of price-fixing and anti-competitive behavior. Analysts say that it is not unusual for the government to investigate the pricing practices of Chinese and international companies. Although most prices in China are set by market forces, the government maintains control over large parts of the economy, including energy and telecommunication prices. In response to the government investigation, several international brands, including Nestlé and Danone, have announced price cuts – as much as 20 percent – on infant milk formula sold in China (Barboza 2013a).

China Central Television also severely criticized Apple's warranty practices and accused Apple of discriminating against Chinese iPhone owners by offering shorter guarantees than in other countries, using refurbished rather than new parts, and shirking after-sale obligations. Gordon Chang (2013) remarks that the Apple accusation appears to be the beginning of a long-term campaign against foreign brands: in 2013 the state targeted Apple and Volkswagen; in 2012 it went after McDonald's and Yum Brands; and Google has been the object of a multi-year effort to undermine its operations in China.

Officials of transnational corporations operating in China complained in mid-2013 that "the Chinese government is using law enforcement to weaken international competitors in commercial sectors where Chinese companies are not strong or have spent very little money to develop their own products" (Barboza 2013b). Thus, Gordon Chang (2013) concludes that Chinese state officials, determined to protect domestic firms, started to take on foreign brands one by one. Under state neoliberalism, the state will do its best to cripple foreign companies and to exclude them from the strategic sectors in order to nurture domestic companies so that they can compete in the global market.

Sixth, whereas there has been a retreat of the state in Western neoliberal countries as market forces play a more important role in the economy, the CCP-controlled state views a pure market economy as excessively volatile and it shows no sign of relinquishing its role of planning for the Chinese economy. Indeed, Premier Li Keqiang has made urbanization the centerpiece of his economic policies (*China Daily* 2013), and China is going to build many new cities, many new housing complexes, many new freeways, and many new subways. According to Li's urbanization scheme, the state can resolve the problem of wasted investment by revving the engine of urbanization, that is, it can engage in a massive investment program related to the need to build infrastructure for all the newly urbanized areas. It is estimated that China will have 300 million people – equivalent to the entire population of the United States – migrating from the countryside to the cities over the next couple of decades. Since city-dwellers earn more and spend more than their rural cousins, urbanization will create a vast body of consumers, boost consumer demand, accelerate China's economic rebalancing, and ultimately propel China to pass the US as the world's biggest economy.

Seventh, the state has further heightened its nationalist credentials. In numerous comments since the start of his tenure, President Xi has highlighted his goal to "rejuvenate the Chinese nation" and to make China prosperous and strong (*fuqiang*), tapping into deep-seated desires in the modern Chinese psyche (Summers 2013). Thus, he is known to be a tough nationalist who will go further than his predecessors in asserting China's territorial claims. He is willing to back the Chinese military in its attempts to assert primacy in the South China Sea over Vietnam and the Philippines and in the East China Sea over Japan. China's aggressive approach to maritime disputes in the South China Sea, to a certain extent, is a response to President Obama's reorientation of US strategic policy toward the Asia-Pacific region.

Finally, despite the great pressure from the liberal faction of the Chinese Communist Party to embark on political reform, Xi's position is a firm "no" to those sorts of liberal proposals.

CONCLUSION

The global capitalist crisis is a period of turbulence, upheaval, political vacuum, and prolonged conflict; it is a period where states, classes, and ethnic groups are trying to redefine their relationship, to realign their configuration, to rethink their development models, and to reset the rules governing access to key resources in the global economy.

As such, we argued that the 2008 global economic crisis initially led to the deepening of state neoliberalism in China. However, when the country's hyper-growth economy eventually slowed down in 2012 during the prolonged global economic crisis, the communist party-state silently discarded its growth model. Thus, it no longer provided a massive stimulus package to jumpstart the economy like it did in 2008. Instead, the new leaders opted for the tightening of credit, the strengthening of market discipline, market liberalization, streamlining of the state bureaucracy, and the opening of the state sector to foreign investment.

Despite adopting a more pro-market policy amidst the call for another wave of neoliberalism reform, however, China is not moving toward the direction of neoliberalism. Instead, it is still moving along the path that we call "state neoliberalism." China's state neoliberalism is different from Western neoliberalism in the following ways.

First, whereas Western neoliberalism aims to serve the interests of the capitalist class, China's state neoliberalism seeks to enhance the survival of the communist state, which was threatened by the 2008 global economic crisis.

Second, whereas the Western neoliberal state has shown signs of retreat from the economy, the Chinese communist party-state continues to intervene deeply in the Chinese economy (through long-term planning and urbanization projects).

Third, whereas the Western neoliberal state has been weakened by public management reforms to downsize state bureaucracy, the Chinese party-state has been strengthened, not weakened, through its mass-line education and anti-corruption campaigns since 2012.

Finally, whereas the Western neoliberal state advocates globalization and the opening of the domestic economy to the transnationals, the Chinese party-state has taken an aggressive stand to protect its strategic sectors from the assault of the transnationals and to heighten its national credentials in territorial disputes in the South China Sea and the East China Sea. Although transnationals are now allowed to enter the strategic sectors, the Chinese state also wants to upgrade and strengthen Chinese companies so they can compete with foreign capital in both the Chinese market and the world economy.

If the Chinese developmental experience is characterized by trial and error, mid-course corrections, and reversals of policies, what is the future trajectory of state neoliberalism in China? The following scenarios seem possible: a return to super-growth developmentalism, a move to neoliberalism, and the consolidation of state neoliberalism.

First, given the fact that China has had a remarkable growth rate over the past three decades, the Chinese might hope that this *hyper-growth model will continue* and China could serve as a growth engine to pull the world out of the global capitalist crisis. However, it seems highly unlikely that China could ever sustain a double-digit growth rate for a long period of time again because of the maturation of its economy, the aging of the Chinese population, and the growing turbulence of the capitalist world economy. Thus, China has already reached the limit of the hyper-growth model and it is unlikely that it will return to the path of hyper-growth developmentalism.

Another scenario is that of *moving back toward neoliberalism.* The major beneficiaries of neoliberalism are those Chinese capitalists who have little connection with the state and have difficulties in getting the state to grant them licenses, in securing loans from the banks, and in attaining protection from corrupt state officials. Thus, those Chinese capitalists who have few links to the state and foreign interests (the transnationals, the World Bank, etc.) would like the state to further liberalize the market, to deregulate the bureaucracy, and to discipline the state enterprises. However, given the strength of the party, the size of the state sector, and the strong interlinkages between the state and the capitalist class (what is called a cadre-capitalist class in So 2003), full-scale market liberalization is going to meet strong resistance from the vested interest in the state bureaucracy and the state enterprises. Unless the state is much weakened by domestic turmoil (e.g. labor or peasant protests) and by the global capitalist crisis, it seems unlikely that China will ever return to the path of neoliberalism.

Thus, the most likely scenario seems to be *the consolidation of state neoliberalism.* This chapter has argued that state neoliberalism was deepened after the 2008 global economic crisis. Selected market forces were introduced into the Chinese economy in order to solve excessive credit creation and misallocation of resources by state enterprises and local governments, yet the communist party-state never intends to move toward full-scale market neoliberalization.

In late 2013, it was reported that although India's economy continued to decline, with a slowing growth rate and depreciation of the rupee, the market had rebounded in China, with factory orders expanding, the trade surplus rising, and borrowing by local government and shadow banking under control, showing the party-state's resolve to keep things on track (Bishop 2013; Bloomberg 2013; *New York Times* 2013). Since China's party-state still has enormous foreign exchange reserves and has successfully dealt with the Asian financial crisis before, there is reason for optimism that the country will be able to pull out of the global capitalist crisis unscathed.

If China does continue to move along the path of state neoliberalism, it could end up in a position that Beverly J. Silver and Giovanni Arrighi (2000, p. 69) envisioned at the turn of the century: "China appears to be emerging as the only poor country that has any chance in the foreseeable future of subverting the Western-dominated global hierarchy of wealth." Whether China succeeds in achieving this will depend, to a large extent, on how global capitalism is able to deal with the unfolding worldwide economic and financial crisis that is now threatening the very survival of the global capitalist system.

PART II | THE CHALLENGES OF CHINA'S GLOBAL RISE ⎯⎯⎯⎯⎯

5 The Challenges of Catching Up: Technological Upgrading and Moving Up the Value Chain

Over the past thirty years, China has attained a remarkable annual growth rate of more than 10 percent and transformed itself into the world's factory. The country's very rapid growth rate is the result of the deepening of its involvement with export-oriented manufacturing. However, by the 2000s, Chinese leaders began to recognize the limitation of this export-led industrial growth and regarded this strategy as insufficient (Appelbaum and Parker 2011).

First of all, much of the industrial production going on in China today involves merely *industrial processing*. Semi-finished or finished components are brought in from overseas locales, usually in nearby Asian nations, assembled into finished products by Chinese workers, stamped as "made in China," and then shipped out to markets in North America and Europe. For example, starting in the 1990s, China's strongest export growth has occurred in electronics, computers, and telecommunication equipment. However, it must be pointed out that all the qualities associated with advanced industry and high-tech products – the knowledge, the innovation, the sophistication – are embedded in the imported components, which for the most part are made outside China by non-Chinese companies. Even when pieces are made in China, this is generally the work of non-Chinese companies. Indeed, even product assembly, an activity we rarely view as a high-tech or high-value endeavor, is done in China by foreign-owned companies (Steinfeld 2010, p. 86).

Second, following this line of argument, Chinese industry, particularly in export-oriented sectors, exhibits extremely high levels of *foreign investment and ownership*. In 2008, foreign-invested enterprises accounted for 55 percent of China's total exports; especially in China's higher tech, higher value consumer product sectors (DVD players, TVs, high-end electronics, microwave ovens, etc.), foreign-invested firms accounted for almost 90 percent of exports in the mid-2000s (Steinfeld 2010, p. 85).

Third, as a result of foreign domination in the export sector, the bulk of profits remained with the transnationals that are manufacturing in China, but the degree of technology transfer – especially with the most advanced technologies – has proven to be quite limited. Adam Segal (2010) explains that for every Chinese-made DVD player sold, the Chinese manufacturer must pay a large royalty fee to the Japanese and Western companies that patented various components of the unit, such as its optical reader. These foreign companies reap substantial profits, but the Chinese take is extremely small – and is shrinking further as energy, labor, and commodity prices rise. Another example is the 30-GB iPod: Yuqing Xing and Neal Detert (2010) report that for every iPod sold in 2006, Apple made a profit of US$321.4, while Foxconn – the Taiwanese subcontractor/manufacturer in Shenzhen (China) – made no more than US$6.50.

Consequently, Cong Cao (2004) notes that in Beijing, the innovative bona fides of China are highly overstated. Cao contends that China is doomed to remain mostly an assembler and processor of foreign technologies, forever trapped in lowest value-added activities. Other Chinese researchers have also identified the following weaknesses: the degree of self-sufficiency of key technology is low; the number of patents is small; the quality of scientific research is unsatisfactory; top-notch scientific talent is lacking; and investment in science and technology is inadequate (Yongnian Zheng and Chen 2006).

Proponents of neoliberalism would argue that China needs more foreign investment, more market liberalization, and more market competition to upgrade its export industrialization. However, twenty years of neoliberal market reforms between 1978 and 1998 in China at best could only bring in industrial processing, while its export sector suffered from the dominance of foreign ownership, minimal profit retention, and little technology transfer. Obviously, this neoliberal path cannot empower China to upgrade technologically and transform itself into an advanced industrial nation.

How, then, could China break its dependence on foreign technology, overcome the challenge of foreign domination in the export sector, move up the value chain in industrial production, and catch up with the West in technological development?

This chapter argues that it is the Chinese communist party-state and its big push in the high-tech sector, not foreign investment or the liberalization of the market, which explains the transformation of China into a technological power in the twenty-first century. In the following sections, we will first examine the various state initiatives to promote high-tech development. Then we will present Dan Breznitz and Michael Murphree's (2011) Run of the Red Queen explanation of why these party-state technological initiatives worked in the Chinese setting.

STATE INITIATIVES TO PROMOTE HIGH-TECH DEVELOPMENT

The Chinese party-state has been keen to promote science and technology policy as the national development strategy since the mid-1980s.

In March 1986, the National High-Tech R&D Program (generally known as the "863 Program") was launched. Implemented during three successive five-year plans, this program provided grants on a competitive basis for applied research in designated sectors. It aimed to bridge China's gap with the world leaders in a select few new high-tech areas, such as biotechnology, electronics, and information and communication technology. Under the 863 Program, about US$200 billion was to be spent on information and communication technologies, of which US$150 billion was earmarked for telecommunication.

In March 1997, the Chinese party-state further launched the National Basic Research Program (generally known as the "973 Program"). The 973 Program was aimed to fund basic research to meet the nation's major strategic needs through innovation studies of major scientific issues related to sustainable development.

In contrast to the 863 Program and the 973 Program, which are characterized by central party-state dirigisme, the National Torch Program (*huoju jihua/guihua*), launched in 1988 during the deepening of neoliberal reforms, was aimed to promote the commercialization of Chinese R&D, that is, the diffusion of new technologies to production and markets (Baark 1991). Sebastian Heilmann and his colleagues (2013) point out that the Torch Program was characterized by decentralized institutional and policy experimentation, an enterprise-dominated financing scheme, as well as a long-standing inclusion of non-state small and medium-sized enterprises (SMEs) in its incubator activities. A major ingredient of the Torch Program was the establishment of *high-tech zones* (HTZs) – often referred to as "science parks," "research parks," "technology parks," or "science and technology industry parks" – where most of the new- and high-technology commercialization efforts were expected to take place.

However, Heilmann and his colleagues (2013) report that the Torch Program has experienced a mission drift: although the program's original goal was to promote domestic R&D and link it to industrial production, it later increasingly concerned itself with FDI acquisition and export business. In other words, as in other neoliberal reform policies, the Torch Program has unintentionally become a strong magnet for FDI and it has further consolidated China's dependence on foreign technology and foreign investment.

Subsequently, in response to this mission drift, the Chinese party-state in 2005 put forward "Medium- and Long-Term Scientific and Technological Development Plan Guidelines for the Period 2006–20" (hereafter abbreviated as MLP). Initiated during the period of the deepening of state neoliberalism, the MLP aimed to foster high-tech development with the ultimate goal of achieving *"indigenous innovation"* (*zizhu chuangxin*) capabilities that would reduce China's dependence on foreign firms for both employment and technology. In this fifteen-year plan, China is effectively pursuing industrial policies designed to make China a high-tech world player, by aiming at the forefront of world technology development, intensifying innovation efforts, and realizing strategic transitions from pacing front-runners to focusing on *"leap-frog"* development in key high-tech fields in which China enjoys relative advantages. In addition, the MLP required China to invest heavily in research and development in advanced technologies, calling for it to become an *"innovation-oriented society"* by 2020, and a world leader in science and technology by 2050 (Appelbaum and Parker 2011).

Given the country's limited resources, the MLP concluded that China should concentrate its public investments where a high payoff was deemed most likely. Four *"science megaprojects"* (nanotechnology, reproductive biology, protein science, and quantum research) were therefore singled out as key areas for funding, along with thirteen *"engineering megaprojects"* (including advanced numeric-controlled machinery; basic manufacturing technology; control and treatment of AIDS, hepatitis, and other diseases; drug innovation and development; core electronic components, high-end genetic chips; etc.), eight *"frontier technology programs"* (advanced energy, advanced manufacturing, aerospace and aeronautics, biotechnology, information technology, laser technology, new materials technology, and ocean technology) and eleven "*key areas*" (agriculture, energy, environment, information technology, manufacturing, national defense, population and health, public securities, transportation, urbanization, and water and mineral resources). A Special Project Office was created with the Ministry of Science and Technology to review proposals, approve funding, and monitor projects.

As we saw in the previous chapter, when the global financial crisis reached China in November 2008, the party-state quickly put forward a 4 trillion yuan (roughly US$586 billion) stimulus package, with "science and technology innovation and industrial structure adjustment" identified as one of its ten investment areas. A 9.3 percent share of the stimulus package was directly channeled into this technological area; some will be channeled directly into the MLP (So 2012; Valigra 2009).

In 2008, China also introduced its High-Tech Certification Management Policy, which slashed corporate taxes from 25 to 15 percent for companies that passed the high-tech certification requirements. Some 20,000 were certified in the next year and a half, although there is evidence that many of these were falsely certified in order to receive the tax breaks (Q. Zhou and Yang 2010).

Another key state initiative in high-tech pursuit was the "1,000 Talents Program" in 2009. The Chinese party-state has long been very active in encouraging overseas Chinese scientists and researchers to return to China. In 1999, the Chinese Academy of Science (CAS) introduced the "*100 Talents Program*." Under this program, awardees received 2 million yuan, enough to buy equipment, fund a laboratory, and supplement the returnee's salary (by 20 percent). In 2002, the Natural Science Foundation set up a "*Distinguished Young Scholars Program*." Under this program, a young experimental researcher received 1 million yuan, while those engaged in theoretical research received 800,000 yuan (Simon and Cao 2010). For university-based scientists and academics, the key award is the "*Cheung Kong Scholar*," founded in 1999 and funded by Hong Kong tycoon Li Ka-shing and the Ministry of Education in China.

Despite the above state initiatives, David Zweig and Huiyao Wang (2013) report that really talented scientists and academics rarely returned before 2007. CAS's 100 Talents Program brought back mostly recent Ph.D. or, at best, post-doctoral fellows. Having worked for many years under their supervisor, most returnees had little experience devising a major research project and directing a research team to complete it. Early returnees have long complained of burdensome paperwork, and excessive time wasted on cultivating personal relations as a means to gain research funding; petty jealousies within work units also complicate their work.

However, the situation has changed since 2007 when the Organization Department of the party-state took a more active role in recruiting talent. The Organization Department put forward two new initiatives. First, it organized local governments and party committees to devise a plan combining socio-economic development and the restructuring of the local economy. Local governments were asked to assess their future scientific and technical needs, and determine whether overseas talent could solve those needs and bring about the economic growth of the local economy. Second, it began the 1,000 Talents Program to supplement the MLP.

Zweig and Wang (2013) explain the process through which the above two initiatives work in China's global searches for overseas talent. First, there is the process of *talent identification*. After localities have assessed their scientific and technical needs and determined whether returnees could solve those needs, the Ministry of Education builds up a dataset of China's needs in education, research, and innovation, and discovers people overseas and in China who are engaged in such work. Education consuls overseas build lists of researchers in their locality, including their specialty and whether they are inclined to return; if so, consuls strengthen links with them and make concrete plans about how to bring them home.

Second, there is the process of *network building*. The Ministry of Education spreads the message on Shenzhou Xueran, its website for overseas study. Returnee organizations (local and abroad) link with expatriate researchers and bring them back bi-annually to meet potential employers. The Ministry of Education also sends delegations of potential employers or investors abroad to meet them. The 1,000 Talents Program, including the "Start-up Fund for Returnees" subprogram, was to be utilized to attract returnees to visit, teach part-time, and join projects.

Third, there is the process of *talent reentry and settlement*. The Ministry of Education was to ease the process of resettling in China for citizens or for long-term residents holding foreign citizenship. Employers are instructed to provide favorable working conditions for the returned entrepreneurs, scientists, and researchers and allow them to assume leadership positions. Livelihood benefits include "Permanent Residence Status for Aliens" and/or multiple entry–exit visas good for two to five years. Employers must find their spouses a job and guarantee their children admission to top schools. They are free to settle in any city of their choice. They receive a one-time subsidy of 1 million yuan and are entitled to medical care and social insurance, including pensions, medical insurance, and work-related injury insurance. They receive housing and food allowances, a subsidy for home leave, and a children's education allowance, all tax free. Their salary, based on consultation, should be reasonable in light of their previous salary overseas. The Ministry of Human Resources and Social Security's Overseas Students and Experts Service Center was instructed to establish a new team to help returnees manage such issues as permanent residence, urban registration, medical treatment, school enrollment of children, and so on.

The party-state is willing to set up a new inter-Ministry team and offer a generous package to returnees because it wants to recruit the following three types of top-notch talent that it failed to recruit in its previous initiatives: (1) international leaders in their fields who have created innovative teams and can make breakthroughs in key technologies; (2) "sturdy" basic researchers who have the ability to make breakthroughs and the potential to become excellent academic leaders who can bring forward newly emerging fields; and (3) core young professors and researchers who can elevate the quality of research and teaching. The assumption is that unless China is able to recruit the very best talent in science and technology, its effort to move the country into the top ranks of innovative societies will not be successful.

THE RISE OF CHINA IN TECHNOLOGICAL INDICATORS

The above state initiatives over the past thirty years seem to have worked fairly well to propel China to become an emerging high-tech power in the twenty-first century. Some of the indicators of China's rise in the pursuit of high technology are as follows:

+ China's *spending on R&D* grew from 0.6 percent of its GDP in 1996 to 1.5 percent in 2010, approaching that of Europe (1.69 percent). While China still falls behind the US (2.85 percent), government policy calls for reaching the US level by 2020 (Breakthrough Institute 2009). One industry forecast describes China's R&D spending since 2000 as "history-making," since it "exceeds and challenges both the US and Europe in terms of the intellectual property rights and the financial and infrastructure commitments it continues to make in science and technology endeavors" (Battelle 2009, p. 24).
+ China has a growing share of *research publications* in virtually every scientific category. Dieter Ernst (2011) reports that China is one of the four leading countries in science and technology publications, with particular strengths in material science (especially nanotechnology, analytical chemistry, and stem cell biology).

+ China has had an increased success rate in generating domestic *patents* through its State Intellectual Property Office (SIPO). In 2008, more than 800,000 patent applications were filed in SIPO, by far the largest number received by any patent office in the world (G. Zhang 2009).

+ China has invested heavily in higher education and a *growing workforce of scientists and engineers*. In 2006, the country had an R&D workforce that included 1.2 million scientists and engineers, awarding more than 19,000 doctorates in those areas, trailing only the US and Russia (Suttmeier 2008).

+ China has experienced rapid growth in *international research collaboration*. Richard P. Suttmeier (2008) points out that the return of overseas Chinese scientists and engineers (so-called "sea turtles") and extensive overseas collaborations have proven to be sources of strength.

+ By the 2010s, Chinese companies seemed to have established a presence in a number of *competitive high-tech industries* as creators of products with brand-name recognition, rather than merely as manufacturers. For example, the Chinese company Suntech, a global multinational that is now the world's third largest solar company (and the world's largest producer of silicon photovoltaic), is based in Wuxi, China. Suntech planned to open a manufacturing plant in Arizona. Applied Materials – the world's largest supplier of solar-manufacturing equipment – announced in December 2009 that it would open an R&D center in Xi'an (Appelbaum and Parker 2011).

In a study of the role of the state in China's development, Alberto Gabriele (2009) concludes that the Chinese state engages in huge and ever-increasing investments in infrastructure, institution, human capital building, R&D, and other areas, on a scale unequalled anywhere else in the world, generating a network of systemic economies which decisively enhance the competitiveness, productivity, and profitability of both public and privately owned/controlled industrial enterprises.

Despite the above impressive indicators in technological development, however, researchers should not get too carried away by China's remarkable achievements and optimistically predict that it will soon catch up with the US in terms of technological development. Indeed, researchers should not overlook the many internal and external obstacles which could easily sidetrack, slow down, suppress, or reverse China's long march to an innovation society and a high-tech power.

INTERNAL AND EXTERNAL OBSTACLES TO CHINA'S TECHNOLOGICAL DEVELOPMENT

To begin with, the Chinese government is still a Communist party-state. It is authoritarian, bureaucratic, and hierarchical. This one party-state can stifle the very innovation that party leaders have made central to their various "indigenous innovation" initiatives. Yasheng Huang (2011) argues that China is now in the midst of one of the most statist periods in its reform era and that there has been a strong turn to a self-defeating industrial policy since the global economic crisis in 2008. Most neoliberal economists would agree with Huang that China's statist industrial policy and areas targeted by state-planners for heavy investment are likely to result in placing government bets (and hence public monies) on losing industries, rather than following the market signals that are more likely to result in fruitful investment decisions.

In addition, the Chinese economy under state neoliberalism is still dominated by the large state-owned enterprises. State enterprises are known to be bureaucratic and conservative. On the other hand, China's emerging private sector generally remains small, under-capitalized, and generally risk-averse.

Furthermore, China's universities and laboratories, too, continue to suffer from a hierarchical structure that stifles innovation and creativity. They remain highly dependent on foreign technology despite the state's strenuous effort to push for "indigenous innovation." China's research culture also is not that conducive to innovation. Cong Cao (2010) points out that misconduct in science is quite common in China. Given the numerous pressures to publish in scientific journals, quantity often trumps quality, and plagiarism and other forms of fraud are widespread. Besides, the Chinese research community is highly critical to the targeted funding of the megaprojects in the recent MLP initiative; Yigong Shi and Yi Rao (2010) remark that the top-down approach of the megaprojects stifles innovation and it is readily apparent that connections with bureaucrats and a few powerful scientists, not the scientific merit of the research proposal, are paramount in getting funding.

Moreover, the lack of a clearly defined property rights regime is a serious obstacle for China to foster the development of a high-tech economy (Breznitz and Murphree 2011). In such an environment, researchers and firms may refrain from committing to extensive, cutting-edge R&D, which is deemed both high risk and long term. This is because they are not sure how much of the fruits of their high-tech innovation they will be allowed to retain in the future.

Aside from the above internal obstacles in the hierarchical Chinese state bureaucracy, the dominance of state-owned enterprises, the culture of doing scientific research, and the lack of a property rights regime, China also faces serious external obstacles in its march to become a high-tech power.

For example, China's MLP and its push to develop "indigenous innovation" are seen by many international technology companies as a "blueprint for technology theft" on a scale the world has never seen before. The US Chamber of Commerce further views the growth of China's domestic patents as *"junk patents,"* filed by private firms and state-owned enterprises largely to satisfy government overseers that their funding has produced results. These patents are also used, at least in the Chamber's view, "to retaliate against foreign companies, which file intellectual property infringement lawsuits offshore that stymie the international expansion plans of Chinese companies. ... These 'junk patents' are proving to be a potent weapon against foreign companies" (McGregor 2010, pp. 26–7).

China's "indigenous innovation" initiative is also criticized as a discriminatory measure against foreign products. In 2009, the Chinese party-state issued Circular 618, which listed a wide range of products for which firms that embodied indigenous innovation were to be given preferential treatment in government procurement (Appelbaum and Parker 2011). According to the US Chamber of Commerce Report, such a "Buy-China Plan" would effectively exclude foreign competition, since few foreign-made products would meet such a requirement. Foreign access was also said to be hampered by a "compulsory certification and standards requirement" as well as "requirements for the disclosure of technology secrets and other proprietary information that serve to exclude foreign products from major Chinese markets" (McGregor 2010, p. 22).

Later, the conflict originated in "indigenous innovation" was elevated to "Chinese industrial espionage" or "Chinese cyber espionage" (Wong and Tatlow 2013). A report issued by the Pentagon in the US accused China of "stealing industrial technology," and warned that the same information-gathering could easily be used for "building a picture of US defense networks, logistics, and related military capabilities that could be exploited during a crisis" (Sanger 2013).

Facing the above internal and external obstacles, how can researchers explain the progress of China's march toward an innovative society? In other words, how could the Chinese party-state overcome the internal and external obstacles to become an emergent high-tech power in the twenty-first century?

THE RUN OF THE RED QUEEN EXPLANATION

Dan Breznitz and Michael Murphree (2011), in their volume entitled *Run of the Red Queen*, convincingly explain the origins of the innovation state in China and how China's current system of innovation is institutionalized and is sustainable for the medium and long term. Breznitz and Murphree's explanation has the following three components.

The first component is that at the global level, *a new system of fragmented production* had emerged at the turn of the twenty-first century, making China's innovative state quite different from that of previous late developers. Before the late twentieth century, the production of goods and services was mostly organized in vertically integrated hierarchical companies located in one country. The task of the state in late developers (e.g. the East Asian NIEs of Taiwan and South Korea) was to concentrate on imitation, utilizing the economies of scale and scope to excel by using the latest technologies developed elsewhere. The aim of the late developers was to develop the capabilities to excel in *novel-production innovation* and become true economic powers. In the past, late developers relied on national champions in the form of conglomerates that tried to master every stage of production.

However, in an era of fragmented production in which each country specializes not only in specific industries but also in specific stages of production, and in which truly novel products are produced or sourced globally without being produced in the countries where they were developed, there are many modes of innovation that contribute to sustainable long-term economic growth.

As China has become the global center for many different stages of production, it has also developed a formidable competitive capacity to innovate in different segments of the research, development, and production chain that are as critical for economic growth as many novel-product innovations. China's accomplishment has been to master the art of thriving in *second-generation innovation* – including the mixing of established technologies and products in order to come up with new solutions – and the science of organizational, incremental, and process innovation. Thus, China's innovation capabilities are not solely in process (or incremental innovation) but also in the organization of production, manufacturing techniques and technologies, delivery, design, and second-generation innovation. Those capabilities enable it to move quickly into new niches once they have been proved profitable by the original innovator. Today, in a world of fragmented production, successful Chinese IT companies have gained global prominence by specializing in specific stages of production and a tighter industrial focus, and China does not need master novel-product innovation in order to achieve sustained economic and industrial growth.

An example of such second-generation innovation is Baidu, the dominant search engine in China, founded in 2000. Baidu's web page bears an undeniable resemblance to Google's, but the resemblance does not end with the visual representation: Baidu's business model and interface mirror those of Google, but it takes advantage of the defined market space and pathway in China it has blazed since the late 1990s. Furthermore, Baidu is not merely an imitator; it has its own innovation capabilities and design strengths. Baidu has built its own proprietary Chinese-language search software and has taken full advantage of local market openings.

The second component of Breznitz and Murphree's explanation is that at the state level, China has created *two innovation systems: one national, and one regional.*

In China, there are two sets of institutions that affect the behavior of Chinese economic actors. The first is the set of central government institutions that govern the national economy. These *central institutions* have been far less reform-oriented than their counterparts at the provincial level. The second set of institutions includes those that effectively separated China into a series of *regional economic fiefdoms*, which both fiercely compete and cooperate with one another and with the center. This dynamic, in which each region develops a unique set of capacities, enables China to dominate at many stages of the fragmented global economy yet inhibits businesses and technical researchers from engaging in cutting-edge, and highly risky, novel-technology and novel-product development.

This central versus local distinction had its origins in the era of state socialism. During Mao's later years, the central leadership continually expanded the role of local economic officials in planning the economy and implementing economic policies at the expense of centralized control.

The economic reforms in post-socialist China since 1978 have further decentralized decision making to the regional level. Building upon the legacy of local planning from the Mao era, reformers gradually increased the authority of local officials, albeit in a piecemeal manner, to experiment, approve projects, and seek foreign investment. Later, *fiscal decentralization* was added to *administrative decentralization*, and localities were permitted to retain a portion of their revenue. Revenue sharing in the Chinese system refers to profits from locally run state-owned enterprises in addition to locally collected national taxes. In essence, the fiscal reforms should be seen as a transfer of partial (or full) property rights from the center to the provinces.

The ability to retain local revenues in the local economy prompted cadres to become increasingly concerned with local development and with the strength of local enterprises, especially since their advancement in the party-state was mostly locally controlled. This led to a deep fragmentation of the Chinese economy into competing economic blocs.

Another important impact on local institutions came from the fragmented and piecemeal nature of the reform process in the 1980s. That decade's story was one of gradually increasing economic or market freedoms in different localities. The historical process, in which each region started its evolution at a different time under different regulations and with different endowments, critically affected the pattern of investment and the type of companies and R&D activities conducted in each region.

As localities became directly responsible for their own revenues, and the local leaders increasingly had the chance to become personally wealthy, many of them became ever more competitive and pursued their own parochial interest, largely independent of national ones. The result has been the creation of strongly policy-innovative and fiercely competitive regions within China. This forced many Chinese companies to think and act locally and offered foreign multinationals the ability to play one region off against another in order to secure the most favorable deal as local government officials competed to attract the largest number of foreign investment projects in order to advance their own careers.

Furthermore, at the national level, the provincial government leaders and city government leaders are judged by the central leadership mostly on the economic growth of their regions. These measures are measured by revenue and job creation.

All the above processes help to explain why the localities are so eager to cooperate with the center's technological initiatives, like the Torch Program, the MLP, and the 1,000 Talents Program. City and provincial governments quickly set up high-tech zones; they warmly welcome local and foreign companies to invest in the zones; and they quickly identify the scientists and researchers they need.

The third component of Breznitz and Murphree's explanation is the *structural uncertainty in China's political-economic system*. In the Run of the Red Queen model (the derivation of which we will explain below), structural uncertainty is defined as an agreement to disagree about the goals and methods of policy, a condition leading to intrinsic unpredictability and to inherent ambiguity in implementation. This ambiguity leads to some tolerance of multiple interpretations and implementation of the same policy. Therefore, structural uncertainty is an institutional condition that guarantees that a plurality of behavior will be allowed in a specific domain, and that none of the actors will know in advance the appropriate ways to conduct themselves.

It is bad enough for technological researchers to work in an environment where their property rights are weak; it is immensely worse to work in an environment where these rights also keep on changing and are applied arbitrarily; worse still, even the rights of businesses to operate in certain markets are never assured and always shifting. Under such extreme structural uncertainty, the great puzzle for social scientists is to explain why some Chinese companies do any R&D at all. Indeed, without the policy of fiscal decentralization and the strong incentive to get rich, it is difficult to explain why the local economic actors (local officials and local entrepreneurs) are so eager to engage in any technological development whatsoever.

Structural uncertainty is the result of the following features of the Chinese political-economic system. The first feature was the need to start reforms in the context of a strong conservative center and a ruling ideology of Maoist socialism. Facing strong opposition from the conservative center, the strategy that the central reformers used was to authorize regional and local agents to experiment with their own interpretations of reform within the limit of obscurely worded policies and pronouncements of the center.

From the first reforms in 1978 to the present, China's central leaders have never laid out detailed reform plans in their pursuit of neoliberalism or state neoliberalism. Instead, they have used vague terms to authorize regional and economic actors to experiment in certain policy or economic areas. Regional leaders have needed to decide whether to implement any changes at all. Authorities who have opted for reform have had to develop a particular interpretation of the ambiguous pronouncements made by the communist leadership and the central government. They also have had to decide what actions the leadership actually desires and permits. High uncertainty has been further augmented by the fact that the time frame of the reforms has been left unspecified, and changes in policy from neoliberalism to state neoliberalism, or from state neoliberalism back to neoliberalism, have come unexpectedly and not infrequently.

This ever-changing environment of extreme uncertainty, with high risks and high gains, has had a far-reaching effect on the behavior of actors. Rational actors have opted to focus on securing short-term gains while trying to minimize risk. Since high-tech R&D, especially novel-product innovation, is both long term and high risk, the particularities of Chinese reform have kept actors from engaging in it.

The second feature of the Chinese political-economic system leading to structural uncertainty is the organization of the bureaucracy. The Chinese bureaucracy is not only vast and complex but also pervaded by numerous cross-allegiances and competing lines of authority. These exist across domains, such as telecommunication technology; within the same agency; between the national, regional, and local layers of bureaucracy; and between the local and central branches of the same bureaucratic organizations. Not surprisingly, it is unclear which organization has final authority over specific domains; and it is not even clear who is in charge of what at each level of the bureaucratic structure. This unwieldy construction is then further muddled by the Communist Party's infusion into every nook and cranny of both the bureaucratic system and industry. In telecommunications, for example, the interaction of policy, party, research, and economic actors forms a multifarious, integrated, and overlapping structure.

This complicated bureaucratic structure instills structural uncertainty in two ways. First, any action or policy implementation must satisfy multiple superiors who often have contradictory roles and preferences. Second, it is impossible for any of the entities involved to know in advance whether a specific action they take will be looked upon favorably by any or all of the bureaucratic agencies that might (or might not) view it as falling under their jurisdiction. As a result, economic actors avoid taking on long-term, high-risk endeavors, preferring actions that lead to immediate, secure, positive material results.

The third feature of the Chinese political-economic system that leads to structural uncertainty is the ambiguous and ever-changing nature of the overarching goal of neoliberalism and state neoliberalism reforms. The reformers themselves, following Deng Xiaoping, have described the entire reform process as "crossing the river by groping for stones" (see chapter 2 above). The inability to define goals and means in neoliberalism and state neoliberalism reform policies clearly infuses the system with a tolerance for contradictions. These, in turn, lead the vast multitude of formal institutions for the Chinese system to interpret goals and the proper mechanisms for achieving them in their own way and in accordance with parochial interests. This uncertainty, again, incentivizes researchers and enterprises to prefer short-term economic growth above all else and to shy away from long-term high-risk activities.

It is therefore imperative to understand the various kinds of structural uncertainties and the areas in which they operate and to trace how they shaped the developmental trajectory of China's high-tech industry, especially with regard to R&D and innovation.

In sum, the emergence of a new global system of fragmented production, together with China's two innovation systems and structural uncertainty, have combined to shape the trajectory of China's path toward an innovative state. The two parallel innovation systems have so far precluded any *novel-product innovation* or any radical technological breakthrough, but they allowed China to thrive in *second-generation innovations, including organization innovation and process innovation.*

Breznitz and Murphree call this course of development China's "run of the Red Queen," a reference to the world of Lewis Carroll's Red Queen in *Through the Looking-Glass,* who, in order to even stay in the same place, had to run as fast as she could (Carroll 2010 [1872]). China shines by keeping its industrial-production and service industries in perfect tandem with its technological frontier. Like the Red Queen, China runs as fast as possible in order to remain at the cusp of the global technological frontier without actually advancing the frontier itself. China developed its Red Queen model by "accident," partly as a result of local experimentation and administrative/fiscal decentralization; and the developmental outcome looks quite different from the declared goal of the central government (which instead aimed at novel-product innovations and technological breakthroughs).

China's economic miracle is not a story of a developmental state carefully orchestrating its industrial upgrading. Rather, it is a story of trial-and-error economic experimentation led by sub-national entities but fashioned by political contestations between conservatives and reformers at the center, between influence-wielding interest groups and the Chinese Communist Party, and between the center and the provinces. China's Run of the Red Queen model is, in essence, a story of how a new fragmented mode of global production in the twenty-first century, a dualistic (national and local) innovation system, and structural uncertainty interact with each other to induce second-generation innovation (including organization and process innovation) without novel-product innovations and technological breakthroughs.

China's party-state, therefore, has erred by pushing for "*indigenous* innovation" and viewing independent mastery of novel-product innovation and new-technology creation as necessary for national wealth and economic security. In the Run of the Red Queen model, there is no urgency for China to master novel-production innovation if the aim is sustained economic growth. This is especially so since China's central government's concern for technology security is anachronistic, failing to take into account the complicated economic interdependence between China and the rest of the world in the new global era of fragmented production. Instead of pushing for "*indigenous* innovation," China should engage in more strategic partnerships and research collaborations with Western multinational high-tech firms.

For example, the China Aviation Industry Corporation (AVC) has entered into a 50–50 partnership with General Electric, a consortium that makes both military and civilian aircraft, to produce aircraft electronic systems. The Shanghai Automotive Industry Corporation (SAIC) has established a joint venture with General Motors (GM) to manufacture and market SAIC's low-cost Wuling microvan in India – a deal that firmly established SAIC in India, which also has a growing motor vehicle market. GM now owns 44 percent of Wuling (SAIC owns half), whose sales amount to nearly a sixth of GM's global vehicle total (Appelbaum and Parker 2011; Oster et al. 2010). Edward S. Steinfeld (2010) points out that it is unwise to assume that indigenous Chinese companies are, by definition, competing head to head with Western multinationals. In this new era of global production, the emerging system of globalized R&D has created a symbiotic relationship between multinational and indigenous Chinese companies. China's response to the hostility of the West in trade conflict and technology theft, therefore, should be the deepening of strategic partnership and research collaboration with Western multinationals.

In the end, we agree with Richard P. Suttmeier (2008, pp. 14–15), who has long tracked China's emergence as a technology leader, that the very notion of the rise of China as a high-tech superpower needs to be recast. Instead of emerging as a national superpower which will soon surpass the US in high-tech, China is better equipped to become a leading presence in global networks of research and innovation. The Run of the Red Queen explanation helps us to understand how the Chinese communist party-state, despite facing so many internal and external obstacles, has successfully responded to the challenge of catching up in terms of technological upgrading and moving up the value chain.

6 The Challenges of Staying in Power

THE EXPLOSION OF SOCIAL CONFLICT AND CIVIL UNREST IN CHINESE SOCIETY

Like other developing countries, China's remarkable economic growth over the past four decades has led to structural dislocation, the rise and fall of social classes, and an increase in social conflict, political protests, and civil unrest. Murray Scot Tanner (2005) reports that political protest rose dramatically over the past decade and is now a daily phenomenon. The Ministry of Public Security (MPS) reported that the number of "mass incidents" (*quntixing shijian*) – an overly broad catch-all term that encompasses the full spectrum of group protests, including sit-ins, strikes, group petitions, rallies, demonstrations, marches, traffic-blocking and building seizures, and even some public mêlées, riots, and inter-ethnic strife –skyrocketed from about 8,700 in 1993 to more than 200,000 in 2011[1] (Feng 2012; Hui and Chan 2011; Page 2011; Roberts and Zhao 2011; Tanner 2005).

How did the communist party-state respond to the explosion of social conflict and civil unrest in Chinese society? Did social conflict and civil unrest lead to any political instability, regime change, or change in the path of development over the past four decades?

This chapter argues that the communist party-state has done a fine job managing the rising social conflict in Chinese society. As a result, the party-state was not only able to meet the challenge of staying in power, but it was induced to adopt the consolidation of the state neoliberalism programs under the Hu/Wen regime at the beginning of the twenty-first century. In what follows, we will first examine how the party-state successfully managed different kinds of social conflict in cities and in the countryside in the late twentieth century, then we will discuss how the recent intensification of social conflict since the 2008 global financial crisis could possibly undermine its legitimacy and capacity.

STATE–WORKER CONFLICT

The Rise of Urban Working-Class Protests

The deepening of neoliberal economic reforms in the late 1990s, such as privatization, deregulation, and marketization, did great harm to the Chinese working class in terms of job security, wages, and entitlements (e.g. housing, healthcare, and education). Subsequently, the Chinese working class responded by engaging in protests, and the number of labor protests has significantly increased over the past three decades. Tim Pringle (2002, p. 1) reports that "almost every week in Hong Kong and mainland China, newspapers bring reports of some kind of labor action: a demonstration demanding pensions; a railway line being blocked by angry, unpaid workers; or collective legal action against illegal employer behavior such as body searches or forced overtime."

According to the official statistics, in 1998, there were 6,767 collective actions (usually strikes or go-slows with a minimum of three people taking part) involving 251,268 people. This represented an increase in collective actions of 900 percent from the 1990s. In 2000, this figure further jumped to 8,247 collective actions involving 259,445 workers (Pringle 2002, p. 2). Given such widespread labor protests, it is no wonder that the Chinese government has identified labor problems as the biggest threat to the country's social and political stability (F. Chen 2000; C.-k. Lee 2000).

However, it must be pointed out that the growing incidence of labor protests has not led to the rise of a labor movement. In general, labor protests in post-socialist China bore the following characteristics (So 2007b, p. 135):

+ *short duration:* less than ten days;
+ *small size:* fewer than 500 people;
+ *compartmentalized:* the protests tended to be isolated from one another and fail to spread from one enterprise to another or from one region/industry to another;
+ *economistic:* mostly involved bread-and-butter issues and seldom raised political issues or structural issues; and
+ *legalistic:* workers went through the existing laws and procedures first before they engaged in collective action. Workers aimed to appeal to local authorities and their protests usually stayed within legal limits.

In short, labor protests in China tended to be "spontaneous, small-scale, short-lived, compartmentalized, economistic, and stayed within legal bounds." In the literature, labor protests were also characterized as "short-lived, economically motivated episodes," "spasmodic, spontaneous and uncoordinated," "spontaneous, leaderless" (Blecher 2002, p. 285; F. Chen 2000, p. 62; C.-k. Lee 2000, p. 50). Obviously, these small-scale, short-lived, spontaneous labor protests failed to generate a national labor movement.

As such, an important research question to be asked is: Why is there no labor movement in post-socialist China? Even though neoliberal economic reforms intensified the structural contradictions confronting Chinese workers, and even though there had been widespread labor protests since the 1990s, why did they fail to generate significant strike waves and protest movements all over China? In other words, despite Chinese workers' participation in labor protests and class struggles, why have they failed to form a class to protect their class interests?

This chapter argues that the communist party-state played a decisive role in shaping the contour of labor protests in post-socialist China. To highlight the decisive role played by the party-state, the following section will examine how the party-state devised policies to create social divisions within the working class, imposed political repression to disorganize workers, set up labor legislation to preempt labor protests, adopted the tactic of accommodation to diffuse such protests, and maintained the moral high ground by shifting the blame to lower-level officials.

Creating Social Divisions within the Working Class

In the Maoist era, there was little significant division among Chinese workers employed in the state sector. In general, all state workers enjoyed stable, secure income, socially provided housing, healthcare, and education, and guaranteed lifetime employment. However, during the neoliberal reform era, a few state policies were devised which resulted directly in the working class's deep social division.

First, there was the division between employed and unemployed workers. In order to ease the pain of unemployment for state workers, the state adopted a policy called "off-duty" (*xiagang*). "Off-duty" workers were those who still maintained "employment relations" with the state enterprises, who were potentially reemployable if business improved, and who still received livelihood allowances amounting to only a tiny fraction of regular income. Yongshun Cai (2002) points out that labor protests were mostly carried out by laid-off workers in the state-owned enterprises, while employed workers and *xiagang* workers seldom offered any support.

Second, there was the division between urban workers and migrant workers. Through the household registration system (*hukou*), the party-state allowed the peasants to leave their farms but not their villages. Thus, the peasants were allowed to work in market towns and urban areas only as temporary migrant workers. They had no right to settle down permanently in these places. A new class of temporary migrant workers, many of them young women known as *dagongmei* (maiden workers), emerged in response to the employment opportunities in the export-processing zone in the southern provinces. An estimated 100 million temporary migrant workers left the countryside to enter towns and cities in search of non-agricultural jobs in the 1990s. This *hukou* system created a *segmented labor market*. Urbanites worked as permanent workers in the state sector or in high-paying primary labor markets which provided healthcare and other benefits, yet rural temporary migrants could only get jobs in the secondary labor market in the private and collective sectors, and picked up jobs with low pay and few benefits.

Such labor market conditions have led to a divided working class. This class division was reinforced by residential segregation and ethnic stereotyping. Temporary migrant workers tended to live in very poor-quality housing in the urban fringe. Migrant housing generally lacked facilities such as electricity, water supply, drainage and sewerage systems, and access lanes for fire prevention. In addition, temporary migrant workers were regarded as outsiders and excluded from local society. Local urban workers assigned many negative ethnic labels to migrant enclaves, including "paradise for thieves and robbers," "camps for prostitutes," "retreats of hunted criminals," and so on. Tensions have been growing between urban workers and temporary migrant workers during the neoliberal era (Taubmann, 2000).

As Ching-kwan Lee (2000, p. 58) points out,

> Local urban workers and migrant workers are not ready allies in forming any class-based movement. Divided by localistic origins (local workers versus outside workers), sociocultural backgrounds (country folk versus urbanites), and age (young versus middle-aged and older), the two groups of workers often find themselves in competition for the same

unskilled and low-paid manufacturing jobs in both the state and the non-state sectors. ... Even when they labor side by side within state-owned factories, conflicts regarding wage rates and work allocations are common.

Imposing Political Repression to Disorganize the Working Class

In order for the working class to form a class, it needs its own organization and its own leaders to concentrate its resources, to disseminate information, to articulate its interests and discourse, to plan strategy and tactics, and so on. However, a fundamental problem for the Chinese working class is that it was disorganized, and its protests were often leaderless. Why was that so?

First of all, although enterprises were supposedly to form labor unions to protect the interests of workers, unions formed in foreign-invested enterprises were mostly "company unions," that is, they were led and staffed by management personnel who were mainly responsible for collecting union fees and organizing birthday parties and recreational events. These union leaders were also salaried shop-floor supervisors or section heads in the factory administration (C.-k. Lee 2000, p. 51). Thus, they were on the side of management rather than on the side of workers when labor conflict broke out.

Similarly, although the All-China Federation of Trade Unions (ACFTU) supposedly takes care of the interests of the workers in state-owned enterprises, Ching-Kwan Lee (2000, p. 55) reports that it proved to be too weak to protect workers' rights. In fact, there is widespread disillusion among rank-and-file workers toward the ACFTU, and most workers turn instead to informal networks for support when their rights are encroached upon. More often than not, official unions are controlled directly by management. Indeed, many studies demonstrate that the ACFTU routinely acts on behalf of the party-state and management and some scholars consider the official unions as simply "state organs" (Taylor and Li 2007) or part of the government bureaucracy (E. D. Friedman 2009) that pursues the interests of the party-state and the employers, rather than the interests of the workers.

In 1989, taking advantage of the rebellious climate in Tiananmen Square, Beijing workers attempted to form a Beijing Workers' Autonomous Federation (BWAF). This attempt greatly frightened the communist party leaders, since the BWAF had the potential to form an alliance between workers and intellectual and human rights dissidents. Subsequently, the BWAF was met with ruthless suppression by the party-state.

In November 1999, the government announced new rules for public gatherings, requiring assemblies larger than 200 to obtain approval from local public security authorities. Gatherings larger than 3,000 would require the approval of security offices from a higher level. Since then, communist party leaders have continued to arrest, convict, and imprison any labor activists who try to form an independent labor organization and start a violent protest, and just to make their intentions clear, they have "ordered cities across the country to augment their anti-riot police" (Eckholm 2001).

Under this repressive environment, Yongshun Cai (2002) reports that workers in labor protests tended not to resort to violent or dramatic forms of action because this would increase the hostility around such protests and would invite suppression by the party-state. This repressive environment also leads to a pattern of *leaderless protest* because being an organizer brings no benefits but just puts the person at risk. If individuals anticipate a threat of violence, they may refuse to assume the leadership role. As some labor activists admit: "We only work as consultants, because organizing is too sensitive. ... We research the workers' situation; find out what ways work best. We only help workers who request help. If they do not request help it is best to keep a distance from them" (Y. Cai 2002, pp. 336–7).

Without organization and leadership, it is difficult to wage large-scale protests over a long period of time. As a result, Chinese labor protests tend to be small-scale, unplanned (spontaneous), and short-lived.

Labor Legislation Designed to Preempt Labor Protests

In addition to bolstering its coercive means of repression, the Chinese state tried to institutionalize labor conflict by setting up a national labor dispute arbitration system. By 1997, some 270,000 labor dispute mediation committees were established at the enterprise level, and 3,159 labor dispute arbitration committees at county, city, and provincial levels. These committees are constituted by a "tripartite principle," with representatives from the state, labor, and employers. During the 1990s, there were 820,000 enterprise mediation cases, while 450,000 cases of labor arbitration were processed (C.-k. Lee 2000, p. 47). A national hierarchy of labor dispute arbitration mechanism attests to the state's attempt to provide institutional channels for the resolution of labor conflicts during economic reforms. The emphasis is on pre-emption and mediation at the enterprise level, with arbitration at the local committee level. Submission of labor disputes to the civil court is the last resort.

In 2007, the party-state passed three new labor laws to strengthen the administrative absorption of labor struggles (Hui and Chan 2011, pp. 164–5). The first of these, the Employment Promotion Law, aims to provide guidelines to local government on how to monitor employment agencies, as well as facilitate occupational training for workers. The second, the Labor Dispute Mediation and Arbitration Law, simplifies the legal procedure of mediation and arbitration, reducing the money and time costs to workers using these procedures. The third, the Labor Contract Law, which is regarded as the single most important of the three new laws, seeks to stabilize employment relations by making it the legal obligation of employers to sign formal labor contracts with workers. Moreover, this law clearly states under what conditions, and with what procedures, employers can legally terminate a labor contract and their penalties if they fail to do so (So 2010a).

As a result, Chinese workers have seized this institutional space to redress grievances and to defend their rights. Most of their disputes are economic in nature, with wages, welfare, and social insurance payments being the most common causes of conflicts. Wage arrears are particularly pronounced in private and foreign-invested firms. Thus, most workers have tried the labor dispute system first to express their grievances; only when they fail to get what they want do they engage in public labor protests. In this respect, the national dispute system has preempted workers from engaging in labor protest and public demonstrations. Had the labor dispute system not been instilled in the 1990s, labor protests would have been more widespread, with the greater likelihood that they would have grown into a massive labor movement.

Adopting the Tactics of Accommodation to Diffuse Working-Class Protest

Although the party-state made it clear that it was determined to suppress any labor protest organized by independent unions which turned violent or was politically oriented, it was also quite willing to accommodate the requests of the labor protests if they were economistic, if they did not engage in any violent behavior, or if they stayed within legal bounds. This accommodation policy by the state greatly influenced the nature of labor protests that emerged in the last decade: labor protests were narrowly confined to the type that is tolerated by the state and have a chance of winning some concessions.

Feng Chen (2000) reports that most of the labor protests by state workers could be labeled as *"subsistence struggles."* It was when neoliberal reforms plunged workers in state enterprises into a subsistence crisis, with their wages unpaid for months, their medical reimbursements denied, and their jobs threatened, that they participated in protests. These workers did not demand a restoration of their previous economic status, but rather chanted or displayed banners with the following slogans:

+ "We Want Jobs";
+ "We Want Food";
+ "We're Not Demanding Fish or Meat, Just Some Porridge";
+ "Not a Yuan in Six Months, We Want Rice to Eat"; and
+ "We Need to Eat, We Need to Survive."

These slogans and banners conveyed the desperation and outrage of the retired or unemployed workers, and also revealed the subsistence form of their demands. The government generally adopted a policy of conciliation and emphasized the use of "persuasion" and "education" to resolve conflicts. Unless the protests turned into riots, local authorities usually dispersed workers not by force but by promises to redress their concerns about subsistence. On the other hand, since this kind of "subsistence struggle" made only local economistic demands (such as the need for emergency relief fund, or to postpone and revise plant closure or relocation decisions during the wave of privatization in the late 1990s), they were not that difficult to meet. A temporary stop-gap measure by local state officials was usually what was needed to silence the labor protest.

The willingness of the state to accommodate the demands of "subsistence struggles" explains why the labor protests were usually short-lived, confined to local areas, and failed to escalate into a large-scale social movement that involved workers from other areas or other industries.

Maintaining the Moral High Ground by Shifting the Blame to Lower-Level Officials

In China's labor protests, local enterprise managers and local government officials, not central government officials, were often the target of attack. In fact, higher-level government officials often punished local officials (or overturned lower-level officials' decisions) in order to silence disgruntled workers. As a result, despite widespread labor protests, the party-state was able to maintain the moral high ground and immunize itself from attack by workers. Corruption and poor management decisions were located at the individual level, instead of at the structural level. It was local officials and enterprise managers who were corrupt and made bad decisions that threatened workers' subsistence level. Higher-level officials in the central state made it very clear that they would not tolerate mistakes committed by lower-level officials. The central state and higher-level officials claimed that they and their economic reforms were blameless for workers' falling living standards and poverty.

In post-socialist China, Marc J. Blecher reports that workers generally accept the hegemony of the state and of the economic reforms, and tend to blame their enterprise managers (rather than the communist party-state or the neoliberal economic system) for their bad luck and poverty. As one worker said during an interview with him:

> Yes, of course it is unfair that my wages are lower and I have to endure wage arrears just because I happen to work in a plant that is not doing well. Does the state have responsibility? The state's policies are good. It is the implementation that is not good. Sometimes middle-level officials mess things up. … Some people just turn bad after becoming officials. (Blecher 2002, p. 291)

By accepting the discourse that it was local or middle-level officials who were at fault, Chinese workers appealed to the central government to solve the problem of corruption or bad management in local government and local enterprises. By taking the moral high ground of the central government for granted, the workers thus seek help from the central party-state rather than challenge its legitimacy. In this respect, labor protests might, at most, lead to the firing of some local or middle-level officials, but will not result in the development of a highly conscious working class that wants to stop or dismantle the ongoing neoliberal reforms.

Rapid Economic Development and Market Hegemony

The state's policies to divide and de-mobilize the workers have been greatly assisted by the rapid economic development of China over the past three decades, which, as we have seen, has recorded an amazing growth rate of 10 percent per year. A booming economy is not conducive to a labor movement, for the following reasons.

A booming economy provides more resources for the state and capitalists to grant concessions to the workers to satisfy their "subsistence struggles." In addition, a booming economy also diverts away from politics the energies of lively, smart people with leadership potential. In Yongshun Cai's (2002) study, the leaders who emerged in the spontaneous labor protest were mostly elite workers who had good social networks. These kind of elite workers were likely to find employment elsewhere in a booming economy, thus they would not risk their careers by continued participation in labor protests.

Furthermore, a booming economy lends further support to market hegemony, that is, the assumption that the economic reforms are good and there can be no return to the Maoist period. If a worker is not doing well, it is due either to bad luck or to lousy enterprise managers. He or she should try to think of a better way to make more money in the booming economy rather than participate in labor protests. In sum, a booming economy lends support to the ideology of neoliberal market competition; it is not conducive to the promotion of a national labor movement that aims to stop or dismantle the neoliberal reforms.

STATE–PEASANT CONFLICT

In the late 1970s, the post-socialist era started with the "*Household Responsibility System*," whereby all the land in the village was sub-divided among peasant households in a manner reminiscent of the land reform of the early 1950s. Since then, peasant households have emerged as the primary unit for agricultural production. The breakup of the communes and the emergence of the Household Responsibility System meant that most peasant households ended up with plots of land that were far too small for mechanization. It also meant that basic infra-structure such as roads and rural irrigation systems, whose upkeep had been the responsibility of the commune, remained in disrepair. Indeed, the majority of the peasants, especially those living in inland provinces or in areas far away from the cities, were to become worse off after the introduction of market reforms.

In the late 1980s, Tiejun Wen (2001) began to theorize and popu-larize the phrase *sannong wenti* (three rural problems), that is, *nongmin* (peasants), *nongcun* (village), and *nongye* (agriculture). In the post-socialist era, peasants are now at the mercy of neoliberal market forces and economic policy which favors exports and cities over the country-side, leading to: *the bankruptcy of the peasants* (due to poverty and the widening of the rural–urban gap); *the bankruptcy of the villages* (after the dismantling of the rural welfare system, the village governments are no longer able to provide basic services like healthcare, education, and welfare); and *the bankruptcy of agriculture* (Chinese agricultural prod-ucts cannot compete with foreign agricultural products after China's entry to the World Trade Organization).

The above three bankruptcies forced the peasants to migrate to the cities to seek a living, leaving only the elderly and the children in the villages. Kam Wing Chan (2013) estimates that about 230 million migrants now work in the city; this migrant-worker labor force has supplied the global economy with the largest ever army of super-exploitable labor. This "unlimited" supply of cheap peasant migrant workers in the late twentieth century laid the foundation for China's economic boom over the past thirty years.

These three rural problems also led to increasing social unrest in the Chinese countryside. Since 1978, there have been two waves of peasant protests. The first wave was against the extraction of arbitrary fees and taxes by local government officials, while the second wave was directed against rural land seizure by local officials and real estate developers.

The first wave of peasant protests, against taxes and fees, started in the 1980s. Patricia Thornton (2004, p. 87) cites a Chinese government report confirming that in 1993 over 1.5 million cases of protests occurred in that year alone, over 6,000 of which were officially classified as "disturbances" (*naoshi*) by the authorities. Of these cases, 830 involved more than one township and in excess of 500 participants; 78 involved more than one county and over 1,000 participants; and 21 were considered to be "extremely large-scale" events, involving more than 5,000 participants. A surprising number of these confrontations turned violent: these incidents of protests resulted in 8,200 casualties among township and county officials; 560 county-level offices were ransacked; and some 385 public security personnel were fatally injured.

The second wave of peasant protests, against illegal land seizure, started in the 1990s. George J. Gilboy and Eric Heginbotham (2004, p. 258) point out 168,000 cases of illegal land seizures were reported by the Ministry of Land Resources in November 2003, twice as many as in the entire previous year. The trend continued to accelerate, with some 2.54 million hectares, or 2 percent of total farmland, lost in 2003 alone. Some 34 million peasants have lost their land entirely since 1987, and the new surge in land transfers certainly indicates an acceleration of that process. China's best-known business and economics magazine, *Caijing*, calls the recent wave of rural land seizure by local officials and real estate developers a new "enclosure" (*quandi*) movement.

There are several distinctive characteristics of peasant protests in post-socialist China. First of all, most of the protests took place in a township and were aimed at an abusive tax collection policy or a land seizure by the township government. Although the incidents might ostensibly appear to be anti-state, it must be stressed that the target was not the central government. In fact, peasants identified themselves with the center, and called upon it for help. In the 1990s, peasants usually began their protests with the slogan "Resolutely unite around the center of the Communist Party headed by President Jiang Zemin and Premier Zhu Rongji."

Moreover, village officials – part of local government – were often found within the leadership ranks of the protests, and they provided the peasant protesters with support (information, networks, and other resources). And despite the fact that violence and clashes occurred during the protests, these were for the most part a result of provocation by the township government. Generally speaking, rural inhabitants wanted nothing more than a peaceful protest, and they usually started their action with a non-violent demonstration.

Examining all these reports of peasant protests in the Chinese countryside cannot but raise a number of questions. Why have so many rural "disturbances" arisen in post-socialist China? Why do peasants target the local township government but not the central state? Why do village officials themselves often join the ranks of those protesting against township government? What is the impact of such agrarian conflict on the Chinese state and the neoliberal path of development since the 1990s?

The Formation of a Bifurcated State

From a peasant's perspective, the central government is "benign" because it cuts taxes to relieve the peasant's burden and increases financial transfers to expand social services to local areas. Moreover, this positive view of the central state apparatus is reinforced by the repeated attempts of the Beijing government to strengthen regulations protecting the peasantry from "exploitation" by corrupt local officials and greedy urban developers. On the other hand, township government is perceived by those at the rural grassroots as malign: not only does the local state impose excessive taxes and fees on the peasantry, it also takes the side of urban developers so as to enrich itself by dispossessing peasants of their land.

Xiaolin Guo (2001) reports that when peasants complained about land expropriation, escalating tuition fees, rising education surcharges, the deterioration of irrigation systems and the environment, they always consciously differentiated the local government from the central government:

> The central policies are good and in favor of us peasants. But when they reach the provincial level, the policies have gone out of shape. The further down, the more distorted the policies become. By the time they reach the village, the policies have completely changed from what they were in the first place. (Guo 2001, p. 435)

Guo (2001, p. 436) further explains the formation of a bifurcation state as follows. The state with which the peasants normally interact is local: the township government. In this structural setting, the relationship of the peasants with the central state is mostly political and symbolic, whereas the relationship with the local state is social and economic. The relationship between the central state and the peasants is maintained at a moral level, whereas that between the local state and the peasants is more tangible and tied to interests in concrete terms. For this reason, the competition for control over economic resources (like land) between the peasants and the local state under the influence of neoliberal capitalism has become a major source of conflict in the Chinese countryside.

Obviously, this split between *a "benign" central* and *a "malign" local state* has profound implications for the pattern of agrarian conflict, including the target, the discourse, the strategy, the leadership, and the outcome of peasant protests. Unless the split nature of the state is inserted into the analysis, it is impossible to clearly understand why peasant unrest is directed only at the township but not at the central government, why village cadres often join such protests, and why this kind of rural agency is unlikely to result in political upheavals and regime transition.

Drawing upon their findings on the first wave of peasant protests, against taxes and fees, Thomas P. Bernstein (2004), Kevin J. O'Brien and Lianjiang Li (2006), Elizabeth Perry (2007), and Patricia Thornton (2004) pointed to the following characteristics of the peasant protests at the turn of the twentieth century.

The Target of Peasant Protests

Among the different levels of government, it is the township government that bears the brunt of peasant anger. As the study by Guo (2001, p. 437) indicates, township government was the main target of village protests, not least because it was the authority that issued notifications of land expropriation, and it was township government officials who deprived villagers of their land by force. In short, both the local state and its staff are the most visible evidence for – and thus the clearest manifestation of – oppression and dispossession experienced by the Chinese peasantry.

Why township officials were invariably singled out in peasant protests is attributed by Bernstein (2004, p. 11) to the fact that the former were under intense pressure to extract funds, both for career reasons and because townships generally were greatly dependent on such economic resources. Given their role in enforcing land expropriations, the physical presence of township officials at the point of conflict also intensified and reproduced the antagonism which subsequently fueled villagers' resistance (Guo 2001).

On the other hand, the central government never appears on the peasants' complaint list and is never directly attacked in peasant protests. Quite the opposite: the central government is often seen as the "ultimate savior" of the Chinese peasant; seeking allies at higher levels of the state is clearly the main strategy of peasant protests. As such, it seems our Chinese case fits nicely with Eric Hobsbawm's (1997, p. 202) observation that "people at the grassroots level confined their struggles to fighting those oppressors with whom they had immediate contact."

The Discourse of Peasant Protests

In keeping with the pattern of this appeal starting from lower levels to authorities at the upper levels, O'Brien and Li (2006) have coined the term "rightful resistance" to describe peasant conflict in the Chinese countryside. Rightful resistance is to defend the rights already granted by the central government, yet often denied by local officials, or rights that peasants believed could be derived from the regime's policies, principles, and legitimating ideology. In the course of undertaking such protests, Chinese peasants endeavor to persuade local officialdom that they are engaged in an entirely legitimate behavior.

The Strategy of Peasant Protests

The term "boundary-spanning" is used by O'Brien (2004) to support the contention that Chinese peasants desire to exploit the gap between rights promised by the central state and rights delivered at the local level. In order to protect themselves, and simultaneously to improve the chances of success, peasant protesters tender impeccably reasonable demands and profess little more than a wish to make the system live up to its promises (what it is supposed to be). This caution, O'Brien points out, is bolstered by the fact that claims made by those protesting are limited in scope. That is, they are doubly circumscribed: parochial and local (i.e. defending the interests of a particular community) protests at the rural grassroots never seek to be national and operate outside the existing political system.

Peasant protests, then, involve "boundary-spanning claims" that sit near the fuzzy boundary between official, prescribed policies and forbidden ones, in a middle ground that is neither clearly transgressive nor clearly contained. Peasants who engage in this type of contention characteristically combine lawful tactics (e.g. collective petitions, seeking audiences with power-holders) with disruptive but not quite unlawful action (e.g. silently parading with lit candles in broad daylight to symbolize the "dark rule" of local leaders). Chinese peasants always behave in accord with prevailing statutes (or at least not clearly in violation of them), and they use the regime's own policies and legitimating myths to justify their action. As a rule, the center is more tolerant and better intentioned than local power officials, which makes it convenient for rightful resisters to invoke commitments from above ignored by local officials.

Furthermore, peasant protesters can find allies, even patrons, at higher levels of the state, as the latter are usually eager to uncover and stop misconduct by their local agents. O'Brien and Li (2006, p. 65) say that "divisions in a multilayered state with formidable principal agent problems thus made rightful resistance possible." The Chinese peasant protesters are especially skillful in exploiting such an opportunity after growing up in such a political structure.

The Leaders of Peasant Protests

Village officials often show up as leaders of peasant protests against the township government. They contribute personal and family networks, organizational expertise, as well as financial resources. Having local government officials as leaders is crucial in explaining the emergence and the persistence of peasant protests in the Chinese countryside over the past three decades. So a key question is: Why are lower-level government officials willing to participate in public protests against a higher-level government in this manner?

To a certain extent, these actions can be interpreted as a product of "rightful resistance." Village government officials legitimated their roles in peasant protests by claiming that they were acting in the name of the center; they were only opposing those township officials who had grossly violated central policies. They saw themselves as upholding the interests of the communist party-state, which were not separable from the peasants' legitimate rights and interests (Bernstein 2004, p. 8).

The Impact of Peasant Protests

In light of the fact that Chinese peasants have a dual concept of the state and that peasant struggles are consequently mainly of the type classified as "rightful resistance," which seldom goes beyond what is permitted opposition, it is highly unlikely that agrarian conflict will lead to political upheavals and regime changes in China.

However, it is also misleading to assert that peasant conflict could not result in any significant impact on macro-structural changes in the Chinese society, politics, and economy. For example, two decades of rightful resistance against local taxes and fees, as O'Brien and Li (2006, p. 124) observe, have "gradually, directly, but surely ... spurred a policy change, namely, a reduction of the fiscal burden." Indeed, it could be argued that the consolidation of state neoliberalism in the early 2010s was the outcome of widespread peasant protests. It was at the height of workers' and peasant protests that the communist party-state formulated the policy of a "harmonious society" and the construction of a "new socialist countryside" under the Hu/Wen regime. In order to pacify the growing peasant unrest in the countryside, the communist party-state wanted to deepen state neoliberalism by abolishing the agricultural tax, increasing expenditure in rural areas by 15 percent, and raising its allocation to the healthcare budget by 87 percent. Peasants were also relieved from the burden of paying for many public services such as miscellaneous fees levied by rural schools (So 2007b).

Since there is also no political upheaval and the Chinese communist party-state is not under imminent danger of an agrarian revolution, the source of shifting the direction of development has to come from the top through the state elites rather than from the bottom through the peasants.

STATE–MIDDLE CLASS CONFLICT

In 1989, Chinese students and intellectuals initiated a robust democracy movement at Beijing's Tiananmen Square which was brutally suppressed by the communist party-state. In December 2008, 300 members of China's middle class signed a document entitled Charter 08. The document called for an entirely new constitution, an independent judiciary, direct elections, freedom of religion, speech, and assembly, and the right to form independent political parties in China. Despite the party-state's efforts to censor the democracy issue, the document obtained more than 7,000 signatures in support from people of all levels and positions in society by February 2009 (So and Su 2011, pp. 135–6).

This Charter 08 incident reignited hope for democratization in China. Since China's remarkable economic growth has given rise to the expansion of the new middle class, Western researchers hope that this class will become a political agent to pursue the democracy project in the country. After all, researchers (C. Li 2010; S. Liu 2009; Unger 2006) point out that a new middle class has begun to form not only on the cultural front (as shown by gated communities and an affluent lifestyle and consumption) but also on the political front. The new middle class is becoming more active in politics. Middle-class professional associations have begun to raise wide-ranging societal concerns that often go beyond their professional boundaries; they also act as members and leaders of various social movements.

For example, the homeowners' resistance movement is a means to defend the consumer rights of the new middle class, to safeguard its privatized lifestyle, and to protect the autonomy of the new middle-class community (S. Liu 2009). This homeowners' resistance movement frequently draws upon the essential resources of the new middle class, like lawyers' familiarity with private property laws, architects' design knowledge about building construction, managers' sophisticated negotiation skills, and former state officials' extensive interpersonal networks and contacts with the news media. With these new middle-class resources behind the movements, homeowners in a middle-class neighborhood could win battles against powerful developers and corrupt local officials. These victories, in turn, have greatly empowered the new middle class.

Similarly, when intellectuals (including writers, scholars, scientists, other professionals, and college students) become more vocal in their demands for a cleaner environment, these new middle-class demands are very hard to suppress. As a result, China's environmental movement has been gaining strength over the past two decades. As environmental activists often expose the institutionalized corruption and the lack of accountability of the entire system of governance, many new middle-class environmental activists have expanded their demands and become closely linked with democracy activists who have agitated for broader political reforms (Economy 2005; S.-h. Lee et al. 1999). So how does the communist party-state respond to the challenge of new middle-class social movements and democratization?

The Party-State and the New Middle Class

During the socialist era between the 1950s and the 1970s, the new middle class had an uneasy relationship with the party-state in China. The Communist Revolution was founded on the support of workers and peasants, and the communist party-state did not trust the middle class. In the Hundred Flowers Campaign and the Cultural Revolution, many new middle-class members were humiliated, downgraded, and sent to the labor camps in the countryside for reeducation.

However, the communist party-state drastically changed its relationship with the new middle class during the post-1978 reform era. In 2002, the Chinese party-state called for "enlarging the size of the middle-income group" (C. Li 2010, p. 11). Instead of taking a hostile stand, the communist party-state is now more amenable to the new middle class, as shown by the following processes.

To start with, the party-state's state neoliberal policies during the past three decades are in harmony with the interests of the new middle class. Policies such as the expansion of higher education institutions, the establishment of high-tech developmental zones, the attraction of foreign investment, and the adoption of an export-led industrialization strategy naturally would enhance the interest of the new middle class because China will need more professors to teach in the universities, more engineers to work on the machines and in the construction industry, more researchers and scientists to work in high-tech industries, more lawyers to handle the legal complications in forming business partnerships with foreign corporations, more social workers to handle the social problems created by the sudden shift from policies of state socialism to those of state neoliberalism, and so on.

In addition, the party-state adopted policies that are particularly aimed to boost the well-being of the new middle class. For example, during the past two decades, the state raised the salary of university professors several times so that these are now much higher than those of average urban workers. University professors are also given very generous housing benefits, such as being allowed to buy an apartment from their work unit (*danwei*) at a discount price, or are given generous housing allowances so they can buy or rent housing in a very nice middle-class neighborhood (S. Liu 2009).

Luigi Tomba (2010b) pointed out that housing subsidization by the party-state played a very important role in the upward mobility of the new middle class. The housing careers of new homeowners had often been kick-started by the subsidized acquisition of a *danwei* dwelling, by the access to subsidies to buy a second apartment, by the access to credit through the "housing provident fund," or through the use of the *danwei* apartment as collateral in a mortgage agreement. Beijing is probably among the clearest cases in which the local party-state used housing policies to boost consumption and build a broad-based, high-consuming, professional new middle class.

Moreover, unlike the situation in Maoist China, where members of the new middle class had to keep their mouths shut or risk political prosecution, the new middle class now feels that it has a voice which is respected by state officials and party leaders. Members of the new middle class are often recruited into think tanks or invited to join consultation committees to offer advice or voice opinions. Irrespective of whether their opinions are accepted by the party-state or not, members of the middle class feel they are respected by the party-state because they have a chance to participate in the decision-making process and believe they could influence policy making through existing political channels (*Dong Fang Zao Bao* 2005).

Finally, there is a "fusion" between the new middle class and the communist party-state. On the one hand, there is a *professionalization of the party leaders* and *state cadres*. For example, in 2006, it was reported that out of the 35,637 communist party members in Beijing Xuanwu District, 12,989 (or 36.5 percent) had the educational qualification of post-secondary or university education (Beijing Xuanwu District 2006).

In order to encourage the professionalization of state officials and party leaders, the party-state implemented a policy of bureaucratic promotion and recruitment: an applicant who has a BA will be appointed as a member; an applicant with a master's degree will be appointed as vice head; while an applicant with a Ph.D. will be appointed as head of a department (Beijing Xuanwu District 2006).

Additionally, the party-state invests a lot of money in sending cadres to advanced nations (like the US) to undergo training. Guangdong Province, for instance, is reported to have spent 100 million yuan in five years to send 300 higher-level cadres overseas for training. The Guangdong government requires that the overseas trainee must be less than 47 years old if he/she is a city-level cadre, must have a university BA, and must have foreign language proficiency equal to a four-year university level. The media reported that upon return from their overseas training, the cadres feel more professionalized and more confident in managing their departments.

On the other hand, members of the new middle class are being recruited into the communist party-state. Since the party has maintained a high degree of support in Chinese society, university students are not deterred from being members of the Communist Party because this could provide an advantage in the job market in both the private and public sectors. Similarly, university graduates and professionals are attracted to enter the state bureaucracy because it instituted a policy which favors the hiring of the applicants with a BA, a master's degree, and a Ph.D. (Nanping Shi 2004).

Democratic Transition from Authoritarian Rule?

What is the implication of the above analysis for the prospects of democratization in China? In many developing countries (e.g. South Korea), democratization emerged when the authoritarian state was overthrown by vocal protests on the street, in which the new middle class acted as leaders and organizers of a "noisy" democratization revolution. The third wave of democratization that Samuel P. Huntington (1991) talks about is full of examples of this *noisy democratization*.

However, it is obvious the Chinese situation is different. Despite the Chinese new middle class getting more politically active, despite incidences of mass disturbances in the countryside and in the cities, and despite many pundits' predictions that the communist party-state would fall after the 1989 Tiananmen Incident, there are few signs to show that the democracy movement is coming alive again or the communist party-state is losing its mandate to rule. It seems that China will not take the route of "noisy democratization," given the fact that the new middle class is moderate and rational and there is a fusion between this class and the party-state. It seems highly unlikely that members of the new middle class would turn themselves into democratic martyrs, sacrificing their superior market position, high status, and comfortable lifestyle to fight and die for the cause of democracy.

But does the new middle class need to adopt a confrontational stance to promote a democratic revolution in China? Does the "communist" party-state need to be overthrown in order to have multiple-party free elections in China? Does democratization in China need to go through a revolutionary phase with open, violent confrontation and abrupt, radical structural changes?

If the above analysis is correct, the Chinese new middle class is actually in a good position to push for another mode of democratization, what can be called *quiet democratization*. Over the past decade, the new middle class has been voicing political issues, raising concerns, and setting up new practices (like expanding the rights of citizenship, implementing the rule of law, enlarging the scope of civil society, pressing for more accountability and transparency from the party-state) that are important in laying the groundwork for democratization. The mode that the new middle class is following is also conducive to democratization. The new middle class's moderate, non-confrontational stand shows that it shares the communist party-state's goal of political stability and avoiding class polarization, and therefore it is not a threat to the established order. Thus, the party-state sees the new middle class as its chief supporter and ally. Coupled with the fusion of membership between the party-state and the new middle class, the new middle class will gradually have a stronger voice in policies. As times go by, party-state policies will gradually reflect the agenda of the new middle class.

In sum, instead of taking a confrontational position to impose democratization on the party-state from below, the new middle class has been quietly laying the groundwork for democratization by working from within the party-state. If the party-state feels empowered by the professionalization of the cadres of the party-state, if the party-state thinks that it has gained strong societal support from Chinese citizens, and if the party-state does not feel any threat to its survival from outside forces, then it is foreseeable in the near future that it could initiate democratization from above so as to consolidate its basis of legitimacy. Should such an event take place, a quiet democratization will emerge in China without any open, noisy confrontation like the third-wave democratic revolution that happened in the Philippines, South Korea, and Eastern Europe.

The above discussion has examined the historical emergence of social conflict and civil unrest in post-socialist China since 1978. It shows that despite the insurgency from the workers, the peasants, and the new middle class, the Chinese communist party-state was not under any serious threat to its survival. Instead of facing any danger of imminent regime collapse, the communist party-state was indeed highly stable.

This chapter has argued that the communist party-state is pretty successful in responding to the challenge of social conflict and civil unrest in Chinese society. First of all, most of the class conflict is deflected toward the local party-state, with the protesters blaming predatory local state officials for their social and economic problems, while the central party-state is seen as benign and thus able to maintain the moral high ground. The party-state also imposes political repression to disorganize the working class and the peasants. It bans any unofficial organization developed by the workers and peasants themselves, leading to a pattern of "leaderless" and spontaneous protest which tends to be of short duration and is not sustainable. It sets up many labor laws to individualize, to economize, and to preempt labor protests. Finally, it adopts the tactics of accommodation to diffuse working-class protests if workers are willing to stay within a legal boundary which is tolerated by the communist party-state. Furthermore, there is a fusion of personnel between the communist party-state and emerging middle-class professionals through the professionalization of party leaders and state officials. Higher educational credentials are built into the recruitment and promotion of officials in the state bureaucracy, and the communist party-state has invested a lot of resources in sending its cadres overseas to undergo professional training.

In sum, despite widespread social conflict and civil unrest among the workers, the peasants, and the new middle class over the past three decades, contemporary Chinese society has been highly stable and the communist party-state was quite successful in efforts to deflect, repress, preempt, or institutionalize various kinds of social conflict and civil unrest up to the late 2000s. It was this successful conflict management that gave the Chinese party-state autonomy and the capacity to design, implement, and deepen the state neoliberalism programs and to make policy adjustments (either to speed up, slow down, or change direction) in mid-course if policies were determined to be not working well.

INTENSIFICATION OF SOCIAL CONFLICT SINCE THE 2008 GLOBAL FINANCIAL CRISIS

However, this favorable situation has been transformed since the outbreak of the global financial crisis in 2008. For example, the subcontractors who run South China factories are highly vulnerable to the fluctuation of orders experienced since the crisis struck. Many factories have carried out retrenchment, unfair dismissals, massive layoffs, stricter factory discipline, and drastic reductions in wages in order to cut the cost of production and to increase productivity.

Workers have responded to this intensified capitalist control and exploitation through protests, demonstrations, sits-in, slow-downs, and so on. In the aftermath of the global financial crisis, a momentous strike wave soon spread across factories, across industries, and even across regions in the summer of 2010 and in 2011. This wave of strikes was highly militant, because Chinese workers were no longer satisfied with defensive struggles (like making sure that they were paid on time and getting back wages owed by their employers). Instead, they were now fighting for higher wages, humane working conditions, and the democratic election of labor union officials, increasingly through direct and, at times, violent confrontation (C. K.-c. Chan and Hui 2012; E. Friedman 2012).

Similarly, Jianrong Yu (2010) has begun to talk about a new pattern of *peasant* protests in the Chinese countryside. First, there has been the emergence of skillful protest organizers, leading to a more organized resistance. O'Brien (2009, p. 26) explains that chronic resistance is a product of skilled protest organizers who know how to shape claims, mobilize followers, orchestrate acts of defiance, and (occasionally) mount actions that transcend the borders of a single community. ... In the face of long odds, these activists have regularly tested the truth of the saying: a big disturbance produces a big result, a small disturbance produces a small result, and no disturbance produces no result.

Second, peasant activists have tended to adopt more spirited defiance in their protests. Learning from their past experience, they have concluded that comparatively tame forms of contention (lodging complaints with a higher level of government) are ineffective, and that forceful, attention-grabbing actions (such as blocking a road or organizing a sit-in) and confrontational tactics (such as surrounding fee collectors as a prelude to driving them off) are needed. Third, violence is also on the rise. Jianrong Yu (2008) has documented the spread of unplanned, "accidental" protests that rapidly take on their own dynamic. These so-called "*anger-venting*" flare-ups are often sparked off by essentially random incidents (e.g. the rumor that a street vendor has been seriously beaten by a rich person or a policeman, or a minor street scuffle between a porter and an individual claiming to be a government official). The protesters and rioters are merely venting their frustrations, feelings of resentment, and anger because they are upset at the local authorities and at the wealthy.

The new middle class, too, is being hurt because of the loss of jobs and financial assets as a result of the global financial crisis and partly due to the rapid rise in housing in urban China. With the tightening of the job market during the economic slowdown, the unemployment rate among college graduates (who are presumed to be members of China's new middle class) is growing. College graduates are frustrated because they not only cannot get good jobs, but also face the challenges of rising prices for housing and other basic services. There is great uncertainty, therefore, as to how many of them can actually make it into the ranks of the new middle class (J. Lin and Sun 2010, p. 230).

New college graduates have earned themselves a nickname, *fengqing* (literally, angry youth). These young Chinese

> often use the internet to vent their frustrations, and that frustration often comes from either their patriotism or their desire to seek what is right, fair, true, and transparent. They care about social issues. And they feel they need to be outspoken, to have their voices heard. And they often use the internet to gain knowledge and have their voice heard. (J. Lin and Sun 2010, p. 235)

Middle-class frustration seems to be on the rise and middle-class members have been more vocal than before in articulating political issues, raising concerns, and setting up new practices that are important in laying the groundwork for citizenship, human rights, and democracy. For example, in early 2013, the anti-censorship street protests against the crackdown of *Southern Weekend* by writers, lawyers, actors, and public intellectuals in the southern city of Guangzhou, and the online outrage that exploded over an extraordinary surge in air pollution in the north, demand something that challenges the very nature of the communist party-state: transparency in the state bureaucracy, the public's right to know, investigative reporting and professional journalism, and the freedom of speech and the press (Shu 2013; E. Wong 2013).

The insurgency of social conflict and civil unrest in Chinese society was finally reflected in the conflict within the communist party. In March 2012, the notions of stability and consensus in China's secretive political system took what may be a big hit by the dismissal of Bo Xilai, the Party Secretary of metropolitan Chongqing. Mr Bo is mostly identified as the charismatic leader of China's new left by the intellectuals and policy wonks who argue that China should use state power to assure social equality and enforce a culture of moral purity and nationalism. Mr Bo's policies in Chongqing, from the mass singing of Mao-era songs to his pitiless anti-corruption campaign, had earned him strong support from the citizens of Chongqing (Wines 2012).

As Yuezhi Zhao (2012, p. 1) points out, Bo was no ordinary Politburo member of the Chinese Communist Party, and his Chongqing model was not just another instance of "decentralized experimentation" so characteristic of the communist policy-making process. What was increasingly at issue, and was emphasized by the press, was the contrast between the two models of development: the "*Guangdong Model*," which symbolized a more neoliberal free market approach, rising inequality, and export-led industrialization since 1978, and the "*Chongqing Model*," which was characterized as looking to revitalize socialist ideas and populist claims in its push toward the direction of state socialist development in the Maoist era. At stake today, then, is not just the fate of Bo, but also China's revolutionary past, the complicated intersections of state socialism, neoliberalism, and state neoliberalism politics, and the unfinished struggle for national development in China.

Since the global financial crisis in 2008, therefore, there has been an intensification of social conflict both in urban areas and in the countryside. As a result, the party-state's capacity and legitimacy seem to be taking a hit. The decreasing ability to manage social conflict can be seen from the fact that the so-called "Stability Fund" increased very rapidly over the past few years. In 2011, the party-state reportedly spent more on internal security (US$111 billion) than on national defense (US$106 billion).

WHITHER CHINA?

The stability of the present communist regime is based upon the assumption that China's remarkable economic development will continue. However, the insurgent social conflict since 2008 has largely eroded the legitimacy of the communist party-state now that this is mainly derived from its economic performance and from its ability to raise the living standard of its citizens (so-called *"performance-based legitimacy"* according to Breslin 2007, p. 44). If China ever runs into any unforeseeable economic breakdown or a prolonged economic slow-down in the near future, this will inevitably reconfigure the asymmetrical power relations between the communist party-state and the insurgent social classes. In this scenario, conflicts in Chinese society will be intensified and the social classes will become more vocal and militant than before, while the autonomy and the capacity of the communist party-state to pursue state neoliberalism will be considerably weakened. As such, the prospect for revolutionary changes in post-socialist China are contingent upon whether the communist party-state in China can continue its remarkable path of economic development and move away from neoliberal capitalism in such a way as to soften its structural contradiction of growing class inequality and class conflict.

The Challenges of Sustainability: Environmental Degradation and Resource Depletion

7

China's rapid economic growth has been attained at a very high cost. Apart from the social conflicts discussed in the previous chapter, the country also faces a very severe environmental challenge, including acute pollution (air, water, and soil), resource depletion, various forms of land degradation, and a diminution of biodiversity. Importantly, some 300 million people in China do not have access to safe drinking water. Among the world's thirty most polluted cities, twenty are in China. Deaths due to air and water pollution were so prevalent in some Chinese villages that they came to be known as "cancer villages," and in 2010 the media and the Internet drew attention to 459 such villages distributed across twenty-nine of China's thirty-one provinces (L. Liu 2010). It has been suggested that annual losses due to water and air pollution amount to US$54 billion, annual direct losses due to desertification total US$7 billion, and losses to crops and forest induced by acid rain cost US$730 million per year, not to mention losses due to mega flooding like the one in 1998, factory closures due to water shortage, and pollution-related healthcare costs (J. Liu and Diamond 2005, p. 1183).

As the previous chapters have emphasized, China's rapid growth was made possible by its reintegration into the capitalist world economy, and, in turn, its bid to become the global factory was largely responsible for the country's environmental degradation and resource depletion.

Owing to the high level of global integration, these environmental challenges affected not only China, but the world at large, arousing social conflicts and diplomatic crises.

This chapter will begin with a discussion of the environmental problem in the state socialist era in the 1950s and the 1960s. Then it will discuss how China's reentry into the capitalist world economy and its hyper-growth model led to the depletion and deterioration of the country's water, land, and air resources, investigating their local and global ramifications. It will then move on to explore the economic underpinnings of the environmental challenges, the positions of the Chinese government, and emerging civil society actors, all with a view to ascertaining the prospect of the country attaining a more sustainable future.

ENVIRONMENTAL PROBLEMS IN STATE SOCIALISM (1950–78)

Some of the factors contributing to China's current environmental challenges can be traced to policies made before the 1978 reforms. For example, the attempt to plant wheat over the grassland of the northeast during the Cultural Revolution (1966–76) continues to affect the country in the form of desertification and dust storms (Marks 2012). A similar case may be made for the erosion of land due to the clearing of forests during the Great Leap Forward (1958–61) (Smil 2004). The population policy adopted until 1970, moreover, which encouraged the Chinese to have as many children as possible, generated a population of some 1.3 billion. With such a sheer number, massive resources would be required to feed, clothe, and house everyone, even if they were to pursue only a frugal existence.

Among the environmental challenges to be examined in this chapter, deforestation stands out as a major problem that deepened during China's state socialist era. Researchers identify two rounds of "great cutting" in the state socialist era (Marks 2012). The first round occurred during the Great Leap Forward, when Mao sought to catch up with the West by releasing the peasantry's productive forces and constructing "backyard steel furnaces." With 600,000 furnaces in operation by October 1958, large numbers of local forests were cleared. The second round pertains to the Cultural Revolution, when food security assumed momentous significance and the whole country was mobilized to adopt the so-called "Dazhai model" of conquering nature. Apart from opening grasslands to the plow and "reclaiming" lakes for cultivation, forests were also cleared for the planting of grains or other crops.

However, it was the country's neoliberal "reform and opening up" policy since 1978 that brought the challenges of sustainability to a head. Not only had deforestation deteriorated, water pollution, air pollution, and other forms of resource depletion were also exacerbated.

ENVIRONMENTAL DEGRADATION AND RESOURCE DEPLETION SINCE 1978

China experienced a period of sustained economic growth and rapid urbanization after the launch of the "reform and opening up" policy. Rapid growth fed the desire for extravagance among the *nouveau riche*[1] and urbanization generated massive problems of sewage and wastage disposal. More important, China's reintegration into the capitalist world economy, its bid to become the global factory, and the adoption of neoliberal policies led to a widespread disregard for environmental issues. Potentially polluting industries producing paper, toys, plastics, fertilizers, refining oil, dyeing, and the like, were established with few environmental safeguards. Tremendous pressure was placed on the country's natural resources so that, since 1978, there has been an intensification of coal use, the construction of hydropower dams, indiscriminate logging, as well as global sourcing of primary commodities. Given the interconnection among various components of the ecological system, the degradation of one aspect can easily lead to the deterioration of another. To comprehend the massive and complex environmental challenges confronting China, the following will examine the deterioration of the country's water, land, and atmospheric resources as well as their global ramifications.

Water Resources and Pollution

China's water resources are in short supply, unreliable, and suffer from a glaring geographical mismatch. According to the UNFAO (2010), China's yearly per capita renewable water resources are rather modest, standing at about 2,000 cubic meters when the global average is approximately 6,200 cubic meters. These moderate resources are aggravated by a mismatch between population density and economic activities. While rainfall concentrates in the southeast, northern China possesses 60 percent of the country's cropland and is home to megacities like Beijing and Tianjin (UNFAO 2010).

In many years, the Yellow River even shows signs of parching up.[2] Water shortage is particularly acute in the cities. According to Jun Ma (2004), it affects 400 of the 600 cities in China, including thirty of the thirty-two largest ones, distributed across every province. Water-stressed areas in China have relied heavily on groundwater in the last few decades, resulting in the drop of water tables by nearly one meter per year in the north China plain, which in the coastal areas led to the added problem of saltwater intrusion (S. Moore 2013). According to one estimate, China's water shortage results in the idleness of 15 percent of its agricultural land and frequent stoppages of its industries (Shapiro 2012).

On top of the question of quantity are the issues of inefficient use and pollution. It has been suggested that water utilization in China suffers from leaky pipes and technological deficiencies so that, on average, a cubic meter of water generates no more than US\$3.5 economic output when the same amount can generate US\$36 in the developed countries (Gleick 2008–9; UNFAO 2010). More serious perhaps is the issue of pollution, which affects rural and urban areas alike.

Aside from agricultural run-off, the lack of wastewater plants, pipe works, and effective management often leaves human and industrial waste largely untreated before discharge. Between September 2006 and 2008, some 130 water pollution incidents were reported by the State Environmental Protection Administration (SEPA, now Ministry of Environmental Protection) (Gleick 2008–9). It has been estimated that water pollution affects 90 percent of China's urban groundwater and 75 percent of rivers and lakes. In 2012, the country's Ministry of Water Resources (2012) reported that some 21.2 percent of water flow in China's ten water systems was ranked category V (the worst in a five-point scale), with the most serious cases concentrating in northeast China, including the Songhua River, Yellow River, Liao River, Huai River, and Hai River (Figure 7.1). Water pollution adversely affects the ecosystem and threatens the lives of many species.[3] It breeds diseases, epitomized in the so-called "cancer villages" mentioned earlier. Similarly, whereas the World Bank estimated some 66,000 deaths in China to be caused annually by water pollution (China Water Risk 2010), the OECD also reported in 2007 that an estimated 30,000 rural children died each year of diarrhea owing to polluted water (Gleick 2008–9).

Water pollution and scarcity not only affected China, but also jeopardized neighboring countries. In 2005, an explosion at a petro-chemical plant in Jilin Province resulted not only in the spill of some 100 tons of benzene substances into the Songhua River, but also the drift of pollutants into Russia's Amur River, generating a major diplomatic crisis (China Water Risk 2010).

Equally serious is the issue of water scarcity. Apart from measures to enhance efficiency and limit overall demand, such as the 2002 Water

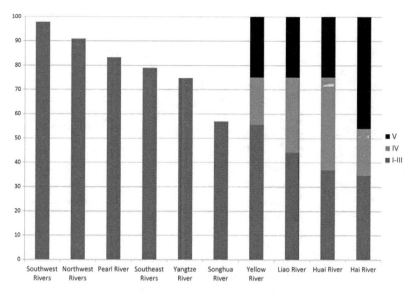

Figure 7.1 Water quality of China's ten water systems, 2012
(*Source:* Ministry of Water Resources 2012)

Law and 2010 "three red lines" policies, the Chinese government initiated various hydraulic projects, including the three-channel South–North Water Transfer Project and the construction of dams of various scales (Marks 2012; S. Moore 2013; World Bank 2009). Just as China's dam building on rivers originating in the Tibetan Plateau in western China impacts on people in India, Nepal, Pakistan, Bangladesh, and Kazakhstan, dams built on the Lancang River and Nu River, which happen to be the upper reaches of the Mekong and Salween Rivers, respectively, affect the downstream states of Laos, Cambodia, Vietnam, Thailand, and Myanmar (Litzinger 2007; Mehtonen 2009; see Figure 7.2). People in these countries were understandably worried that their water supplies would be adversely affected (Leitsinger 2010).

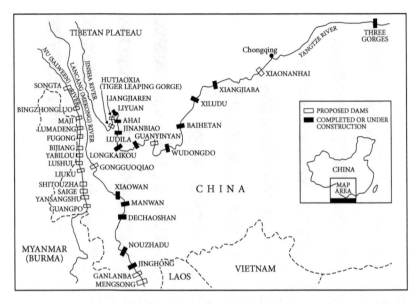

Figure 7.2 Proposed and completed dams on the Nu, Lancang, and Jinsha rivers
(*Source:* Wells-Dang 2012, p. 138, reproduced with permission of Palgrave Macmillan)

Land: Resource Depletion and Deforestation

Like water, other natural resources have also become severely depleted and land has been gravely polluted in China. Rapid industrial growth requires the massive input of energy and raw materials, leading to the depletion of aluminum, coal, copper, iron, lumber, petroleum, tin, and other resources. Industrial pollution and urbanization have, together with other processes, resulted in the loss of 8.2 million hectares of arable land since 1997, such that the country's arable land per capita only amounts to 40 percent of the world average (UNOHCHR 2010).

In turn, the scarcity of arable land has led to the intensive use of fertilizers in China, the per hectare usage of which amounts to 2.5 times the global average, worsening the country's pollution and generating severe problems of food safety.[4] Over-cultivation, over-grazing, deforestation, and other natural or non-natural forces have also led to desertification, salinization, and other forms of land degradation (Berry 2003).

All the above dimensions are of momentous significance. Instead of attempting a broad overview, the following will focus on deforestation, a process that epitomizes the global scale and contradictory repercussions of China's resource depletion.

Deforestation accelerated in the initial phase of neoliberalism between 1978 and 1988, both because the "household responsibility system" prompted smaller holders to reap short-term timber wealth and because rural households raced to take advantage of the regime's permission to construct new homes. This is what researchers identified as the third round of "great cutting" in China. The fourth round of "great cutting" occurred in the post-1992 era when neoliberalization deepened. Specifically, rapid industrial growth prompted massive logging not only among contracted-out collective forestland, but also among state-owned forest companies that cleared forested mountains in western Sichuan, northwestern Yunnan, and the Qinling Mountains in China's northeast[5] (Marks 2012: 287; see also Hays 2008).

Things appeared to have come to a head in 1998. The excessive flooding of the Yangtze River in that year was attributed to deforestation, which denuded mountain slopes and led to sedimentation of riverbeds. The communist party-state proceeded to ban logging (Marks 2012; Shapiro 2012, pp. 42–3). It also stepped up its reforestation effort, which, according to some observers, contributed to the "comeback" of the world's forests (Hays 2008; D. Liu 2009).

Notwithstanding disagreements over the success of reforestation in China, the country's ban on logging has been largely successful[6] (D. Liu 2009; Marks 2012). However, despite this ban, China's furniture, flooring, and paper industries have grown rapidly, facilitated mainly by imports of lumber and pulp. Indeed, China has imported a lot of resources that became depleted in the course of industrialization, with many observers finding the scale and modes of imports controversial or even alarming (Moran 2010). This issue will be examined further in the next chapter. Suffice to mention here that primary-commodity imports as a share of China's total imports rose from 21 percent in 1995 to 35 percent in 2008, with fuels and ores taking the largest share. In 2009, China's imports of oil seeds constitute 40 percent of the world imports, metalliferous ores 39 percent, and pulp and waste paper 31 percent (Dahlman 2012, p. 159).

Focusing on timber, it is notable that China's imports tripled between 1997 and 2009, and the country is presently the second largest importer of logs, with Indonesia, Myanmar, Cambodia, and Russia serving as the main suppliers (Marks 2012, p. 288). Yet, as an investigative report in the *Washington Post* graphically exposed, some of the logs in Southeast Asia were harvested illegally and, through China's furniture factories, found their way into the homes of consumers visiting Western stores such as Home Depot and IKEA (Goodman and Finn 2007). The recent growth of China's furniture and flooring industries has thus been built on the environmental degradation of the country and other less developed ones.

Air Pollution

China has also suffered from deteriorating air quality since 1978, though some improvements have been made in the years after 2000. A 1999 World Resources Institute report found the level of total suspended particulates (TSP) and sulfur dioxide (SO_2) in most Chinese cities to far exceed the World Health Organization guidelines. However, drawing upon the Air Pollution Index (API) released by the Ministry of Environmental Protection since 2000, Canfei He and his colleagues (2012) argue that the overall trend of air quality in urban China actually improved in the decade between 2001 and 2011.

Specifically, "for those 42 cities reporting API values throughout the entire period of study, the annual median API decreased from 78.81 in 2001 to 63.36 in 2011, and the number of days with API greater than 150 fell substantially, from 24.95 days to 5.23 days" (He et al. 2012, p. 759).

Air pollutants in China consist mainly of sulfates, ozone, black carbon, desert dust, and mercury. These are generated by coal-fired power plants, automobile exhaust, and desertification[7] (Shapiro 2012). To fuel industrial growth, China requires an enormous supply of electricity. Even with the aggressive effort to build hydropower dams, the country continues to get 80 percent of its electricity from coal-fired power plants, burns about 6 million tons of coal on a daily basis, and constructs on average one new coal-fired power plant per week (Marks 2012, p. 314). Chinese coal mines, smaller ones in particular, tend to turn out coal of inferior quality. The use of inferior and unwashed coal generates massive fine particulate pollution. In turn, inefficient burning discharges carbon dioxide and sulfur dioxide into the atmosphere. In 2009, China surpassed the United States to become the world's biggest emitter of carbon dioxide and, by extension, the top contributor to global warming (Marks 2012, pp. 312–13; see also Smil 2004).

A second major source of air pollution comes with the expansion in car ownership and use of low-grade gasoline. Indeed, there is *prima facie* evidence to suggest that China is developing a car culture not unlike that of the United States. Some 14 million cars were manufactured in China in 2009, with only a small portion destined for export. Highway mileage also doubled between 2001 and 2010 to reach some 23,000 miles. The sheer number of automobiles presents immense challenges to air quality. Worse still, given the government's policy of suppressing the prices of oil, gas, and diesel fuel, and the pressure of the now-privatized oil companies to operate at a profit, they are inclined to source low-quality crudes, resulting in the widespread utilization of low-quality and pollutant-laden diesel by trucks in China. The sulfur content of diesel sold in China is said to be 130 times of those sold in the US and Europe, generating poisonous fumes that choke the country's city dwellers (Marks 2012, pp. 314–15).

The final source of atmospheric pollution is dust storms. Over-grazing, deforestation, and similar factors have exacerbated the extent of desertification in China. Dust storms on average struck northwestern China once every thirty-one years between AD 300 and 1949, but this increased to almost once every year after 1990. The huge dust storm of 1993 alone killed more than a hundred people (J. Liu and Diamond 2005).

Like other environmental issues, China's air pollution has a global dimension. Significantly, air pollutants and dust storms have been found to impact Japan, South Korea, and parts of North America. The extent of particulate air pollution impacting the United States tends to be highest during the springtime, when China's dust storms are most intense (Bradsher and Barboza 2006; Shapiro 2012, p. 3).

ATTAINING SUSTAINABILITY: ECONOMIC IMPERATIVES, STATE POLICIES, AND SOCIAL ACTORS

China's "reform and opening up" policy and its adoption of state neoliberalism after 1978 brought the country's environmental challenges to a head. The following will examine the environmental implications of the country's insertion into the capitalist world economy, the party-state's efforts at environmental management and preservation, as well as the roles of the emerging civil society.

Insertion into the Capitalist World Economy

China's reintegration into the capitalist world economy after 1978 and its bid to become a global factory were major factors underlying the strains on the country's natural resources. To further understand the global dimension of China's environmental problem, the following will examine the industry of electronic waste recycling in Guiyu County located on the southeastern coast of China.[8]

From the early 1990s, old computers and other electronic products shipped from the United States and elsewhere in the world and, in recent years, dumped by consumers in major Chinese cities were sent to small workshops in Guiyu for the salvaging of precious metals using primitive methods of breaking and burning. While the industry produces a humble income for peasant workers, generates profit for capitalists involved in all links in the "e-waste" commodity chain, provides a cheap way out for electronics manufacturers from their producer responsibility, and enables consumers around the world to purchase and discard their electronics products at a stunning pace, Guiyu County has become so polluted that, in 2002, the level of lead in its water was 2,400 times above the WHO drinking guidelines. The central government issued a ban in 2000 on the import of e-waste, yet the industry remains in operation (Puckett and Smith 2002; F. Wang et al. 2013).

For businessmen in China and around the world, the desire for profit, which is part and parcel of capitalism, underlies their environmental oversights. They have no scruples in shifting the cost of pollution to the developing countries so long as it can reduce the production cost. In turn, Chinese peasants, workers, and consumers have been blinded by destitution, the dire need for survival, and the thirst for small comforts that consumption can provide. Ignorance and technological deficiencies have rendered them indiscriminate. In a country where civil society is suppressed and poorly developed, it is up to party-state officials, as gate-keepers, to provide the necessary regulation and surveillance.

The Response of the Communist Party-State

The role of the party-state in China's environmental preservation is complex, to say the least. In the first place, most environmental issues are global in dimension. Whatever the national priorities, China as a member of the international community has to respond to the latter's concern. Over the years, China has participated in many international programs and, by 2005, had signed over fifty conventions, agreements, and protocols on environmental protection. The latter include the 1987 Montreal Protocol on Substances That Deplete the Ozone Layer, the 1989 Basel Convention on the Control of Transboundary Movements of Hazardous Waters and Their Disposal, and the 1997 Kyoto Protocol. Participation in these global organizations and signing of such international treaties since the 1950s require the country to draft new laws and set up new institutions, thus enhancing its capacity for environmental protection[9] (Economy 2004; Qu 2005).

In the second place, despite changes in the communist party-state's priorities, it has over time introduced an increasing number of more specific legal provisions on environmental protection. At the height of neoliberalization promoted during much of the time between 1978 and 2002, the party-state introduced the Law on the Prevention and Control of Atmospheric Pollution (1995), the Law on the Prevention and Control of Water Pollution (1984), and, above all, the Environmental Impact Assessment Law (2002), which allows ordinary citizens to participate in the governmental assessment of major projects that might have significant environmental impacts (Economy 2004, pp. 101–5; Shapiro 2012, pp. 65–7). Other legal provisions, such as the 1984 Forest Law, the 1991 Law of Water and Soil Conservation, and the 2002 Water Law, were also introduced.

With the introduction of state neoliberalism between 2003 and 2012, the party-state gave higher priority to environmental preservation, contending that sustainable development was essential for the attainment of a harmonious society. Plans and policies on renewable energy and climate change were made in 2005 and subsequently incorporated into the Twelfth Five-Year Plan issued in 2011[10] (Xia et al. 2010). Among other things, the plan pledges to reduce energy intensity by 16 percent between 2011 and 2015 by building on the 20 percent reduction attained between 2006 and 2010. Guidelines for pollution control and prevention on the eight major rivers and lakes were also issued jointly by the Ministries of Environmental Protection, Water Resources, Agriculture, Housing and Urban–Rural Development, Industry and Information Technology, and the National Development and Reform Commission, so that the Twelfth Five-Year Plan's objective of rapid urbanization can be attained without endangering water security (Shapiro 2012, pp. 63–4). Strenuous efforts have also been made to build wastewater treatment plants in Shaanxi Province and Guangzhou (Gleick 2008–9).

In the third place, China attained at most sporadic and controversial success in the matter of environmental preservation despite its impressive list of legal provisions. There are two major reasons for this. First, some policies were poorly designed and their implementation generated unintended consequences. As an example, the country used the construction of hydropower dams as a strategy to achieve the 2005 goal of increasing the share of renewable energy. However, even if the hydropower dams could be beneficial, they also generated grave ecological risks, massive social dislocations, and enormous human suffering. In particular, when local governments from poor regions used dam construction to generate an income, the concern with sustainability often became overshadowed.

Second and more fundamental, effective implementation of even well-intended policies was sometimes compromised by the institutional structure of the party-state and the fact that, like most policies made at the national center, they relied on local governments for implementation.

For one thing, environmental challenges tend to be multifaceted and do not normally fall under the jurisdiction of a particular branch of the government. In China, among the twenty-seven Ministries and Commissions under the State Council, the Ministries of

Environmental Protection, Water Resources, Agriculture, Housing and Urban–Rural Development, Science and Technology, and Land and Resources all exercise authority over some aspects of environmental issues. Together with differences in the domains of their core concern, confusions, omissions, and even contradictions in policies made in relation to the environment are only to be expected (Shapiro 2012, p. 62; cf. Gleick 2008–9). Just as important, the Ministry of Environmental Protection in China is plagued by a lack of resources. It has a core staff of just a few hundred, making it one of the smallest ministries in the country (Economy 2004, pp. 105–12).

For another thing, typical of China's state administration, while the Ministry of Environmental Protection designs and carries out policies at the central level, local Environmental Protection Bureaus (EPBs) are responsible for policy implementation at the provincial, county, and township levels.[11] Sometimes, lower-level officials suffer from inadequate management training and are impaired by the lack of proper communication from the center to implement the policies (see Trac et al. 2007, p. 287). More fundamentally, the small size of the Ministry has intensified its reliance on the equally under-staffed local EPBs, which, under China's administrative practice, have to answer both to the Ministry of Environmental Protection and to local governments (Economy 2004; W. Li et al. 2012; Marks 2012).

Local governments, as chapter 3 suggests, were placed under considerable financial pressure by the 1994 fiscal reform such that they felt it necessary to provide a congenial economic environment so as to generate sufficient tax income. This has not been helped by the central government's practice to evaluate local officials by the local economy's growth rate (Y. Zheng and Qian 1998). President Hu's "Scientific Outlook on Development" has not fundamentally altered the practice, and many political leaders continue to believe in the strategic significance of industrial development and the possibility of developing first and cleaning up later.

Together with China's rampant corruption, local EPBs have been under much pressure to approve the operation of mines and factories without proper environmental impact assessments and to employ a "light-touch" approach to regulation and surveillance afterwards (Jahiel 1997; T. Ma 2009; X. Ma and Ortolando 2000). The tendency for local government officials to overlook day-to-day violations of environmental protection laws often persists until the ill effects of pollution or environmental deterioration culminate in a crisis that eventually draws the attention of the media and the central government.

The Response of Civil Society

While the prospects for China making material strides in environmental preservation and sustainable development are grim, there is one cause for optimism. In particular, this involves the awakening of the general public, the emergence of a nascent civil society, and, under some circumstances, certain forms of synergy between the civil society and the party-state.

As in other circumstances, the communist party-state finds protesting citizens worrisome and social organizations threatening. Hence, it has always preferred to deal with protesters directly as individuals and put obstacles in the way of setting up social organizations. Despite the party-state's oppression, however, "protests" in relation to the environment have risen drastically over the years. It was reported by the Ministry of Environmental Protection that "environmental complaints" made via letter or in person increased from 370,000 in 2001 to 616,000 in 2006, whereas environmental disputes increased from 51,000 in 2004 to 128,000 in 2005 (T. Ma 2009). Working through official statistics and comments from the Minister for Public Security and the Deputy Minister of the Ministry of Environmental Protection, Tianjie Ma (2009) reports, in addition, that the number of rural "mass incidents" jumped from about 10,000 a year in 1994 to 74,000 in 2004, of which 5,000 were related to environmental issues. Villagers' attempts to protest the sources of pollution have led some scholars to suggest the emergence of a certain environmental consciousness among the Chinese (Jun 2000; W. Li et al. 2012).

Apart from petitions and mass incidents, which have mostly been initiated by individuals affected by pollution, another important player is the environmental NGOs. In China, to register as a social organization is difficult. To get registered, an organization needs the sponsorship of a government office and has to demonstrate its access to a "legitimate" source of funding. Hence, even though some 440,000 social organizations were registered by 2010, many more were not (Shapiro 2012, p. 106).

The mid-1990s saw the emergence of a certain political space in China for environmental NGOs. Since then, some 2,000 such organizations have been registered throughout the country, though observers consider no more than forty to be active (J. Schwartz 2004). Among the more notable groups are Green Earth Volunteers, Green Watershed, Wild China, and Global Village of Beijing[12] (Economy 2004; Shapiro 2012, pp. 112–16). NGOs from the grassroots apart, observers also identify a category of "semi-NGOs," a prominent example of which is the Center for Legal Assistance to Pollution Victims, founded in 1998 and housed at the Chinese University of Political Science and Law (Marks 2012, p. 324).

China also fashions a form of "government-organized non-governmental organizations" (GONGOs), which receive funding from and are supported by government agencies or officials. Examples include the All-China Environment Federation, founded in 2005 under the patronage of SEPA and the China Environmental Protection Foundation established in 1993 by Qu Geping, then director of SEPA (Shapiro 2012, p. 120). Most of them are conservative in orientation, although a few have sought greater autonomy over time.

Finally, international environmental groups have also been active in China. The first to make a presence in the country were China Development Brief and the World Wide Fund for Nature (WWF).[13] Later examples include Conservation International, Nature Conservancy, Natural Resources Defense Council, Environmental Defense, World Resources Institute, Greenpeace China, and Friends of the Earth (Shapiro 2012).

However, apart from the obstacle to registration, activist groups face other constraints. They are in need of trained staff, lack independent funding, and have limited or no access to actual data. They are also put under close scrutiny, are subject to censorship in the information they disseminate, face the threat of imprisonment when found to disclose reports classified as secret by the government, and can be punished for public assemblies they organize (Marks 2012, p. 323; J. Schwartz 2004; Shapiro 2012).

Despite these constraints, environmental NGOs in China, working individually or in the form of a network, have played vital roles in exposing pollution and other environmental threats. Depending on the case in question, they might draw upon government reports or undertake the investigation themselves.[14] Where appropriate and feasible, they work closely with concerned journalists and the media in general to publicize problems. Newspapers such as *China Youth Daily* and *Southern Weekend*, radio stations, and nationwide television networks such as CCTV played a strategic role during the early days, whereas the new media (webpages, text-messaging, blogs, and micro-blogs) have taken on utmost significance in recent years[15] (G. Yang 2009; G. Yang and Calhoun 2008). In exposing the ravages, environmental NGOs seek to capture the attention of the government and the general public, and in some cases to educate and involve the community. In recent years, they have also relied on the new media (text-messaging, for instance) to urge interested individuals to "take a walk" together, as in the rally on June 1, 2007 to oppose a planned petro-chemical (paraxylene) plant at Xiamen (known as the Xiamen PX Project) (W. Li et al. 2012). All these actions are performed with a view to placing pressure on business corporations and the government, local ones in particular, urging them to comply with national legislation or international treaties, where applicable.

Some environmentalists have also resorted to litigation as a means to defend their rights. One of the semi-NGOs mentioned earlier, the Center for Legal Assistance to Pollution Victims, for instance, has fielded more than 10,000 inquiries and won hundreds of cases since its founding in 1998. The case of *Changjian Zhang v. Rongping Chemical Plant* (in Fujian) was lauded as one of the ten most influential lawsuits in China in 2005 (W. Li et al. 2012; Shapiro 2012, pp. 110–27).

Finally, despite the government's aversion to all forms of social activism, it appears to be more tolerant of public participation in environmental matters, especially when compared with political issues like democratization. As Elizabeth C. Economy (2004) explains, the NGOs provide helpful services like environmental education for the general public and surveillance at no extra administrative cost of violations to environmental laws by business firms and local governments. As such, some forms of synergy have emerged between the environmental NGOs and the government. On the one hand, enlightened government officials have sometimes taken initiatives to help worthy causes. Qu Geping, when serving as the director of SEPA, persuaded government departments to support a national media campaign to expose polluters around the country. For fifteen years from 1993 when the campaign was initiated, some 220,000 such stories were reported (Shapiro 2012, p. 67).

On the other hand, and more crucially perhaps, a "partnership" has emerged between three crucial actors on environment problems: environmental NGOs first take the initiative to expose the problem; the mass media then provide publicity and arouse societal concern; and the central government then intervenes by urging policy change, compensation, or caution in implementing developmental projects, as outlined above.

A notable case concerns the proposal to build thirteen dams over the Nu River, which was announced in August 2003. Environmentalists were much aroused, in part because the area had recently been declared a UNESCO World Natural Heritage site. Together with a number of academics, NGO leaders spoke out against dam construction in a seminar organized by SEPA a month later. Their views were reported widely by the media, and also found support within SEPA itself. With these and other efforts, the anti-dam advocates eventually outstripped the provincial government and hydropower corporations by drawing the attention of Premier Wen Jiabao, who was disturbed by the "high level of social concern" and ordered the project's suspension in April 2004 (Litzinger 2007; Mertha 2008; Wells-Dang 2012; G. Yang 2004). Even though particular NGOs might have used different mobilization and advocacy strategies, the general pattern can be found in many other cases[16] (Wells-Dang 2012, p. 149).

CONCLUSION

China's scanty natural resources have come under great strain in the course of the hyper-growth model of neoliberal development, which aims to promote economic growth at any cost. The above discussion has highlighted some ways in which the country's water, land, and atmospheric resources became depleted or polluted. These problems exacted grave human costs on the Chinese. We have already seen the shocking degree of pollution to China's river systems, the long-term devastation of the country's groundwater, the scope of deforestation, the high level of air pollution, and the heavy costs they exact on people's health.

The communist party-state's efforts to address some of these challenges, such as the construction of hydropower dams, the South–North Water Transfer Project, the ban on logging, and the reforestation campaigns have produced indeterminate benefits accompanied at times by heavy social costs. The ecological and human risks attending these environmental challenges and their proposed solutions affect not only the Chinese, but many other people both in the neighboring countries and elsewhere around the world.

Forces underlying China's environmental challenges are complex. Apart from the country's natural endowment, population size, and changing consumption habits, its insertion into the capitalist world economy and the pursuit of neoliberal development at all costs is arguably the most important threat. Even though China has sought to move into high-technology sectors in recent years, it remains the case that it has attained rapid industrial development and become the global factory by tapping into the country's inexpensive labor and cheap resource inputs. As the case of Guiyu has made clear, the grave transgression of environmental standards is a main reason for inexpensive resource inputs. From this perspective, owners and managers of business enterprises that constitute all links in the global commodity chains profited from China's pollution, and consumers are but accomplices in the environmental disasters.

However, it is the communist party-state's "collusion" with the capitalists' pursuits that defines China's environmental challenges. The party-state has over time become more receptive to ideas of environmental preservation, as vindicated in its adoption of the Scientific Outlook on Development in 2003. The reorganization of SEPA into the Ministry of Environmental Protection, and the encouragements given to various environmental NGOs and GONGOs are just as significant. However, even though some material progress has been made, China's efforts to clean up pollution, carry out reforestation, and implement environmental preservation laws have only been partially successful.

The reasons for environmental policy failures, as suggested in the previous section, involve both policy conflicts, on the one hand, and institutional fragmentation and poor administrative capacity, on the other. Above all, the fact that local Environmental Protection Bureaus are answerable both to the Ministry of Environmental Protection and to local governments, and that local officials continue to be evaluated according to their economic performance of promoting high growth rates, sends out confusing and contradictory messages. These structural contradictions hinder the fulfillment of environmental protection goals, while encouraging government and business actors to collude and plunder the environment.

The emergence of environmental "mass incidents" and environmental NGOs suggests the rise of a certain degree of environmental consciousness among the general public, and, to some extent, their concerns have found a common purpose with the Chinese authorities. However, the party-state's preoccupation with growth at all cost and with continued domination over the country will ultimately circumscribe the endeavors of the NGOs. In as much as the opportunity for autonomous organization, independent investigation, and free dissemination of information has been taken away from these environmental NGOs, their ability to investigate the corporations and local governments as well as place pressure on them will be much limited.

Whether China is able to meet the challenge of environmental degradation and resource depletion, therefore, depends on whether the communist party-state is able to overcome its obsession with the growth-at-all-cost model of neoliberalism, whether it is willing to liberate and strengthen civil society (including the mass media, the NGOs, and social movements), and whether it is willing to streamline the state bureaucracy and to empower the Environmental Protection Bureaus. Time is running out. If the Chinese authorities do not take decisive steps in the near future and continue the hyper-growth model for another two or three decades, the environmental destruction may reach a point of no return and it may become difficult for the country to repair its damaged environment, restore the ecological balance, and promote sustainable development.

8   The Challenges of Global Rivalry: Resource Competition and Territorial Disputes

After three decades of rapid economic growth, China is a formidable player in the capitalist world system. While continuing to serve as a "global factory," the country has become more dynamic in exploring economic opportunities and forthright in defending its political and cultural interests. This newfound confidence on the part of China, however, has sometimes been met with mistrust and apprehension from other core states in the world. Above all, the country's aggressive attempts recently to expand its outward direct investments have caused concern among the US and various Western European countries, the economies of which still flounder in the shadow of the 2008 global economic crisis. China's efforts to defend its territorial rights also aroused the concerns of its neighbors and the Western states in general. In the words of David Shambaugh (2011, p. 7),

> 2009–2010 will be remembered as the years in which China became difficult for the world to deal with, as Beijing exhibited increasingly tough and truculent behavior toward many of its neighbors in Asia, as well as the United States and the European Union. Even its ties in Africa and Latin America became somewhat strained, adding to its declining global image since 2007.

The view that China has become more assertive, if not aggressive, in the economic and politico-military domains is linked to the notion of "the rise of China," which has been a topic of fervent discussion since

2008. Scholars raise the following questions: Is China bidding to replace the United States and become the next global hegemon? Will the contention escalate into violent confrontations? Will China behave just like an imperialist: expropriating resources in its economic rise, and using its nascent economic and military might to deprive and dominate its less developed neighbors? Questions such as these have increasingly defined the global political environment, and now may delimit the options for China and undermine the country's endeavors. In these ways, global rivalry becomes another challenge in China's rise.

To understand the nature of China's global rivalry, the following will examine the economic, military, political and cultural dimensions[1] of the country's rise. Owing to the overwhelming apprehensions related to the economic and military dimensions, more attention will be paid to them. Then discussion will move on to examine China's avowed disinterest in being a global hegemon, the international community's perception of the country's intentions, and their implications for its future.

THE RISE OF CHINA: ECONOMIC DIMENSIONS

China's vast foreign exchange reserves (US$2.65 trillion) and its seemingly inexorable economic growth even amidst the worst economic depression since World War II have led analysts like Morgan Stanley's Stephen Roach to ask the question, "Can China save us?" (Pettis 2010; N. Schwartz 2009). Such analysts hope that a strong economy will boost China's imports and allow the country to become the new growth engine of the world economy. There are signs that this scenario is, in part, coming true.

China's Outward Investments and Resource Competition

Over the years, China's conglomerates and sovereign wealth funds found overseas investments an invaluable opportunity to generate higher profits, seek technological advancement, and secure resource inputs that the country either lacked or had exhausted or polluted in its thirty-some years of rapid growth (W. Jiang 2009). The policy of *"go global"* was adopted in 2000 as part of the Tenth Five-Year Plan, and the 2008 financial crisis presented a perfect opportunity for expanding such investments. Zhang Guobao, head of China's National Energy Administration (CNEA), for instance, was noted for saying in 2009 that the slowdown reduced the price of international energy resource assets and favored the CNEA's search for overseas resources (Klare 2010). In 2010, Chinese leaders gave priority to outbound investments that could "expand markets for Chinese companies, obtain critical know-how and technology, and secure resources for China's internal growth" (Scheltema et al. 2012). Energy, energy conservation, raw materials, biotechnology, agriculture, services, high-end manufacturing, and innovative technologies are the privileged sectors.

To facilitate global procurement, the communist party-state has mobilized the China Development Bank (CDB) and other institutes to provide low-interest, long-term loans to major Chinese resources firms. In 2009, for instance, China National Petroleum Corp (CNPC) was promised a loan of US$30 billion over a five-year period by the CDB to support its asset acquisition abroad (Klare 2010).

China's overseas direct investment (ODI) started to grow in 2005 and its pace accelerated after 2008. From an annual total of less than US$3 billion before 2005, the amount reached US$60 billion in 2010, a time when the financial tsunami hit the world (Rosen and Hanemann 2012). The amount increased further to reach US$87.8 billion in 2012. Resource-rich countries such as Australia, Canada, South Africa, and the United States historically captured most of the investments. After 2008, the interest in South Africa waned, whereas investments in Indonesia, South Korea, Britain, Germany, France, and especially the United States surged[2] (National Bureau of Statistics 2014a).

The Heritage Foundation, which uses firm-level data to generate its own estimate for the period between January 2005 and July 2012, has found that Australia and the United States top the list of China's ODI destinations at the values of US$45.3 billion and US$42 billion, respectively (Scissors 2012). Other major destinations include Brazil (US$25.7 billion), Indonesia (US$23.3 billion), Nigeria (US$18.8 billion), Canada (US$17.2 billion), and Iran (US$17.2 billion). According to the Heritage Foundation, the vast majority of such investments in the post-2008 period have gone into energy and power. Despite China's interest in technology and agriculture, ODI in these sectors remains much less prominent (Scissors 2012).

China's post-2008 drives for procurement, whether through ODI or otherwise, have been well documented. To name a few examples, the CDB in 2009 loaned US$10 billion to Petrobras, Brazil's state-controlled oil company, to develop deep offshore fields in return for a promise to supply China with up to 160,000 barrels of Brazilian crude oil per day. In the same year, CNPC signed an agreement with the government of Myanmar to build and operate an oil pipeline that will run from Myanmar to the Chinese province of Yunnan. The 460-mile pipeline will permit China-bound tankers from Africa and the Middle East to unload their cargo in Myanmar on the Indian Ocean, thereby avoiding the long voyage to China's eastern coast via the Strait of Malacca and the South China Sea, an area dominated by the US Navy (Klare 2010). Again in 2009, Sinopec acquired Canada's oil company Addax for US$7.5 billion, while China Minmetals purchased Australia's O.Z. Minerals with US$1.38 billion (Yao 2009). Moving beyond energy and natural resources, China's Geely Automobiles acquired the Volvo subsidiary from Ford Motors in early 2010. The acquisition of one of Europe's most celebrated brands suggests that China has not only emerged as the world's largest auto market, but also moved a step closer in its ambitions to produce for the global auto market (Bradsher 2010b).

The rapid surge of China's outward direct investments must be understood in the context of its latecomer status. The country's stock of ODI, valued at US$365 billion at the end of 2011, ranks lower than Belgium, the Netherlands, and Spain (Rosen and Hanemann 2012). China's US$42 billion worth of ODI to the United States made between 2005 and June 2012 amounted to no more than 2 percent of the US's total stock of inward foreign investment (*Economist* 2013). Similarly, although China's investments in Africa increased from US$70 million in 2003 to US$5.5 billion in 2008, on average the country contributed only 5 percent of the annual ODI flow into the continent, whereas the United States and the European Union constantly contributed over 30 percent (Ali and Jafrani 2012). In the words of *The Economist* (2013) magazine, "China is still far from buying up the world."

China's ODI in Developed Economies: Competition and Security Threat

As it is, China's global buying spree has already aroused much apprehension. With the country becoming a major customer and patron for energy and mineral producers, some fear that it will receive the political allegiances once given to the US, Japan, and Western Europe (Klare 2010). More important, many developed Western countries seem to believe that China has bought too many of their nations' companies and that this presents security if not cultural threats.

The United States seemed unprepared for China's surging interest in overseas investments and now expresses much concern over their security implications. The defeat suffered by China's offshore oil company CNOOC in the politically charged bidding war over the California-based Unocal in 2005 was emblematic (Rosen and Hanemann 2012). Restrictions over other sectors, such as telecommunications and advanced technology in general, are equally striking.[3] Of course, some observers disagree. They contend that the United States has become more open to investments from China. The Obama administration is said to have stood firmly "against calls to use national security reviews for foreign investment as a protectionist tool" and recently approved proposals in sensitive areas like power generation, shale gas development, and aviation (Rosen and Hanemann 2012).

The green light given by the US authorities for CNOOC to acquire Canada's Nexen for US$15.1 billion in 2012 was particularly significant. Once again, some observers contend that the transaction was deemed admissible only after technological breakthroughs in horizontal drilling and fracking as well as oil price increases, which unlocked the United States' unconventional oil and gas potential, and promised that the US will now surpass Saudi Arabia as the world's largest oil producer (Tu and Livingston 2013). Similarly, IBM's consent to sell its PC business to Lenovo in 2004 was based on the consideration that PC production was neither profitable nor "cutting edge" in the strict sense of the term (Rosen and Hanemann 2012).

China's ODI in Developing Economies: Neo-colonialism?

The more serious and indeed acrimonious criticisms are directed at China's investment in Africa (Campbell 2008; Horta 2008a, 2008b; Jauch 2011). In 2006, Britain's Foreign Secretary, Jack Straw, first used the notion "*neo-colonialism*" to describe China's activities in Africa. In 2011, the US Secretary of State, Hillary Clinton, also warned of neo-colonialism and that Africa should be wary of (Chinese) investors that only seek to extract natural resources and deal with African elites, rather than bring benefits to all citizens (Quinn 2011). Lamido Sanusi, the governor of Nigeria's central bank, contended in 2013 that China was not unlike "the US, Russia, Britain, Brazil and the rest" in its interest in Africa's raw materials and markets rather than a real contributor to the continent's industrial development (Sanusi 2013). In short, China has been "accused of sweeping up natural resources,...and in the process destroying local industrial capabilities, engaging in corrupt practices, employing imported Chinese (prison) labor, and undermining attempts by northern governments and international institutions to promote good governance and better labor and environmental standards" (Kaplinsky 2012, p. 24).

However, such criticisms are not entirely justified. First, as Raphael Kaplinsky (2012) explains, Chinese investments in Africa are diverse and changing. The investors include large state-owned enterprises run by the central government, enterprises owned by provincial governments, private firms of various sizes, and Chinese migrants. Hence, the criticism that "whereas China has a policy for Africa, Africa does not have a policy for China" is mistaken, glossing over differences among divergent African countries and industrial sectors, and treating China as an undifferentiated unit (W. Jiang 2009; Strauss and Saavedra 2009).

Second, contrary to the belief that China invests primarily in Africa's natural resources, Shimelse Ali and Nida Jafrani (2012) estimate that in 2009 only 29 percent of China's investments in the continent, compared to nearly 60 percent of US investments there, went into mining. In the same year, more than half of China's ODI in Africa, especially to those non-resource-rich countries, went to manufacturing, finance, and construction. Furthermore, observers also suggest that most African assets held by China's national oil companies are of a size and quality of little interest to, or indeed already relinquished by, international oil companies (Hanson 2008). A similar case has also been made regarding China's acquisition and holding of Africa's agricultural land (Cotula et al. 2009; see also Brautigam and Tang 2009).

Third, oil-producing countries from Sudan to Venezuela profited not only from rising oil prices at the time the agreements were signed, but also from direct trade and investment agreements with China. Investment from Chinese oil companies often goes beyond mere oil extraction and includes investment in refining capacities and petro-chemical industries as well as infrastructure that are unrelated to the oil industry.

Lastly, instead of contributing to the monopolization of resources, studies by the Peterson Institute for International Economics[4] found that Chinese investments tend to go into emerging resource firms and thus have enhanced competition in the sector. Furthermore, although Chinese firms studied by the Institute do not support the Extractive Industries Transparency Initiatives or other groups devoted to the enhancement of good governance, and firms established earlier have been fined for the violation of health, safety, and environmental standards, enterprises established more recently are more attentive to concerns of the local community (Moran et al. 2012, p. 30). Indeed, Wenran Jiang (2009) went so far as to contend that Chinese investors violated environmental rules owing to miscommunication rather than deliberate oversight.

THE RISE OF CHINA: THE MILITARY DIMENSION

Apart from the massive overseas direct investments, much apprehension has also been expressed over China's aggressive behavior toward its neighbors, the rapid rise in its military budget, and its lack of transparency in matters of national defense. The country's territorial disputes over the Spratly Islands and the Diaoyu/Senkaku Islands will be examined as a handle by which to understand the nature of China's "military rise."

Territorial Disputes: The Spratly Islands and the Diaoyu/Senkaku Islands

Historically, China was entangled in territorial disputes with India, Japan, the Philippines, the Soviet Union, and Vietnam, among others.

Even as China sought to settle or suspend some of these conflicts, those concerning the Spratly Islands and the Diaoyu/Senkaku Islands have become more fiery in recent years. The reasons, according to some observers, can be attributed both to the islands' natural resource endowment and to their strategic geopolitical significance.

The Spratly Islands are a group of some 750 reefs, islets, atolls, and islands that spread over 425,000 square kilometers of the South China Sea. China, Brunei, Malaysia, the Philippines, Taiwan, and Vietnam have all claimed sovereignty over part of or the entire archipelago. Though not inhabited, the Spratly Islands possess rich fishery resources, are believed to hold substantial oil and natural gas reserves, and are positioned strategically on the most important sea lanes connecting the Pacific and Indian Oceans (Table 8.1).

While the security of and rights to use sea routes were originally the focus of contention, the discovery of crude oil around the Spratly Islands in the 1970s intensified the competitive claims for territorial and maritime sovereignty. Countries in the region advanced historical and legal arguments to make their claims. Pre-modern records and maps, archaeological evidence, as well as modern cartographic attempts by Western colonial powers were mobilized. In turn, regional powers also appealed to legal documents such as the 1951 San Francisco Peace Treaty, the 1982 United Nations Convention on the Law of the Sea, and the 2002 ASEAN Declaration on the Conduct of Parties in the South China Sea.[5]

Despite these efforts, the competing claims remain unsettled. Open conflicts between China, the Philippines, and Vietnam occurred in 1974, 1988, and the latter years of the 1990s, involving gunfire at and arrests of fishermen by patrolships and naval vessels of the various governments. Although the South China Sea was peaceful in much of the first decade of the twenty-first century with the countries making their competing submissions to the United Nations, confrontations that involved China, the Philippines, and Vietnam surfaced again in

Table 8.1 China's territorial disputes[a]

	Spratly Islands	Diaoyu/Senkaku Islands
Claimants	PRC, Taiwan, Vietnam (complete); Malaysia, Philippines (part); Brunei (part: fishing zone)	PRC, Taiwan, Japan
Geopolitical significance	Oil, natural gas, fisheries, shipping links, Strait of Malacca	Oil, natural gas, fisheries, shipping links
Current administration	PRC, Taiwan, Malaysia, Philippines, and Vietnam	Japan
Notable conflicts and developments	1974: PRC–Vietnam Conflict 1988: PRC–Vietnam Conflict 1992: PRC–Vietnam Conflict 1995: PRC–Philippines Conflict (Mischief Reef) 1998: Vietnam–Philippines Conflict (Tennent Reef) 2002: ASEAN Declaration of Conduct 2009: Malaysia and Vietnam joint submission to the UN 2009: PRC protested Malaysia's and Vietnam's joint submission and issued official note on the nine-dash line 2011: Philippines protested the PRC's nine-dash line 2011: PRC protested joint Vietnam–India oil exploration 2012: Philippine warship stopped Chinese fishing vessels around the Scarborough Shoal, with protest actions from both sides ensuing 2015: The Philippines and Vietnam criticized China for its rapid land reclamation within the Spratly Island group. The ASEAN Summit, held in Malaysia in late April 2015, also issued a statement criticizing the reclamation activities; China, in turn, charged the Philippines and Vietnam with undertaking unauthorized reclamation	1971: Chinese overseas[b] protested the US's handover of administration to Japan 1978: Japanese right-wing group built lighthouse 1979: PRC and Japan agreed to shelve the issue 1990: Chinese overseas protested lighthouse recognition 1996: Japanese right-wing group built new lighthouse; protests by Chinese overseas 2010: Collision between Chinese fishing boat and Japan's Coast Guard 2012: Japanese government purchased three disputed islands 2012: China's marine surveillance vessels patrol the Islands regularly

Notes:

[a] Adapted from Shelly Zhao (2011).

[b] "Chinese overseas" refers to Chinese in Hong Kong, Taiwan, and around the world.

2010, 2011, 2012, 2014, and the first months of 2015, when this chapter was last updated.

Turning to the Diaoyu/Senkaku Islands, referring to their respective Chinese and Japanese names, they are a group of islets and islands located northeast of Taiwan and southwest of the Ryukyu Islands. Like the Spratly Islands, the Diaoyu/Senkaku Islands also possess rich fishery resources, are believed to hold substantial oil and natural gas reserves, and are situated upon strategic sea links. China and Japan are the main contenders making competing claims over these Islands (Table 8.1).

China traces its historical claim to the Diaoyu Islands to the early fifteenth century and, along with Taiwan, placed them under the naval defense district of Fujian Province during the Ming and Qing dynasties (Xiang 1961; B. Xu 2011). With the signing of the Treaty of Maguan on April 17, 1895, subsequent to China's defeat in the Sino-Japanese war, Taiwan became Japan's colony and, with it, gained control over the Diaoyu Islands, which were then administered as part of the Toucheng Township of Yilan County, Taiwan.

Japan, for its part, traces its historical claim to the Senkaku Islands to the eighteenth century and declared its control over them on January 14, 1895, a few months before the signing of the Treaty of Maguan. In 1945, when Japan was defeated by the United States in the Pacific War, the country relinquished its hold over the colonies in accordance with the Cairo and Potsdam Declarations as well as the San Francisco Peace Treaty. Despite this, the Diaoyu/Senkaku Islands were not returned to China along with Taiwan. Instead, they came under American administration as part of the United States Civil Administration of the Ryukyu Islands and, in 1972, the United States turned over the Islands' administration to Japan[6] in accordance with the Okinawa Reversion Treaty passed by the US Senate in 1971.

Both the mainland Chinese and Taiwan governments protested that decision. However, bogged down by their own problems – the Cultural

Revolution on the mainland and loss of UN membership in the case of Taiwan – the protests by both Chinese governments were only lukewarm. In May 1979, when China embarked on economic reform, Deng Xiaoping expressed the view that China and Japan should shelve the sovereignty dispute over the Diaoyu Islands, and work together to develop their resources. Nevertheless, the Chinese overseas in Hong Kong, Taiwan, and elsewhere around the world were indignant. They staged massive protests in 1971 and intermittently thereafter when Japan took actions that were deemed provocative.

In 2012, both the Tokyo Metropolitan and Japanese governments announced their plans to purchase three of the Diaoyu/Senkaku Islands from the Kurihara family. In response, protesters from Hong Kong commandeered a fishing boat to stage a protest and succeeded in landing forcibly on the Diaoyu Islands on August 15, 2012. Violent demonstrations also broke out in mainland China. The Japanese government closed the deal on September 11, 2012, declaring that it only intended to exercise orderly management of the dispute. Apparently seeing the move as a violation of the agreement to "shelve the issue," China's Foreign Ministry objected, saying Beijing would not "sit back and watch its territorial sovereignty violated." In response to Japan's breach of goodwill, China began to send its marine surveillance vessels to patrol the islands regularly.

The US: Pivot toward the Pacific and Rebalancing toward Asia

If China and its East and Southeast Asian neighbors were the main players in the disputes over the Diaoyu/Senkaku Islands and the Spratly Islands, the dynamics are somewhat altered with the entrance of the United States into the scene. In 2010, the US Secretary of State, Hillary Clinton, defied China's expressed wish of keeping the Spratly Islands disputes off the ASEAN Region Forum agenda and addressed the issue, declaring it the US's national interest to see a resolution of the rival claims through a collaborative diplomatic process by all claimants in the absence of coercion (Dosch 2011).

As for the Diaoyu/Senkaku Islands, the US government has emphasized repeatedly that it does not take sides on the sovereignty dispute. However, since the Islands have been under Japan's administration, it views the issue to be covered by the US–Japan Treaty of Mutual Cooperation and Security. This reassurance leads Japanese politicians and security scholars to believe they hold a strong position.

More generally, the Obama administration announced in 2011 its *pivot toward the Pacific and rebalancing toward Asia*. According to a report prepared by the US Congressional Research Service, the goal of the policy shift "is to promote US interests by helping to shape the norms and rules of the Asia-Pacific region, to ensure that 'international law and norms be respected, that commerce and freedom of navigation are not impeded, that emerging powers built trust with their neighbors, and that disagreements are resolved peacefully without threats or coercion'" (Manyin et al. 2012, p. 1). Among other things, the pivot involves negotiations to form a nine-nation Trans-Pacific Strategic Economic Partnership (TPP) free trade agreement, to authorize new troop deployments to Australia and new naval deployments to Singapore, to establish new areas for military cooperation with the Philippines, and to strengthen the US military presence in East Asia in a way that renders it more broadly distributed, more flexible, and more politically sustainable. According to Mark E. Manyin and his colleagues. (2012), the perceived importance of Asia-Pacific for the United States' economic future, China's growing military capabilities and assertiveness and its implications for the US's ability to project power in the region, as well as the winding down of US military operations in Iraq and Afghanistan all underlie this strategic shift.

It has also been suggested that many countries in the region have "encouraged the United States to step up its activity to provide a balance to China's rising influence" (Manyin et al. 2012, Summary).

Making a similar point, Henry Kissinger (2011, p. 511) contends that it would be hard for countries within the region, which have seen the wax and wane of the Chinese empires, to be nonchalant about China's growing power and historical record.

China's Military Capability

Regardless of the territorial disputes, to what extent has China's military capability posed a threat? To begin with, there is little doubt that China commands a substantial military capability and its military budget has grown rapidly in recent years. However, the country is hardly a match for the United States and it would take a very long time for it catch up.

For instance, of the estimated 10,000 nuclear warheads in 2013 worldwide, China owned about 250, whereas the United States and Russia possessed 4,650 and 4,480, respectively (Kristensen and Norris 2013). Similarly, even though China can rely on some fifty small diesel-electric submarines and ten nuclear ones to deny US surface vessels access to the South China Sea, they are ill suited for extended deployments into the Pacific or Indian Oceans. By contrast, the fifty-five nuclear attack submarines owned by the US are so quiet that they can operate freely in Chinese coastal waters (Cote 2011). Furthermore, in 2012, China was "the last of the five permanent members of the United Nations Security Council [after the United States, the United Kingdom, France, and Russia] to own an aircraft carrier" (J. Li 2013). Moreover, as a training carrier, this vessel, the *Liaoning*,[7] can in no way contribute to an immediate enhancement of the country's war-making capability (Cheng and Paladini 2012).

More generally, China's military budget registered double-digit growth yearly between 1989 and 2008. Citing an estimate made by a 2010 Pentagon report, Joseph Nye (2011, p. 184) suggested that China's total military expense amounted to US$150 billion or 2 percent of its gross national product. In the same year, however, the United States' budget was US$719 billion or 4 percent of its gross national product. Experts believe that the US advantage will be maintained for a long time. For even if China's total military expense was to increase to US$185 billion by 2025, it would still be no more than a quarter of the current US military expenditure (Nye 2011, p. 184). The country can hardly challenge the United States' military capability, which encompasses the entire world. The latter was demonstrated in 2011 when the US mounted a major military operation in Libya at the same time that it made war simultaneously in Afghanistan and Iraq.

THE RISE OF CHINA: THE POLITICAL DIMENSION

China has also become more and more active in global affairs. David Shambaugh (2009) listed the following activities to indicate the rise of China in the international political arena:

+ China has played a particularly vital role in the Six-Party Talks process concerning North Korea's nascent nuclear program.
+ China has participated in the "5 + 1" United Nations Security Council "quintet" concerning Iran's nuclear program.
+ China has also ramped up its contributions to UN peacekeeping operations – contributing at present 2,155 personnel in a dozen locations, making China the fourteenth largest contributor in the world but first among Security Council members.
+ China has become a major contributor of aid to poor African and other developing countries.

The increase in China's global presence has led American leaders to talk about "strategic dialogues," "strategic and economic dialogues," and "strategic reassurance" when they deal with Chinese leaders. The world press is also starting to speak of the G2 (the United States and China) as countries that effectively wield world power. Noting the irony, Immanuel Wallerstein (2010) remarks on the difference between the present situation and that of the late 1960s when China spoke of the United States and the Soviet Union as the "two superpowers" against whom everyone else should unite.

However, the political rise of China has not been met with gracious accommodation, and its "strategic" relationship with the United States is hardly one of harmonious accord. China differs vastly from the US in its approach to international affairs and, more than once, the country's foreign policies have challenged the existing global institutional arrangements constructed after World War II under US leadership (Buzan 2010).

First, China clings to the Westphalia vision of international relations and is inclined to defend its sovereign rights over its internal affairs. This is at odds with the international order put together by the United States, which bolsters the right for international organizations to uphold human rights, democracy, environmental sustainability, and intrude into the internal affairs of individual countries, if necessary. China has protested numerous times about the United States' criticisms of its human rights record, and the country's *Human Rights Record of the United States*, issued annually since 1998, is an effort to mimic and thus expose the hypocrisy of the US.

More fundamentally, China advocates the democratization of international affairs, which not only voices the interests of many developing countries, but also threatens to attenuate American influence. As part of this effort, the country strives to build various international institutions and platforms for policy discussion and implementation. Apart from the Forum on China–Africa Cooperation, the country also plays a strategic role in the Boao Forum for Asia. The New Development Bank, founded by China alongside Brazil, Russia, India, and South Africa to balance the influence of the World Bank and the International Monetary Fund, is the latest of such examples. Nevertheless, it remains the case that China heads a very limited number of international organizations and is hardly in a position to set the international agenda.

THE RISE OF CHINA: THE CULTURAL DIMENSION

On the cultural front, Jeffrey Wasserstrom (2010b) points out that China is now engaging in an ongoing "re-branding" drive. It aims to foster the image of China as a place that has combined humanistic traditions (represented by Confucius) with impressive strides toward economic modernity. The re-branding drive can be seen in the image presented in the opening ceremony of the 2008 Beijing Olympics and the establishment of government-funded "Confucius Institutes" around the world. All these re-branding efforts strive to demonstrate how dramatically China has changed and that it is again a central player in world affairs (Wasserstrom 2010b). They also aim to differentiate today's China from the China of Mao's day, the Communism of the Soviet Union, and its nakedly repressive neighbors like Myanmar and North Korea (see also Clark 2011; Nye 2011).

Commenting on a recent dialogue between Confucian and African thinkers in South Africa, funded by China's Confucian Institute, Daniel A. Bell (2010) remarks that such dialogues are relatively new. Now that China has found greater wealth, it can afford to fund dialogues that develop China's "soft power" and explore political alternatives to Western values and Western models of development.

As discussed in chapter 1, before the 2008 global economic crisis, the term "China Model" (or "Beijing Consensus") was used to represent an alternative economic development model to the neoliberal "Washington Consensus," which was a US-led plan for reforming and developing the economies of small, third world countries (Ramo 2004).

With the unfolding of the 2008 crisis, the mass media and policy circles began to talk about the China Model to celebrate not only China's fast-paced development but especially its rapid recovery.

In the 2010s, when China is making inroads in Africa, the Middle East, and Latin America for raw materials and minerals, and as Chinese state enterprises are encouraged to extend their investments into other parts of the world, the China Model is put forward to provide an ideological foundation to clear the way for the above-mentioned overseas adventures of the Chinese state and Chinese transnationals. As Arif Dirlik (2004, p. 2) remarks, the China Model "appears, more than anything, to be a sales gimmick – selling China to the world, while selling certain ideas of development to the Chinese leadership."

Developing and post-socialist countries are buying into this China Model because they are highly dissatisfied with neoliberalism's Washington Consensus, shock therapy, and Structural Adjustment Programs (Rodrik 2006). The former Brazilian leader, Lula da Silva, for example, expressed his admiration for China and its ability to globalize without giving up its autonomy and sovereignty (Dirlik 2004).

Once again, however, although the China Model holds some appeal for the developing and post-socialist countries, China has not made many inroads in consolidating other aspects of its soft power. Significantly, just as the Chinese state has attained great success in establishing its Confucius Institutes – numbering some 400 branches by 2014 – the initiative has also aroused a fury of criticisms and protests from academics and researchers, leading to the closure of the Institute in some cases. For instance, the University of Chicago closed its Confucius Institute in mid-2014 in accordance with a petition waged by more than 100 faculty members. They pointed out that, by prohibiting the hiring of individuals with particular religious and political beliefs and by limiting the course content to "politically neutral" issues, the

Institute had infringed human rights and circumscribed academic freedom. Pennsylvania State University and the McMaster University are other cases in point.

CHINA AS AN "ASPIRING HEGEMONIC POWER"?

Thirty years of rapid economic growth hardly allowed China to build up much political, military, and cultural power on top of its economic prowess. The global economic crisis is a period of turbulence and upheaval; it is a period when states, classes, and ethnic groups can find the room to redefine their relationships, to realign their configurations, and to reset the rules governing their access to key resources in the capitalist world economy. We argue that China's communist party-state was able to seize the opportunity of the 2008 global economic crisis not only to strengthen its economy, but also to expand its political power and influence and become more assertive in the interstate system. In addition, China tried to articulate a new set of values and a new model of development to challenge the United States' universal values and the so-called "Washington Consensus" model of development.

At the same time, we have also seen that, despite China's surging economic performance, there is still a long distance between China and the United States in terms of military, political, and cultural power. Hence, even though "the rise of China" is a historical process, not a single event, we think that, if it happens at all, it will take a long time before China can unseat the United States and assume the latter's position as the incumbent hegemonic state – a position the US has assumed since the second half of the twentieth century.

Nonetheless, it remains the case that this is a highly turbulent period that can easily lead to conflicts and confrontations. To address this matter, the following will examine two important elements, namely,

China's avowed intentions and the reactions of the international community.

China's Intentions

"Peaceful development" is the official policy that has defined China's global intentions since 1978 when the "reform and opening up" policy was initiated. Before examining its main tenets, however, it is notable a certain "triumphalist view" has emerged in recent years (Keith 2012; Kissinger 2011; Shambaugh 2011).

The so-called "triumphalist view" is best exemplified by China's best-selling books: Xiaojun Song and his coauthors' *Unhappy China* (2009) and Mingfu Liu's *The China Dream* (2010). Emerging in the aftermath of the 2008 global economic crisis, these books contend that the economic edge of Western society is massively overstated and that China should "shake off its self-doubt and passivity, abandon gradualism, and recover its historic sense of mission by means of a 'grand goal'" (Kissinger 2011: 505). In addition to economic ascendancy, these authors believe China should also assert itself politically.

Although this triumphalist view may have reflected the position of certain factions within the ruling bloc, it has been criticized severely by the communist party-state. *Peaceful development* is the official line advocated by generations of Chinese leaders. Deng Xiaoping made it clear in 1974 when he spoke at the United Nations that China will never become a superpower. Over time, even though some Chinese leaders have become "confident enough to reject, and even on occasion subtly mock, American lectures on reform ... [its] foreign policy aimed primarily for a peaceful international environment (including good relations with the United States) and access to raw materials to ensure continued economic growth" (Kissinger 2011, p. 490).

The idea of a *"peaceful rise"* was articulated formally by Chinese leaders and academics as the country's guiding principle subsequent to a series of lectures and study sessions between 2003 and 2006 on the rise and fall of great powers.[8] The principle affirms China's determination to not follow the footsteps of the great powers in history, but to seek "incremental reforms and the democratization of international relations" in its search for a new international political and economic order (B. Zheng 2005). The term "peaceful rise" was revised later to become "peaceful development," and the principle has been reaffirmed by President Hu Jintao in a speech delivered at the United Nations (Hu J. 2005), State Councilor Dai Bingguo in a speech given at the Conference on Interaction and Confidence-building Measures in Asia (CICA) (Dai 2010), as well as the State Council's 2011 White Paper on China's Peaceful Development (State Council 2011).

Dai (2010) made it eminently clear that China's "peaceful development" was not a tactical statement. The country was not seeking to bide time so as to gain hegemony. China did not intend to dominate Asia or to displace the United States as the world's preeminent power. Even as there was an apparent increase in military tension between China and Japan over the Diaoyu/Senkaku Islands after September 2012, the Chinese administration as well as the People's Liberation Army remained adamant on the country's commitment to peace and harmony. On February 4, 2013, a Political Commissar of the General Logistics Department of the People's Liberation Army made it very clear that China's main objective is economic growth, not war (Y. Liu 2013). The point was also reiterated in a Government Report delivered by Premier Wen Jiabao on March 5, 2013. In his own words, "We will continue to hoist the flag of peace, development, cooperation and mutual benefit; tread unwaveringly the way of 'peaceful development'; uphold resolutely a foreign policy of independence, autonomy and peace; promote perpetual global peace and mutual prosperity"[9] (Wen J. 2013).

Challenges to China's Hegemonic Aspiration

Despite China's avowed commitment to peaceful development and its disadvantage as compared to the United States in economic, military, and cultural power, the power transition theory continues to predominate among many China observers. The reason, as Henry Kissinger (2011, pp. 518–21) reminds us, may be likened to the argument put forth by Eyre Crowe in 1907 in relation to the emergence of Germany. For Crowe, it did not really matter whether Germany was pursuing conventional diplomacy to advance its interests or seeking a general political hegemony, thereby threatening the independence of its neighbors and, ultimately, the existence of Britain. Regardless of Germany's real purposes, once Germany succeeded in building a powerful navy, this would present an *objective threat* to Britain. Given the stakes on hand, formal assurance from Germany was hardly sufficient to dispel the suspicions.

Extrapolating Crowe's logic to the China–US relationships, the high risks associated with an emerging China render it quite difficult for the United States and other countries to trust in its good faith. The noise of the "triumphalist view" has only reinforced this suspicion. Regardless of China's avowed objectives, the country presents a latent threat to the US, and US leaders can hardly be expected to take the prospect kindly. There are good reasons to fear that "China would try to push American power as far away from its borders as it could, circumscribe the scope of American naval power, and reduce America's weight in international diplomacy" (Kissinger 2011, p. 521).

China's neighbors are also unlikely to view its ascending economic and military capability with ease. Unfortunately, perhaps in confirming the self-fulfilling prophecy, the United States' policy of "pivot to the Pacific," which in a way can be seen as its attempt "to organize China's many neighbors into a counterweight to Chinese dominance"

(Kissinger 2011, p. 521), has only deepened the mutual distrust and exacerbated the tension-ridden situation (cf. Yan 2013).

It is within this context of deep distrust that observers have dismissed China's declared intentions and objective evaluation of the country's material power resources, acceding instead to "the rise of China" discourse. The lack of trust and fear of China's ambitions color the assessments of the country's outward investments and territorial disputes, hence the apprehension and one-sided criticisms. If a strong China is invariably an aggressive China, its efforts to strengthen its economy will necessarily reinforce its military ambition. In turn, China's efforts to defend (or reclaim) its territorial rights must be driven by greed and state-induced nationalist fervor rather than justified by historical disputes and so must be censured accordingly. The US-led international order, in prevailing over the setting of agendas and shaping of values, also plays a major role in consolidating if not steering the critical evaluation of China.

In short, despite China's capability and avowed intentions, the apprehension over its military ambition has not been alleviated. China's values and agenda for the international system have also been at odds with those of the US-led international institutions. These concerns reinforce each other and exacerbate the various criticisms over China's expansion in overseas investments and attempts to defend its territorial rights.

CONCLUSION

As Ian Clark (2011, p. 25) suggests, whether China can attain a "peaceful rise" is not for China alone to decide, but depends equally upon the accommodation of other powers in the inter-state system. While we are not suggesting that China's expansion in overseas investments and involvements in territorial disputes are faultless, we also contend that such efforts have been subject to inaccurate, excessive, and one-sided criticisms. In turn, we argue that such prejudices can be traced to the apprehension over China's military ambitions and concern with China's departure from the agenda and values upheld by the US-led international institutions.

For the purpose of the present discussion, the apprehension and concern generate additional challenges to China as it seeks to attain further economic and social advancement in the capitalist world economy. At the very least, the need for military build-up, induced in part by the threats from the United States and its allies, will drain the needed resources that should be deployed to address the challenges to China's social and economic development. Further economic development will also be frustrated by failures to secure raw materials, consumer markets, or investment opportunities in other parts of the world. While the future depends in part on whether the United States chooses to be belligerent or play a more constructive role in shaping a new, more multilateral global order, China may also deflect the suspicions and proceed with economic construction by becoming more transparent with respect to its military activities and working with other countries to build a more inclusive global economy and polity (Buzan 2010).

In less than forty years, China has attained remarkable economic growth and drastically transformed from a poor third world country in 1978 to a world economic powerhouse in the twenty-first century. This volume has the following goals: first, to trace the historical process through which this development miracle has taken place; second, to delineate its distinguishing features: what we called state socialism, neoliberalism, and state neoliberalism; and, third, to examine how the communist party-state has been able to overcome the various developmental challenges, including the challenges of technology upgrading, staying in power, sustainability, and inter-state rivalry.

Chapter 1 spells out our state-centered approach to China's post-socialist development. Even though we agree with the neoliberal and social explanations that entrepreneurship, market institutions, and family are indeed crucial factors for China's remarkable post-1978 economic development, we argue that researchers need to bring the state back in. Specifically, we examine how the metamorphosis of the communist party-state enabled it to overcome the bureaucratic inefficiency of a planned economy, to seize the golden opportunity offered by the neoliberal transformations of the capitalist world economy in the late twentieth century, to mobilize market forces in local society, to unleash the entrepreneurial potential in the Chinese family, and to propel China into an economic powerhouse. The chapter also spells out the idea of "state neoliberalism" and highlights its differences from the developmental state as well as the neoliberalism as practiced in

Western capitalist countries and introduced by the former socialist countries of Eastern Europe.

Part I includes three chapters that examine the historical process of China's socialist and post-socialist development. Chapter 2 starts with a discussion of the characteristics of Chinese state socialism in the 1950s and 1960s. Unlike the interpretation offered in much literature on China, chapter 2 argues that state socialism left an important legacy for the post-1978 reforms. Despite the policy failures of the Great Leap Forward and the Cultural Revolution, it was during the Great Leap Forward that the state mobilized millions of peasants to construct dams, reservoirs, and large-scale irrigation systems for the communes. It was also during these socialist experiments that commune and brigade enterprises were set up and, through their operation, local officials learnt to take initiatives, gained managerial experience, and accumulated human capital. These infrastructural and institutional foundations made possible the rapid increase in agricultural productivity, the speedy emergence of rural entrepreneurs, and enabled local forces to play an important role in China's post-1978 development.

Chapter 2 also argues that it is the interplay between several global, political, and historical factors that explains China's critical transition in 1978. The fading of the Cold War, the rise of the neoliberal globalization project, and the effort by the East Asian newly industrialized economies (NIEs) to relocate their industries provided the precondition. Inside China, growing dissatisfaction with income stagnation and political alienation made the Chinese population more receptive to try a new path of development; and the emergence of an undercurrent against ultra-leftism served to mobilize the support of middle-class professionals and former disgraced state officials against the Maoists. Historical factors, which included the passing of Mao and other senior revolutionary leaders in the mid-1970s, helped to clear the way for the reforms; and even though the reforms were initially very moderate, they soon drove China onto a slippery path with no return.

Chapter 3 then reviews China's experiment with neoliberal capitalism between 1979 and 2008. Unlike other socialist states in Eastern Europe, China's reform was started with local support, without commensurate political change, and initially involved the decollectivization of agriculture and certain levels of marketization and proletarianization. It was gradual, marked by salient policy reversals, yet overseen by the party-state at all stages.

Despite the restraints of reform, *neoliberal* practices had already generated enough contradictions to lead to the showdown of the 1989 Tiananmen Incident. In the three-year interim after 1989, the party-state recentralized its administrative and fiscal capacity, injected massive funding for research and education, and provided support to strategic state enterprises, or, in other words, experimented with what we call *state neoliberalism.*

However, given robust economic growth between 1978 and 1989, the rise of living standards among the Chinese population, and support from the local officials, it was impossible to further encroach on the market. Having reconsolidated its administrative and fiscal capacity, the party-state deepened neoliberalism between 1992 and 2003. Among other things, it privatized state enterprises, bankrupted many small and inefficient SOEs, laid off millions of state workers, and opened many economic sectors to foreign investment.

The decade-long deepening of neoliberalism culminated in widespread petitions and protests, which, in turn, prompted the party-state to change its course again during the leadership transition in 2003. The Hu/Wen regime launched the politics of harmonious society, strived for balanced development, introduced more policies for social protection, or in other words *consolidated "state neoliberalism."*

Chapter 4 examines how China took advantage of the 2008 global economic crisis and sought to further consolidate state neoliberalism, resulting in the expansion of the state sector, the strengthening of state capacity, and the realignment of social forces in society. Although state neoliberalism had jumpstarted the Chinese economy in the short term (2008–12), it also produced many structural problems. With the global economic crisis continuing into the 2010s and signs of deceleration in economic growth emerging in China during 2012–13, the decade-long leadership transition once again presented an opportunity for the newly elected President Xi Jinping and Premier Li Keqiang to respond to calls for policy change and launch another wave of neoliberalization.

Part II examines four challenges faced by China in its bid for hypergrowth over the past forty years. Chapter 5 deals with the challenge of technology upgrading. It reports that, up to the end of the 1990s, neoliberal reform merely brought China up to the level of industrial processing, while its export sector suffered from the dominance of foreign ownership with little profit retention and little technology transfer. Like some developmental states, the Chinese state launched "big push" policies to transform China into a technological power in the twenty-first century. However, the policies did not work as intended. Instead, the structural uncertainty and the dualistic (national and local) innovation system interacted with the new fragmented mode of global production to induce second-generation innovation (including organization innovation and process innovation) within China without attaining novel-product innovation or technological breakthrough.

Chapter 6 deals with the challenge for the communist party-state to stay in power. China's remarkable economic growth over the past four decades led to structural dislocation and an increase in social conflict. Chapter 6 reports that, relying on policies introduced under the Hu/Wen regime to consolidate state neoliberalism, the communist party-state did a fine job managing the rising social conflicts among the peasants, the workers, and the new middle class. However, with the intensification of social conflicts since the 2008 global financial crisis, the legitimacy and capacity of the communist party-state could be undermined in the near future.

Chapter 7 deals with the challenge of environmental degradation. It documents how China's bid for hyper-growth depleted and gravely polluted the country's water, land, and atmospheric resources. Despite an increase in the party-state's sensitivity to environmental concerns, policy conflicts and institutional fragmentation undermined China's efforts to clean up pollution, reforest, and implement environmental preservation laws. Similarly, despite the emergence of environmental NGOs, their endeavors remain circumscribed given the party-state's preoccupation with growth at all cost and with continued domination over the country.

Chapter 8 examines the challenge of global rivalry, detailing the tensions surrounding China's outward direct investments and its territorial disputes over the Spratly Islands and the Diaoyu/Senkaku Islands. These tensions reflect China's rise in global economic, political, and cultural domains as well as the tendency for it to become assertive in international affairs. Together, these sharpened the difference in values and agenda between China and the US-led international institutions, gave rise to apprehension over China's military ambitions despite the country's capabilities and avowed intentions, and, with the US's new pivot policy towards Asia-Pacific, threatened to intensify the rivalry within the inter-state system in the future.

THE CHARACTERISTICS OF THE CHINESE PATH OF DEVELOPMENT

State-Led Development

Similar to many East Asian NIEs, China's development is also state-led. China benefited from its socialist legacy by inheriting a strong communist party-state which was apt to mobilize societal resources for developmental goals. Among other things, the state sets up five-year development plans, nurtures and protects large and strategic state enterprises, undertakes many mega-infrastructure projects, injects massive funding for education and technology research, and works tirelessly to achieve macroeconomic stabilization.

However, unlike the East Asian developmental states, the development experience of the Chinese state has been permeated by central–local dynamics, a great dose of gradualism and experimentation, and a deliberate effort to introduce neoliberalization while upholding the socialist ideology from the beginning.

Decentralization and Bottom-Up Development

The path of development in China has been distinguished by its decentralization policies and local initiatives. Benefiting from the state socialist legacy of localized administration as well as brigade and commune enterprises, local governments and township and village enterprises played a pivotal role in China's capitalist development. Administrative and fiscal decentralization policies, furthermore, generated both the institutional foundation and immense incentives (and pressures) for these local actors to capture market opportunities. Inter-local competitions, moreover, encouraged the less developed regions to copy and catch up with the more developed ones, hence injecting an invaluable source of dynamism into the economy. This also helps to explain why the Chinese local economy was so competitive in the early 1980s even though the communist party-state had yet to institute legal reforms to safeguard private property.

The importance of local governments and their interactions with the state center had exerted other far-reaching impacts on China's path of development. First, local support had provided a "counterweight" to the conservatives and allowed China to undertake economic reforms without initiating political ones, hence enabling the country to travel a path distinct from the one followed by the Soviet Union and Eastern Europe. Second, inter-local competitions have interacted with the communist party-state's policies to determine the trajectory of development. In the case of technology upgrading, even though the central government poured resources into research and development, as noted above this did not result in novel-product innovation or new technology creation. Instead, structural uncertainties interacted with the concerns of local governments, leading the latter to collaborate with foreign enterprises and engage in organization and process innovation. Third, the central–local relationships also provided a specific way for the Chinese communist party-state to tackle or perhaps deflect social and political conflicts that emerged in the course of capitalist development. Specifically, labor, land, and environmental conflicts were often tackled by local governments and enterprises, with the central government taking the moral high ground and assuming the role of the final (and benevolent) arbitrator when necessary. Thus far, this strategy has allowed the communist party-state to deflect the core conflicts (state-orchestrated neoliberal development) and contain the tensions within and damages to the system.

Gradualism and Zig-Zag Development

Unlike the "big bang" approach in Eastern Europe, the path of China's development has been a gradual, adaptive process without a clear blueprint. China's neoliberal market reforms have proceeded by trial and error, with frequent mid-course corrections and reversals of policy. In other words, the Chinese economic reforms were not a complete project that was settled in the first stage, but were an ongoing process with many adjustments, whether two steps forward and one step backward, or one step forward and two steps backward. In China, there was no rapid leap to free prices, currency convertibility, or the cutting of state subsidies; nor was there massive privatization and the quick selling off of state enterprises. This gradualist, cyclical approach of the Chinese post-socialist transition was quite different to the "big bang" and "shock therapy" approaches practiced in Eastern Europe, which called for the dismantling of the centrally planned economy and the building up of neoliberal market institutions as quickly as possible.

State Neoliberalism

Part and parcel of the bottom-up approach and gradualism, China's path of development is a hybrid that we have called "state neoliberalism." State neoliberalism consists of an uneasy combination of different contradictory elements that defies any easy characterization. Although we have already discussed the concept of state neoliberalism in chapters 1 and 3, it is still worthwhile recalling the key features here.

First and most fundamentally, state neoliberalism signifies the tendency for the communist party-state to promote neoliberalism as part of its strategy to facilitate national development. Apart from launching many standard developmental state supports, the Chinese state endorsed neoliberalism so that an increasing number of commodities were subjected to market principles, workers and natural resources were exposed to ruthless capitalist exploitation, and many state enterprises in the non-strategic sector were privatized. In so doing, China also differed from the West in that the state rather than capitalists were behind the neoliberal turn. Indeed, before the initiation of policy change in state socialist China in 1978, market relations were strongly suppressed by the state, property was predominantly state-owned or collectively owned, market institutions were rudimentary, and a capitalist class was practically non-existent. The communist party-state laid the groundwork for the emergence of neoliberalism by generating room for the rise of market relations, the emergence of a capitalist class, and for a long time played an instrumental role in the imposition of blatant neoliberal practices. Unlike the West, where profit served as the ultimate motive, the ebb and flow of neoliberal practices in China was in part governed by the communist party-state's overriding concern for its survival and continued leadership.

Second, the notion of state neoliberalism was also coined to highlight the state's continued appeal to socialism while pursuing neoliberal practices and, hence, acute tensions and contradictions that arose. As in most societies, neoliberal practices give rise to conflicts between the dominant social groups and subordinate ones such as workers, peasants, and the middle class. In China, this was complicated by the party-state's gradual and hesitant policy changes. Hence, for a long time, the emerging business class remained weak, needed to take heed of state policies in order to delineate its market strategies, and often depended on the state for survival. Similarly, the dispossessions of the workers and peasants have until now been incomplete and peasants have only partially turned into workers (i.e. there has been partial proletarianization). On top of this, the communist party-state continues to declare itself the defender of peasants and workers and, so long as it sustains this façade, it has found it difficult to defend neoliberal policies at the ideological level. As a result, social actors and segments of the state elite whose material and cultural interests were hurt by the neoliberal reforms could well use the inherent contradictions of state-initiated neoliberal reforms to challenge the party-state itself.

Third, the term "state neoliberalism" was also coined to highlight the policy changes and reversals that China has experienced, which were perhaps expected given the acute contradictions and the communist party-state's determination to stay in power. As such, the term depicts an ongoing process rather than an attained condition.

In sum, China's path of post-socialist development is characterized by the centrality of the state, decentralization and a bottom-up approach, gradualism and a zig-zag path of development, and state neoliberalism. Given such a historical product, how did the communist party-state respond to the four developmental challenges that it encountered over the past forty years?

RESPONSES TO DEVELOPMENTAL CHALLENGES

Part II shows that the communist party-state did a fine job if the challenges were congruent with the goals of economic development and political stability.

Thus, the party-state succeeded in upgrading China's technology, moving the country up the value chain, and making it an emerging high-tech power in the twenty-first century. China's R&D was "history-making," since it "exceeds and challenges both the US and Europe in terms of the intellectual property rights and the financial and infrastructure commitments it continues to make in science and technology endeavors" (Battelle 2009, p. 24). China's share in scientific publications and co-authored articles has exploded, catapulting it to become the second largest source country behind the US. In terms of total patenting activities, China has overtaken South Korea and Europe, and is catching up with the US and Japan (Ernst 2011). By the 2010s, Chinese companies seemed to have established a presence in a number of *competitive high-tech industries* as creators of products with brand-name recognition, rather than merely as manufacturers. Even if China was not yet at the frontier of cutting-edge research and had not achieved novel-product innovation, it had done very well in terms of organization and process innovation.

Likewise, the communist party-state is surprisingly able to stay in power, despite the presence of widespread social conflict and civil unrest among workers, peasants, and the new middle class to challenge the party-state over the past three decades. Chinese society is politically stable and the communist party-state was quite successful in deflecting, repressing, preempting, or institutionalizing the different kinds of social conflict and civil unrest up to the early 2010s. It was this successful conflict management that gave the Chinese party-state autonomy and the capacity to design, implement, and deepen the state neoliberalism programs and to make policy adjustments (either to speed up, slow down, or change course) in mid-course if it detects that the policies are not working well.

Insofar as China is able to upgrade its technology and the communist party-state manages to stay in power, it out-performs the Eastern European former socialist countries. However, the communist party-state is unable to overcome the developmental challenges that contradict the goals of rapid economic growth.

Even though the party-state has over time become more receptive to ideas of environmental preservation, set up regulations to protect the environment, and worked with selected environmental NGOs, China has continued to experience very serious environmental degradation. So long as China gives high priority to economic development, local state officials will be induced to "collude" with capitalists in their quests for lower cost and higher profit even if this entails plundering the environment.

Finally, the communist party-state has only done moderately well in managing the challenge of global rivalry. China's global quest for more resources inevitably puts it in conflict with neighbors and the existing power-holders in the inter-state system. So far, the communist party-state has not been very successful defending against Western charges that its investments in Africa amount to neo-colonialism, while the hostility among its East Asian neighbors (Japan, Vietnam, the Philippines) is escalating, with sporadic confrontations between patrol ships and battleships. China heads a very limited number of international organizations and is hardly in a position to set the international agenda.

A question worthy of asking, then, is whether the Chinese path of development can be copied by other developing countries to attain a commensurate rate of economic growth.

CAN THE CHINA MODEL BE COPIED?

What this book has tried to show is that there is, in fact, no easily identifiable path (or "model") that captures China's developmental experience over the past forty years. The Chinese path is highly ambiguous in the sense that it is a hybrid and uneasy combination of contradictory elements: state-led development versus decentralization and a bottom-up approach, neoliberalism versus state neoliberalism, and so on.

To the extent that a Chinese path can be described, it concerns *process* rather than a blueprint or policy prescription. As Sarah Cook (2010) remarks, the China experience is one of pragmatism, experimentation, and gradualism, looking for successes, keeping what works, and discarding what does not. This approach is reflected in widely cited slogans of the Chinese communist party-state, such as "seeking truth from facts," "crossing the river by groping the stones," and Deng Xiaoping's comment that it doesn't matter whether a cat is black or white, so long as it catches mice.

What is distinctive in China's developmental experience, therefore, is less an ideological set of policy prescriptions than a flexible process of adaptation to rapid changes within specific political and institutional contexts in a changing capitalist world economy. As such, can third world developing countries copy China's *flexible process of adaptation?*

This flexible process of adaptation presupposes a strong state machinery that has the capacity not only to carry out its policies, but also to adjust them if necessary. It also presupposes that the state has a high degree of autonomy in the sense that other social classes and political groups are too weak to capture the state for their own interests. For example, since the capitalist class was almost completely wiped out during the Cultural Revolution, it was too small, too weak, and too dependent on the party-state at the initial phase of the reforms to capture state power. Similarly, when the party-state responded to growing labor unrests and other popular struggles by pursuing state neoliberalism, the nascent capitalist class was powerless to stop the policy change.

In short, unless third world developing countries have a state as strong and as autonomous as the Chinese communist party-state, they will not be able to copy the "flexible process of adaptation" of China.

Before ending, we want to raise one final set of questions: Where is China heading in the forthcoming years of the twenty-first century? Will it rise up to become the center of accumulation of the capitalist world economy?

WHITHER CHINA?

The fact that the communist party-state has managed the challenges quite well during the initial phase of development since 1978 does not mean that the road for Chinese development will be all smooth from now on. After going through an *initial phase* of what can be called *"catching up"* over the past forty years, China now has reached a turning point and will move on to a mature phase of what can be called *"rising power"* in the twenty-first century. This mature phase will involve the following set of new challenges:

• *The challenge of maintaining the hyper-growth rate.* China has attained truly remarkable economic growth over the past three decades, but there are currently signs that its economy is slowing down. The global economic recession is continuing, the country is beginning to use up its valuable resources, its environment is reaching the point of ecological breakdown, its population is aging and its workforce is shrinking, and it is unable to achieve novel-product innovation and move up to the top of the value-added hierarchy in the commodity chain. China needs an annual 8 percent GDP growth rate in order to provide enough jobs for the new job seekers every year, or it will have to face considerable grievances and social unrest from the unemployed young generation. But as the Chinese economy matures, it will be a real challenge to continue the 8 percent growth rate for another decade or two.

+ *The challenge of hegemonic struggle.* The global search for raw materials (especially energy), markets, talents, and capital will inevitably bring China into conflict with major world powers. We have already noted in chapter 8 how China's investments in Africa, the Middle East, and Latin America have raised many eyebrows in Europe and North America. Hostility with China's neighbors (Japan, Vietnam, and the Philippines) has also intensified over time, which is not helped by the US's policy of pivot toward the Pacific and rebalancing toward Asia. In addition, US pundits and politicians have explored measures to prevent or to delay the rise of China. As China's economy becomes more global, the hegemonic struggles between China and Western powers are bound to become more acute.

One aspect of the hegemonic struggle concerns whether China will suffer from a premature death like that experienced by Japan. Japan was a very promising global power in the 1980s. However, when the country acceded to US pressure to raise its currency at the Plaza Accord in 1985, it went into a decade-long recession and ceased to be an engine to power the capitalist world economy. Trying to avoid Japan's mistake, China has resisted the pressure from the US and other European states to raise its currency value. It remains to be seen whether China can hold its position as the pressure for currency revaluation increases with the deepening of the 2008 global economic crisis (Palat 2010).

+ *The challenge of changing class structure, the changing power base of the party-state, and power sharing.* Rapid economic growth has resulted in the expansion of both the capitalist class and the new middle class. These rising classes will inevitably seek more power and influence, thus challenging the authority of the communist party-state. At the same time, peasants and workers – as the traditional socio-economic base of the communist party-state – have been subjected to increasing exploitation and suppression. Whether the state neoliberal strategies will continue to succeed in deflecting their dissatisfaction and gaining support for the party-state remains to be seen.

More fundamentally, the party-state has so far avoided making any changes to the political structure. Given the growing unrest in civil society and the expansion of the capitalist class and the middle class, the party-state will be under increasing pressure to initiate political restructuring, democratic reforms, and power sharing with other social classes. These changes are likely to involve radical structural changes, arouse acute political conflicts, and entail high stakes. Minxin Pei (2008), for one, is quite pessimistic about the structural transformations as he talks about the possibility of political decay and a possible "trapped transition."

Since global economic crisis is a period of uncertainty, it is hard to predict whether the rise of China will continue. What we know for sure is that the country has now moved from the initial phase of "catching up" to the mature phase of "rising power." How China handles the above new challenges will play a significant role in determining its historic fate in the near future. Furthermore, whatever its future role might be, the country's bid for global ascendance will trigger more conflicts, more uncertainties, and more chaos in the global economy of the twenty-first century.

Notes

Chapter 1 Introduction

1 Oi (1992) seems to disagree with Whyte (2009) and thinks that the communist bureaucracy, as it was, could handle developmental tasks without a major overhaul. We take issue with this.

Chapter 2 Socialist Foundation and the Critical Transition to State Neoliberalism

1 Much scholarly research has been devoted to explaining why, unlike Europe, China did not experience capitalist development and why the country followed a socialist route to modernity. Exemplary studies here include Hamilton (1985), Johnson (1962), B. Moore (1966), and Skocpol (1979).

2 This population figure is actually for 1953 (Coale 1984).

3 Agricultural processing and other sideline industries were transferred to the urban areas after 1954, depriving the peasants in many ways of their sources of cash income (Selden 1993, p. 78).

4 Notably, the repayment of Soviet debt began in earnest in 1955 (Reiitsu 1982, p. 243).

5 In turn, 18 percent worked in urban collectives, 24 percent in rural collectives, 5 percent as urban temporary workers, and 11 percent as rural temporary workers (Walder 1986, p. 41).

6 Fairbank (1986, p. 300) talked about the Great Leap's attack on bureaucratic centralism, which correlated with the granting of greater managerial power to local cadres.

7 China's total population as of 1958 was 660 million (Kung and Lin 2003).

8 Of course, a centralized economic system had its advantages. It "bequeathed a strong organizational framework, as well as a large task-force of people who were capable of mobilizing popular energies, who thought in strategic terms and who viewed themselves as members of a team rather than individuals" (Nolan and Ash 1995, p. 984, n. 15).

Chapter 3 State Neoliberalism: The Political Economy of China's Rise

1 Decollectivization was aided by two rounds of grain procurement price increases that amounted to some 20 percent.

2 According to Yasheng Huang (2010, p. 5), TVE "include enterprises sponsored by townships and villages, the alliance enterprises formed by peasants, other alliance enterprises and individual enterprises."

3 Shirk (1993, p. 15) examined the policy-making institutions and processes in China and suggested that "the trajectory of Chinese industrial reforms over the decade…was shaped by consensus decision-making" that gave even lower-level bureaucrats the power of veto, thus making for China's slow and gradualist reform in the 1980s.

4 According to Shen and his colleagues (2012, pp. 9–11), the central state's share of revenue declined from 33 percent in 1988 to 22 percent in 1993, whereas the share of local expenditure increased from 45 percent in 1981 to about 72 percent in 1993. The central state's effort to change sector ownership and introduce new levies had also led to the emergence of a climate of distrust between central and local governments.

5 It has also been translated as "tax sharing scheme."

6 Lu (2002) and his colleagues classified the social classes according to the control of economic resources, ownership of social (networks) and cultural (education) capital, and taking into account variations in the quantity and quality of such capital. He used a ten-class classification. The classes not mentioned in the text include national and social administrators (2.1 percent), managers (1.5 percent), clerical employees (4.8 percent), as well as the unemployed and underemployed (31.1 percent). See Lu (2002, Table 14) for details.

7 Mass disturbances were defined as "any riots, demonstrations, and protests that involved more than 100 people" (Human Rights in China 2006).

8 Karl Polanyi (1944) argues that the dynamism of modern capitalist society is characterized by a "double movement": there is an incessant movement of market relations to engross land, labor, and capital; and because the market price cannot resolve all social contradictions, a countermovement of protests emerges as the society seeks to protect itself.

Chapter 6 The Challenges of Staying in Power

1 The report lists approximate totals as follows: 8,700 (1993); 10,000 (1994); 50,000 (2002); 58,000 (2003); 60,000 (2006); 80,000 (2007); 127,000 (2008); 180,000 (2010); 200,000+ (2011).

Chapter 7 The Challenges of Sustainability: Environmental Degradation and Resource Depletion

1 One of the first decrees issued by Xi Jinping when he became China's President in 2013 was to curb lavish banquets at official functions (Zhuang 2013).

2 In 1997, the Yellow River failed to reach the Eastern delta for 226 days.

3 The Yangtze River dolphin, for instance, is practically extinct.

4 Apart from the excessive use of fertilizers, the use of forbidden pesticides, preservatives and additives, as well as industrial pollution, resulted in crises of confidence in rice, pork, chicken, fish, egg, milk, and other food products in China. A scandal that assumed international proportion concerns the addition of melamine into milk products, which was exposed in 2008. To date, Chinese parents remain so affected that they refuse to feed their babies with milk powder produced (or even imported) by firms in China. They purchase infant milk powders in vast quantity from Hong Kong, the UK, New Zealand, and Germany, prompting these governments to impose quotas on such purchases (An and Wang 2013).

5 A film, *Cutting Down Tibet*, made by a Tibetan in secret, shows logging camps in southern Tibet with trucks loaded with trees 10 feet in diameter (Hays 2008).

6 Illegal logging and slash-and-burn agriculture is still said to consume 5,000 kilometers of virgin forest every year (Shapiro 2012).

7 Toxins released by industrial plants may be considered another factor causing China's air pollution. However, most scholars appear to regard coal and automobiles to be far more significant (He et al. 2012).

8 The recent study by Feng Wang and his colleagues (2013) suggests that the industry has spread to Zhejiang Province.

9 International organizations are said to have shaped China's policy agenda on the environment. (The point will not be elaborated here, but see Economy 2004: chapter 6.)

10 These efforts were heralded by the Medium- and Long-Term Plan for Renewable Energy, passed in 2007, which requires that 15 percent of China's energy come from renewable sources by 2020 (Shapiro 2012, p. 63), as well as the 2011 White Paper on China's Policies and Actions for Addressing Climate Change, issued by the State Council, which lays out plans for cutting carbon emissions (Shapiro 2012, p. 49).

11 This "division of labor" in state administration is also called *tiao-kuai*, or the branch-and-lump system.

12 Economy (2004, pp. 136–7) suggests that China's environmental NGOs have three "objectives": conservation, urban renewal, and democracy.

13 WWF is the abbreviation of the World Wildlife Fund in the US and Canada, but its registered name in Hong Kong is "World Wide Fund for Nature."

14 Ma Jun, author of *China's Water Crisis* and founder of the Institute for Public and Environmental Affairs (IPE), for instance, has posted information released by the Ministry of Environmental Protection on the IPE website to put pressure on global firms operating in China (Shapiro 2012, p. 117).

15 As Marks (2012) suggests, environmental activists are sometimes journalists or other media personalities, and they might choose to wear different hats depending on the situation.

16 Another example would be Green Watershed's effort to expose the poverty and hardships suffered by farmers affected by the construction of dams on the Lancang River (Shapiro 2012, p. 117). In both cases, reportage in the national media captured the attention of the central government, which in turn urged the provincial governments to tackle the issues.

Chapter 8 The Challenges of Global Rivalry: Resource Competition and Territorial Disputes

1 Our discussion is necessarily selective. The exchange rate of the renminbi, for example, while important, will not be dealt with here.

2 China's National Bureau of Statistics (2014a) shows that Asia, especially Hong Kong and Singapore, capture the lion's share of China's cumulative ODI. However, the Heritage Foundation study by Scissors (2012) suggests that they refer to investments in Hong Kong's and Singapore's financial markets, meaning that the final destinations are elsewhere. China's official statistics are also at odds with those presented by Rosen and Hanemann (2012) and Ali and Jafrani (2012). Please refer to the discussion below.

3 As of March 29, 2013, the US government also forbade all its offices to acquire/install Chinese-made telecommunication equipment, allegedly for reasons of national security, although the shares of Huawei, China's premier telecommunications equipment manufacturer, and Lenovo, China's premier computer hardware company, are majority owned by the general public (*Mingpao News* 2013).

4 The study was about Latin America and not Africa as such.

5 The 1982 United Nations Convention on the Law of the Sea (UNCLOS III) specifies a 12-nautical-mile territorial sovereignty boundary from a nation's coastline as well as a 200-nautical-mile creation of exclusive economic zones (EEZs). As for the ASEAN Declaration, it commits the signatories to

resolve the disputes by peaceful means and in accordance with universally recognized principles of international law.

6 In the years after 1972, Japanese built lighthouses and other small constructions on the Islands. In 1979, the Japanese government sent an official delegation to spend four weeks on one of the islands to study the ecosystem and marine life there.

7 The carrier was developed on the basis of an incomplete ex-Soviet Varyag purchased from the Ukraine in 1998.

8 The study sessions were also consolidated into *The Rise of Great Powers*, a twelve-part film series aired on Chinese national television in 2006.

9 The authors' translation.

References ——————————————————

Aivazian, Varouj A., Ying Ge, and Jiaping Qiu. 2005. "Can Corporatization Improve the Performance of State-Owned Enterprises Even Without Privatization?" *Journal of Corporate Finance* 11: 791–808.

Ali, Shimelse and Nida Jafrani. 2012. "China's Growing Role in Africa: Myths and Facts." *International Economic Bulletin* (February 9), online: http://carnegieendowment.org/ieb/2012/02/09/china-s-growing-role-in-africa-myths-and-facts/9j5q.

An, Baijie and Xiaodong Wang. 2013. "Li Calls for Action on Baby Milk." *China Daily* (June 1), online: usa.chinadaily.com.cn/china/2013-06/01/content_16554275.htm.

Appelbaum, Richard P. and Rachel Parker. 2011. "*China's Move to High-Tech Innovation: Some Regional Policy Implications.*" Paper presented to the Worldwide Universities Network conference on "The Asia-Pacific, Globalism, and Global Governance," University of Leeds (May 12–13).

Baark, Erik. 1991. "Fragmented Innovation: China's Science and Technology Policy Reforms in Retrospect." Pp. 531–45 in *China's Economic Dilemmas in the 1990s: The Problems of Reforms, Modernization, and Interdependence*, edited by Joint Economic Committee, Congress of the United States. Armonk, NY: M. E. Sharpe.

Barboza, David. 2009. "Obama Begins First Visit to China." *New York Times* (November 15), online: www.nytimes.com/2009/11/16/world/asia/16shanghai.html.

Barboza, David. 2010a. "China Passes Japan as Second-Largest Economy." *New York Times* (August 15), online: www.nytimes.com/2010/08/16/business/global/16yuan.html?pagewanted=all&_r=0.

Barboza, David. 2010b. "Report Warns of Risks to China's Bank System." *New York Times* (July 14), online: www.nytimes.com/2010/07/15/business/global/15yuan.html.

Barboza, David. 2010c. "China Shift away from Low-Cost Factories." *New York Times* (September 15), online: www.nytimes.com/2010/09/16/business/global/16factory.html?pagewanted=all.

Barboza, David. 2010d. "China's Booming Internet Giants May Be Stuck There." *New York Times* (March 23), online: www.nytimes.com/2010/03/24/business/global/24internet.html?gwh=CAB9405012C253E6567C4689FAE1A08E&gwt=pay.

Barboza, David. 2013a. "Tetra Pak Comes Under Scrutiny in China." *New York Times* (July 5), online: www.nytimes.com/2013/07/06/business/global/tetra-pak-comes-under-scrutiny-in-china.html?_r=0&gwh=0BF49302148AC9DB7D0449056CB672C3&gwt=pay.

Barboza, David. 2013b. "China Arrests British Adviser Hired by GlaxoSmithKline." *New York Times* (August 21), online: www.nytimes.com/2013/08/22/business/global/police-in-china-arrest-british-executive.html?gwh=68B30EAC28BF8841BB89D38ED787021E&gwt=pay.

Battelle. 2009. "Global R&D Funding Forecast." *R&D Magazine* (December), online: www.rdmag.com/digital-editions/2009/12/2010-r-d-magazine-global-funding-forecast.

Beijing Xuanwu District. 2006. *Beijing Xuanwu District Nian Shu (Year Book of Beijing Xuanwu District)* (no longer online).

Bell, Daniel A. 2010. "Developing China's Soft Power." *New York Times* (September 23), online: www.nytimes.com/2010/09/24/opinion/24iht-edbell.html.

Berberoglu, Berch. 2012. "Introduction: The Global Capitalist Crisis and Its Impact on a World Scale." *International Review of Modern Sociology* 38(2): 163–8.

Bernstein, Thomas P. 1999. "Farmer Discontent and Regime Responses." Pp. 197–219 in *The Paradox of China's Post-Mao Reforms*, edited by Merle Goldman and Roderick Macfarquhar. Cambridge, MA: Harvard University Press.

Bernstein, Thomas P. 2004. "Unrest in Rural China: A 2003 Assessment Report." *CSD Working Papers*, University of California, online: https://escholarship.org/uc/item/1318d3rx.

Berry, Leonard. 2003. *Land Degradation in China: Its Extent and Impact*. Commissioned by Global Mechanism, with support from the World Bank, online: rmportal.net/library/content/frame/land-degradation-case-studies-02-china/at_download/file.

Bishop, Bill. 2013. "Market Rebound in China Shows Beijing's Resolve." *New York Times* (September 9), online: http://dealbook.nytimes.com/2013/09/09/market-rebound-in-china-shows-beijings-resolve/.

Blecher, Marc J. 2002. "Hegemony and Worker's Politics in China." *The China Quarterly* 170: 283–303.

Bloomberg. 2013. "China Local Debt May Top Estimates, Former Minister Says." *Bloomberg News* (April 7), online: www.bloomberg.com/news/2013-04-06/china-local-debt-may-top-estimates-former-minister-says.html.

Bradsher, Keith. 2009a. "Bowing to Protests, China Halts Sale of Steel Mill." *New York Times* (August 17), online: www.nytimes.com/2009/08/17/business/global/17yuan.html?_r=0&gwh=60F9AB9EB9F3DA2FD2F4A74C963B797B&gwt=pay.

Bradsher, Keith. 2009b. "China Racing Ahead of US in the Drive to Go Solar." *New York Times* (August 25), online: www.nytimes.com/2009/08/25/business/energy-environment/25solar.html?gwh=C505DB6034342D5D5520806EBBCA93CD&gwt=pay.

Bradsher, Keith. 2010a. "On Clean Energy, China Skirts Rules." *New York Times* (September 8), online: www.nytimes.com/2010/09/09/business/global/09trade.html?_r=2&partner=TOPIXNEWS&ei=5099.

Bradsher, Keith. 2010b. "Ford Agrees to Sell Volvo to a Fast-Rising Chinese Company." *New York Times* (March 28), online: www.nytimes.com/2010/03/29/business/global/29auto.html?_r=0&gwh=071415B4562170E1749FB47638310B57&gwt=pay.

Bradsher, Keith and David Barboza. 2006. "Pollution from Chinese Coal Casts Shadow around Globe." *New York Times* (June 6), online: www.nytimes.com/2006/06/11/business/worldbusiness/11chinacoal.html?pagewanted=all&gwh=05560D14C608754203173464822831lA&gwt=pay.

Bramall, Chris. 1993. *In Praise of Maoist Economic Planning: Living Standards and Economic Development in Sichuan since 1931.* Oxford: Clarendon Press.

Brautigam, Deborah A. and Xiaoyang Tang. 2009. "China's Engagement in African Agriculture: 'Down to the countryside.'" *The China Quarterly* 199: 686–706.

Breakthrough Institute. 2009. *Rising Tigers and Sleeping Giant: Asian Nations Set to Dominate the Clean Energy Race by Out-Investing the United States.* New York: The Breakthrough Institute, online: http://thebreakthrough.org/blog/Rising_Tigers.pdf.

Breslin, Shaun. 2007. *China and the Global Political Economy.* New York: Palgrave Macmillan.

Breznitz, Dan and Michael Murphree. 2011. *Run of the Red Queen: Government, Innovation, Globalization, and Economic Growth in China.* New Haven: Yale University Press.

Browne, Andrew and Norihiko Shirouzu. 2010. "Beijing Pressures Japanese on Wages." *Wall Street Journal* (August 29), online: http://online.wsj.com/news/articles/SB10001424052748704342504575459582891999498.

Buckley, Chris. 2004. "Let a Thousand Ideas Flower: China Is a New Hotbed of Research." *New York Times* (September 13), online: www.nytimes.com/2004/09/13/technology/13china.html.

Buckley, Chris. 2013. "China Takes Aim at Western Ideas." *New York Times* (August 19), online: www.nytimes.com/2013/08/20/world/asia/chinas-new-leadership-takes-hard-line-in-secret-memo.html?pagewanted=all.

Buzan, Barry. 2010. "China in International Society: is "Peaceful Rise" Possible?" *The Chinese Journal of International Politics* 3: 5–36.

Cai, Fang, Albert Park, and Yaohui Zhao. 2008. "The Chinese Labor Market in the Reform Era." Pp. 167–214 in *China's Great Economic Transformation*, edited by Loren Brandt and Thomas G. Rawski. Cambridge: Cambridge University Press.

Cai, Hongbin and Daniel Treisman. 2006. "Did Government Decentralization Cause China's Economic Miracle?" *World Politics* 58(4): 505–35.

Cai, Yongshun. 2002. "The Resistance of Chinese Laid-Off Workers in the Reform Period." *The China Quarterly* 170: 327–44.

Cai, Yongshun. 2005. "China's Moderate Middle Class: The Case of Homeowners' Resistance." *Asian Survey* 45(5): 777–99.

Campbell, Horace. 2008. "China in Africa: Challenging US Global Hegemony." *Third World Quarterly* 29(1): 89–105.

Cao, Cong. 2004. "Zhongguancun and China's High-Tech Parks in Transition." *Asian Survey* 44(5): 647–88.

Cao, Cong. 2010. "A Climate for Misconduct," in "Will China Achieve Science Supremacy?: The Opinion Pages." *New York Times* (January 18), online: http://roomfordebate.blogs.nytimes.com/2010/01/18/will-china-achieve-science-supremacy/?_php=true&_type=blogs&_r=0#cong.

Carroll, Lewis. 2010 [1872]. *Through the Looking-Glass and What Alice Found There.* Boston: Adamant Media.

Chan, Anita, Richard Madsen, and Jonathan Unger. 1992. *Chen Village under Mao and Deng.* Berkeley: University of California Press.

Chan, Chris King-chi and Elaine S. Hui. 2012. "The Dynamics and Dilemma of Workplace Trade Union Reform in China: The case of Honda workers' Strike." *Journal of Industrial Relations* 54(5): 653–68.

Chan, Kam Wing. 2003. "Migration in China in the Reform Era: Characteristics, Consequences, and Implications." Pp. 111–35 in *China's Developmental Miracle: Origins, Transformations, and Challenges*, edited by Alvin Y. So. Armonk, NY: M. E. Sharpe.

Chan, Kam Wing. 2013. "Cities of Dreams." *South China Morning Post* (January 19), p. A15.

Chang, Gordon G. 2013. "Did China Just Declare War on Apple? Sure Looks Like It." *Forbes* (March 24), online: www.forbes.com/sites/gordonchang/2013/03/24/did-china-just-declare-war-on-apple-sure-looks-like-it/.

Chen, Feng. 2000. "Subsistence Crises, Managerial Corruption, and Labor Protests in China." *The China Journal* 44: 41–63.

Chen, Kuan, Hongchang Wang, Yuxin Zheng, Gary H. Jefferson, and Thomas G. Rawski. 1988. "Productivity Change in Chinese Industry: 1953–1985." *Journal of Comparative Economics* 12(4): 570–91.

Cheng, Joseph Y. S. and Stefania Paladini. 2012. "Battle Ready? Developing a Blue-Water Navy – China's Strategic Dilemma." Pp. 255–83 in *China: a New Stage of Development for an Emerging Superpower*, edited by Joseph Y. S. Cheng. Hong Kong: City University of Hong Kong Press.

China Daily. 2009. "China's Model Creates Economic Miracle." *China Daily* (October 17) (no longer online).

China Daily. 2010. "Rising Labor Costs Trigger Industrial Relocation." *China Daily* (July 6), online: www.chinadaily.com.cn/business/2010-07/06/content_10069557.htm.

China Daily. 2013. "Premier Calls for New Urbanization Strategies." *China Daily USA* (September 10), online: usa.chinadaily.com.cn/business/2013-09/08/content_16952310.htm.

China CSR. 2006. "*UNDP Wins Honor at China Poverty Eradication Awards,*" online: www.chinacsr.com/en/2006/10/18/792-undp-wins-honor-at-china-poverty-eradication-awards/.

China Water Risk. 2010. *China's Water Crisis, Part I*, online: http://chinawaterrisk.org/wp-content/uploads/2011/06/Chinas-Water-Crisis-Part-1.pdf.

Chinability. 2014. "GDP Growth in China 1952–2011," online: www.chinability.com/GDP.htm.

Chu, Kathy. 2010. "China Posed to Replace Japan as World's No. 2 Economy." *USA Today* (August 17), online: www.usatoday.com/money/world/2010-08-16-china-japan-gdp_N.htm.

Chu, Yin-wah. 2007. "Land Rights Protests in Mainland China: A Preliminary Analysis of Their Meanings and Political Significance," presented at the Thirty-First Annual Political Economy of the World-System Conference: "Asia and the World-System," St Lawrence University, Canton, New York, May 10–12.

Clark, Ian. 2011. "China and the United States: A Succession of Hegemonies?" *International Affairs* 87(1/January): 13–28.

Coale, Ansley J. 1984. "Rapid Population Change in China, 1952–1982," *Committee on Population and Demography Report No. 27*. Washington, DC: National Academy Press.

Cook, Sarah. 2010. "China's Development Model: What Is There to Learn?" International Institute of Social Studies, online: www.iss.nl/fileadmin/ASSETS/ iss/Documents/DevISSues/DevISSues11_1_May_09_web_final_new.pdf.

Cote, Owen R. 2011. "Assessing the Undersea Balance between the US and China." SSP Working Paper (February), online: http://web.mit.edu/ssp/pub lications/working_papers/Undersea%20Balance%20WP11-1.pdf.

Cotula, Lorenzo, Sonja Vermeulen, Rebeca Leonard, and James Keeley. 2009. *Land Grab or Development Opportunity? Agricultural Investment and International Land Deals in Africa*. London: IIED/Fao/IFAD.

Cumings, Bruce. 1987. "The Origins and Development of the Northeast Asian Political Economy." Pp. 44–83 in *The Political Economy of the New Asian Industrialism*, edited by Frederic C. Deyo. Ithaca, NY: Cornell University Press.

Dahlman, Carl J. 2012. *The World under Pressure: How China and India Are Influencing the Global Economy and Environment*. Stanford: Stanford University Press.

Dai Bingguo. 2010. "Stick to the Path of Peaceful Development," speech delivered at the Third Summit of the Conference on Interaction and Confidence-Building Measures in Asia (CICA), *Beijing Review* (December 27), online: www. bjreview.com.cn/quotes/txt/2010-12/27/content_320120.htm.

Ding, Xue Liang. 1994. *Gongchan zhuyi hou yu Zhongguo (Post-Communism and China)*. Hong Kong: Oxford University Press.

Dirlik, Arif. 2004. "Beijing Consensus: Beijing 'Gongshi': Who Recognizes Whom and to What End?" online: www.ids-uva.nl/wordpress/wp-content/ uploads/2011/07/9_Dirlik1.pdf.

Dong Fang Zao Bao. 2005. "Zhuan jia jian yan 3G pai zhao fa fang, jian yi yin wai zi yu min ying zi ben (Expert Suggest to Set up a 3G License to Attract Both Foreign Capital and Local Capital)." *Dong Fang Zao Bao* (April), online: http://tech.sina.com.cn/t/2005-04-26/1718594488.shtml.

Dosch, Jorn. 2011. "The Spratly Islands Dispute: Order-Building on China's Terms?" *Harvard International Review* (August 18), online: http://hir.harvard. edu/archives/2841.

Eckholm, Erik. 2001. "Chinese Officials Order Cities to Bolster Riot Police Forces." *New York Times* (January 30), online: www.nytimes.com/2001/01/30/ world/chinese-officials-order-cities-to-bolster-riot-police-forces.html.

Economist. 2006. "Asia: Dreaming of Harmony; China." *The Economist* (October 21), 381(8500): 76.

Economist. 2013. "The Expanding Scale and Scope of China's Outward Direct Investment." *The Economist* (January 19), online: www.economist.com/news/china/21569775-expanding-scale-and-scope-chinas-outward-direct-investment-odi-lay-hee-ho.

Economy, Elizabeth C. 2004. *The River Runs Black.* Ithaca, NY: Cornell University Press.

Economy, Elizabeth C. 2005. "China's Environmental Challenge." *Current History* 104(683): 278–83.

Edin, Maria. 2003. "State Capacity and Local Agent Control in China: CCP Cadre Management from a Township Perspective." *The China Quarterly* 173: 35–42.

Ernst, Dieter. 2011. "Testimony of Dr Dieter Ernst." *East–West Center News* (June 18).

Evans, Peter B. 1995. *Embedded Autonomy: States and Industrial Transformation.* Princeton: Princeton University Press.

Fairbank, John King. 1986. *The Great Chinese Revolution, 1800–1985.* Cambridge, MA: Harvard University Press.

Feng, Chongyi. 2012. "Auspicious Time for Change in China." *The Financial Review* (October 13), online:www.misaustralia.com.au/p/lifestyle/review/auspicious_time_for_change_in_china_qA0Esy9xb547BYwAu1uV2N.

Fewsmith, Joseph. 2008. *China since Tiananmen: From Deng Xiaoping to Hu Jintao.* New York: Cambridge University Press.

Ford, Peter. 2010. "Foreigners Doing Business in China Feel Boxed Out: Report." *Christian Science Monitor* (June 29), online: www.csmonitor.com/World/Asia-Pacific/2010/0629/Foreigners-doing-business-in-China-feel-boxed-out-report.

Friedman, Eli. 2012. "China in Revolt." *Jacobin: A Magazine of Culture and Polemic* (issue 7–8), online: https://www.jacobinmag.com/2012/08/china-in-revolt/.

Friedman, Ellen David. 2009. "US and Chinese Labour at a Changing Moment in the Global Neoliberal Economy." *The Journal of Labor and Society* 12(2): 219–34.

Friedman, Thomas. 2009. "Lost There, Felt Here." *New York Times* (November 15), online: www.nytimes.com/2009/11/15/opinion/15friedman.html?_r=0.

Gabriele, Alberto. 2009. "The Role of the State in China's Industrial Development: A Reassessment." *Comparative Economic Studies* 52(3): 325–50.

Gilboy, George J. and Eric Heginbotham. 2004. "The Latin Americanization of China?" *Current History* 103: 256–61.

Gleick, Peter H. 2008–9. "China and Water." Pp. 79–100 in *The World's Water 2008–2009,* edited by Peter H. Gleick, Oakland, CA: Pacific Institute, online: www.worldwater.org/data20082009/ch05.pdf.

Goldstein, Steven M. 1995. "China in Transition: The Political Foundation of Incremental Reform." *The China Quarterly* 144: 1105–31.

Goodman, Peter S. and Peter Finn. 2007. "Corruption Stains Timber Trade." *Washington Post* (April 1), online: washingtonpost.com/wp-dyn/content/article/2007/03/31/AR2007033101287.html.

Goswami, Rahul. 2010. "A Pearl River Tale, Power and Pride in China." *Energy Bulletin*, August 28.

Gough, Neil and David Barboza. 2013. "Credit Tightens in China as Central Bank Takes a Hard Line." *New York Times* (June 20), online: www.nytimes.com/2013/06/21/business/global/china-manufacturing-contracts-to-lowest-level-in-9-months.html?_r=2&.

Guan Xinping. 2000. "China's Social Policy: Reform and Development in the Context of Marketization and Globalization." *Social Policy and Administration* 34: 115–30.

Guo, Xiaolin. 2001. "Land Expropriation and Rural Conflicts in China." *The China Quarterly* 166: 422–39.

Hamilton, Gary G. 1985. "Why No Capitalism in China?" *Journal of Developing Societies* 2: 187–211.

Hannum, Emily, Jere Behrman, Meiyan Wang, and Jihong Liu. 2008. "Education in the Reform Era." Pp. 215–50 in *China's Great Economic Transformation*, edited by Loren Brandt and Thomas G. Rawski. Cambridge: Cambridge University Press.

Hanson, Stephanie. 2008. "China, Africa, and Oil." *Council on Foreign Relations Report* (June 6), online: www.washingtonpost.com/wp-dyn/content/article/2008/06/09/AR2008060900714.html.

Hart-Landsberg, Martin. 2010. "The US Economy and China: Capitalism, Class, and Crisis." *Monthly Review* 61(9): 14–31.

Hart-Landsberg, Martin and Paul Burkett. 2005. *China and Socialism: Market Reforms and Class Struggle*. New York: Monthly Review Press.

Harvey, David. 1990. *The Condition of Postmodernity: An Enquiry into the Origins of Cultural Change*. Oxford: Blackwell.

Harvey, David. 2005. *A Brief History of Neoliberalism*. New York: Oxford University Press.

Hays, Jeffrey. 2008. "Deforestation and Desertification in China," online: http://factsanddetails.com/china/cat10/sub66/item389.html.

He, Baogang. 2003. "The Making of a Nascent Civil Society in China." Pp. 114–40 in *Civil Society in Asia*, edited by David C. Schak and Wayne Hudson. Aldershot: Ashgate.

He, Canfei, Teng Zhang, and Wang Rui. 2012. "Air Quality in Urban China." *Eurasian Geography and Economics* 53(6): 750–71.

Heilmann, Sebastian, Lea Shih, and Andreas Hofem. 2013. "National Planning and Local Technology Zones: Experimental Governance in China's Torch Program." *The China Quarterly* 216: 896–919.

Hiro, Dilip. 2010. "America Is Suffering a Power Outage … and the Rest of the World Knows It." *Huffington Post* (September 23), online: www.huffington-post.com/dilip-hiro/america-is-suffering-a-po_b_736567.html.

Hitotsubashi University Team. n.d. "The Historical National Accounts of the PRC, 1952–1995," online: www.ier.hit-u.ac.jp/COE/Japanese/online_data/china/china.htm.

Hobsbawm, Eric J. 1997. *On History*. New York: The New Press.

Horta, Loro. 2008a. "Food Security in Africa: China's New Rice Bowl." *China Brief* 9(11), online: www.jamestown.org/single/?no_cache=1&tx_ttnews%5Btt_news%5D=35042#.VUtQe3l0zwo.

Horta, Loro. 2008b. "The Zambezi Valley: China's First Agricultural Colony?" *The Center for Strategic and International Studies* (June 8), online: http://csis.org/publication/zambezi-valley-chinas-first-agricultural-colony–.

Howell, Jude. 2006. "Reflections on the Chinese State." *Development and Change* 37(2): 273–97.

Howell, Jude and Jenny Pearce. 2001. "Civil Society and Market Transition: The Case of China." Pp. 123–46 in *Civil Society and Development*. London: Lynn Rienner.

Hsing, You-tien. 1998. *Making Capitalism in China: The Taiwan Connection*. New York: Oxford University Press.

Hu Jintao 2005. "Build towards a Harmonious World of Lasting Peace and Common Prosperity," statement by H. E. Hu Jintao, President of the People's Republic of China, at the United Nations Summit, New York (September 15), online: www.un.org/webcast/summit2005/statements15/china050915eng.pdf.

Hu, Zuliu and Moshin S. Khan. 1997. "Why Is China Growing So Fast?" *IMF Economic Issues* 8, online: www.imf.org/EXTERNAL/PUBS/FT/ISSUES8/issue8.pdf.

Huang, Yasheng. 2008. *Capitalism with Chinese Characteristics: Entrepreneurship and the State*. Cambridge: Cambridge University Press.

Huang, Yasheng. 2010. "China Boom: Rural China in the 1980s." *Asia Society: The China Boom Project*, online: chinaboom.asiasociety.org/essays/detail/212.

Huang, Yasheng. 2011. "Rethinking the Beijing Consensus." *Asia Policy* 11(January): 1–26.

Huang, Yiping. 2013. "'Likonomics' Policies in China." *East Asia Forum* (July 7).

Hui, Elaine S. and Chris King-chi Chan. 2011. "The 'Harmonious Society' as a Hegemonic Project: Labour Conflict and Changing Labour Policies in China." *Labour, Capital and Society* 44(2): 154–83.

Human Rights in China. 2006. "January 2006: China Responds to Increasing Social Unrest with Greater Repression." *Trends Bulletin* (no longer online).

Hung, Ho-Fung. 2009. "America's Head Servant? The PRC Dilemma in the Global Crisis." *New Left Review* 60: 5–25.

Huntington, Samuel P. 1991. *The Third Wave: Democratization in the Late Twentieth Century.* London: University of Oklahoma Press.

Hussain, Athar. 2005. "Preparing China's Social Safety Net." *Current History* 104(683): 683–722.

Insurgent Notes. 2010. "Wildcat Strikes in China." *Insurgent Notes* (June 17), online: http://insurgentnotes.com/2010/06/wildcat-strikes-in-china.

Jahiel, Abigail R. 1997. "The Contradictory Impact of Reform on Environmental Protection in China." *The China Quarterly* 149: 81–131.

Jauch, Herbert. 2011. "Chinese Investments in Africa: Twenty-First Century Colonialism?" *New Labor Forum* 20(2): 48–55.

Javers, Eamon. 2009. "Is China Headed Toward Collapse?" *Politico* (November 10), online: www.politico.com/news/stories/1109/29330.html.

Jefferson, Gary H. and Jian Su. 2006. "Privatization and Restructuring in China: Evidence from Shareholding Ownership, 1995–2001." *Journal of Comparative Economics* 34(1): 146–66.

Jiang, Chengcheng. 2010. "Why Foreign Businesses in China Are Getting Mad." *Time* (September 9), online: http://content.time.com/time/world/article/0,8599,2017024,00.html.

Jiang, Wenran. 2009. "Fuelling the Dragon: China's Rise and Its Energy and Resources Extraction in Africa." *The China Quarterly* 199: 585–609.

Johnson, Chalmers A. 1962. *Peasant Nationalism and Communist Power: The Emergence of Revolutionary China, 1937–1945.* Stanford: Stanford University Press.

Johnson, Chalmers A. 1995. *Japan, Who Governs? The Rise of the Developmental State.* New York: W. W. Norton & Company.

Jolly, David. 2013. "World Economy Growing Unevenly, OECD Says." *New York Times* (September 3), online: www.nytimes.com/2013/09/04/business/global/world-economy-growing-unevenly-oecd-says.html?gwh=31FE72D225416506B2F9A91CA614609B&gwt=pay.

Jun, Jing. 2000. "Environmental Protests in Rural China." Pp. 197–214 in *Chinese Society: Change, Conflict, and Resistance*, edited by Elizabeth J. Perry and Mark Selden. New York: Routledge.

Kahn, Joseph. 2006. "A Sharp Debate Erupts in China over Ideologies." *New York Times* (March 12), online: www.nytimes.com/2006/03/12/international/asia/12china.html?pagewanted=all&_r=0.

Kaplinsky, Raphael. 2012. "No Simple Pattern to Chinese Foreign Investment." *East Asia Forum Quarterly* (April–June): 24–6.

Keith, Ronald C. 2012. "New History inside Hu Jintao's Foreign Policy: 'Harmony' versus 'Hegemony.'" Pp. 235–53 in *China: A New Stage of Development for an Emerging Superpower*, edited by Joseph Y. S. Cheng. Hong Kong: City University of Hong Kong Press.

Kiely, Ray. 2008. "Poverty's Fall/China's Rise: Global Convergence or New Forms of Uneven Development?" *Journal of Contemporary Asia* 38(3): 353–72.

Kissinger, Henry. 2011. *On China*. New York: Penguin.

Klare, Michael T. 2010. "China's Global Shopping Spree: Is the World's Future Resource Map Tilting East?" *TomDispatch.Com* (April 1), online: www.tomdispatch.com/blog/175226/tomgram%3A_michael_klare,_shopaholic_china.

Konai, Janos. 1986. "The Hungarian Reform Process: Visions, Hopes and Reality." *Journal of Economic Literature* XXIV(December): 1687–737.

Kristensen, Hans M. and Robert S. Norris. 2013. "Global Nuclear Weapons Inventories, 1945–2013." *Bulletin of the Atomic Scientists* 69(5): 75–81.

Krugman, Paul. 2013. "This Age of Bubbles." *New York Times* (August 22), online: www.nytimes.com/2013/08/23/opinion/krugman-this-age-of-bubbles.html.

Kung, James Kai-sing and Justin Yifu Lin. 2003. "The Causes of China's Great Leap Famine, 1959–1961." *Economic Development and Cultural Change* 52(1): 51–73.

Kuroda, Haruhiko. 2009. "China's Policy Response to the Global Financial Crisis." *China Development Forum* (March 22), online: www.eastasiaforum.org/2010/01/24/chinas-response-to-the-global-financial-crisis.

Lam, Willy. 2009. "Hu Jintao's Great Leap Backward." *Far Eastern Economic Review* (January/February): 19–22.

Lee, Ching-kwan. 2000. "Pathways of Labour Insurgency." Pp. 41–62 in *Chinese Society: Change, Conflict, and Resistance*, edited by Elizabeth J. Perry and Mark Selden. New York: Routledge.

Lee, Ching-kwan. 2007. "Is Labor a Political Force in China?" Pp. 228–52 in *Grassroots Political Reform in Contemporary China*, edited by Elizabeth J. Perry and Merle Goldman. Cambridge, MA: Harvard University Press.

Lee, Su-hoon, Michael Hsin-huang Hsiao, Hwa-jen Liu, On-kwok Lai, Francisco Magno, and Alvin Y. So. 1999. "The Impact of Democratization on Environmental Movements." Pp. 230–52 in *Asia's Environmental Movements:*

Comparative Perspective, edited by Yok-shiu Lee and Alvin Y. So. Armonk, NY: M. E. Sharpe.

Leitsinger, Miranda. 2010. "Drought Grips Parts of China, Southeast Asia Amid Dam Concerns." *CNN* (April 7), online: edition.cnn.com/2010/WORLD/asiapcf/04/06/china.mekong.river.thailand.laos/index.html.

Li, Cheng. 1994. "University Networks and the Rise of Qinghua Graduates in China's Leadership." *Australia Journal of Chinese Affairs* 32: 1–30.

Li, Cheng. 2010. "Introduction: The Rise of the Middle Class in the Middle Kingdom." Pp. 3–31 in *China's Emerging Middle Class*, edited by Cheng Li. Washington, DC: Brookings Institution Press.

Li, Jingrong. 2013. "The Liaoning Aircraft Carrier" (September 28), online: www.china.org.cn/chinese/2012-09/28/content_26665015.htm.

Li Keqiang. 2013. "China Will Stay the Course on Sustainable Growth." *Financial Times* (September 6), online: www.ft.com/cms/s/0/03377ccc-16e0-11e3-9ec2-00144feabdc0.html.

Li, Wanxin, Jieyan Liu, and Duoduo Li. 2012. "Getting Their Voices Heard: Three Cases of Public Participation in Environmental Protection in China." *Journal of Environmental Management* 98: 65–72.

Lin, Jing and Xiaoyan Sun. 2010. "Higher Education Expansion and China's Middle Class." Pp. 217–44 in *China's Emerging Middle Class*, edited by Cheng Li. Washington, DC: Brookings Institution Press.

Lin, Justin Yifu. 1988. "The Household Responsibility System in China's Agricultural Reform." *Economic Development and Cultural Change* 36(April/Supplement): S199–224.

Lin, Justin Yifu. 2011. "China and the Global Economy." *China Economic Journal* 4(1): 1–14.

Lin, Justin Yifu, Ran Tao, and Minxing Liu. 2006. "Decentralization and Local Governance in China's Economic Transition." Pp. 305–27 in *Decentralization and Local Governance in Developing Countries: A Comparative Perspective*, edited by Pranab Bardhan and Dilip Mookherjee. Cambridge, MA: MIT Press.

Lin, Yimin. 2003. "Economic Institutional Change in Post-Mao China: Reflections on the Triggering, Orienting, and Sustaining Mechanisms." Pp. 29–57 in *China's Developmental Miracle: Origins, Transformations, and Challenges*, edited by Alvin Y. So. Armonk, NY: M. E. Sharpe.

Lippit, Victor D. 1974. *Land Reform and Economic Development in China*. White Plains, NY: M. E. Sharpe.

Lippit, Victor D. 1982. "Socialist Development in China." Pp. 116–58 in *The Transition to Socialism in China*, edited by Mark Selden and Victor D. Lippit. Armonk, NY: M. E. Sharpe.

Litzinger, Ralph A. 2007. "In Search of the Grassroots Hydroelectric Politics in Northwest Yunnan." Pp. 282–99 in *Grassroots Political Reform in Contemporary China*, edited by Elizabeth J. Perry and Merle Goodman. Cambridge, MA: Harvard University Press.

Liu, Dachang. 2009. "Reforestation after Deforestation in China." Pp. 90–105 in *Good Earths*, edited by Abe Ken-ichi and James E. Nickum. Kyoto: Kyoto University Press.

Liu, Jianguo and Jared Diamond. 2005. "China's Environment in a Globalizing World." *Nature* 435(June): 1179–86.

Liu, Lee. 2010. "Made in China: Cancer Villages." *Environment* (March/April), online: www.environmentmagazine.org/Archives/Back%20Issues/March-April%202010/made-in-china-full.html.

Liu, Melinda. 2007. "Beijing's New Deal." *Newsweek* 149(13): 26.

Liu, Mingfu. 2010. *Zhongguo Meng: Hou Meiguo shidai de daguo siwei yu zhanlue dingwei (The China Dream: Great Power Thinking and Strategic Posture in the Post-American Era)*. Beijing: Zhongguo Youyi Press.

Liu, Shuo. 2009. "The Ordinary Middle Class in an Ordinary Community: The Formation of the New Middle Class in China." Unpublished dissertation, Department of Sociology, Chinese University of Hong Kong.

Liu, Yuan. 2013. "Quebao zangluejiyu, Zangzeng si zuihou xuanxiang (Assure Strategic Opportunity, War as the Last Option)." *Global Times* (February 4), online: opinion.huanqiu.com/opinion_world/2013-02/3614115.html.

Loo, Becky and Sin Yin Chow. 2006. "China's 1994 Tax Sharing Reforms: One System, Different Impact." *Asian Survey* 46: 215–37.

Lowrey, Annie. 2013. "IMF Tells China of Urgent Need for Economic Change." *New York Times* (July 17), online: www.nytimes.com/2013/07/18/business/global/imf-tells-china-of-urgent-need-for-economic-change.html?pagewanted=all&_r=0.

Lu, Xueyi (ed.) 2002. *Dangdai Zhongguo Shehui Jieceng Yanjiu Baogao (Research Report on Social Stratification in Contemporary China)*. Beijing: Shehui Kexue Wenxian Chubanshe.

Ma, Jun. 2004 [1999]. *China's Water Crisis*. Norwalk, CT: EastBridge.

Ma, Tianjie. 2009. "Environmental Mass Incidents in China: Examining Large-Scale Unrest in Dongyan, Zhejiang." Pp. 33–49 in *China Environment Series 10 (2008–2009)*. Washington, DC: Woodrow Wilson Center.

Ma, Xiaoying and Leonard Ortolando. 2000. *Environmental Regulation in China: Institutions, Enforcement, and Compliance*. Lanham, MD: Rowman & Littlefield.

McGregor, James. 2010. *China's Drive for "Indigenous Innovation": A Web of Industrial Policies*. US Chamber of Commerce Global Regulatory Cooperation Project, online: www.uschamber.com/sites/default/files/reports/100728chinareport_0.pdf.

McMillan, John and Barry Naughton. 1992. "How to Reform a Planned Economy: Lessons from China." *Oxford Review of Economic Policy* 8: 781–807.

McNally, Christopher A. 2012. "Sino-capitalism: China's Reemergence and the International Political Economy." *World Politics* 64(4): 741–76.

Manyin, Mark E., Stephen Daggett, Ben Dolven, Susan V. Lawrence, Michael F. Martin, Ronald O'Rourke, and Bruce Vaughn. 2012. "Pivot to the Pacific? The Obama Administration's 'Rebalancing' Toward Asia." Congressional Research Service Report # R42448, online: www.fas.org/sgp/crs/natsec/R42448.pdf.

Marks, Robert B. 2012. *China: Its Environment and History*. New York: Rowman & Littlefield.

Mehtonen, Katri. 2009. "The Linkages between Poverty, Environment and Trans-boundary Water Management in Southwest China's Yunnan Province." Pp. 198–226 in *Good Earths*, edited by Abe Ken-ichi and James E. Nickum. Kyoto: Kyoto University Press.

Mertha, Andrew. 2008. *China's Water Warriors: Citizen Action and Policy Change*. Ithaca, NY: Cornell University Press.

Mingpao News. 2013. "The US Bans Government Procurement of China's Telecommunications Products." *Mingpao News* (March 29), p. A17.

Ministry of Water Resources. 2012. *2012 Zhongguo Suijiyuan Gongbao (2012 Annual Report of China's Water Resources)*, online: www.mwr.gov.cn/zwzc/hygb/szygb/qgszygb/201405/t20140513_560838.html.

Montinola, Gabriella, Yingyi Qian, and Barry Weingast. 1995. "Federalism, Chinese Style: The Political Basis for Economic Success." *World Politics* 48(1): 50–81.

Moore, Barrington, Jr. 1966. *Social Origins of Dictatorship and Democracy*. New York: Penguin.

Moore, Scott. 2013. "Issue Brief: Water Resource Issues, Policy and Politics in China." Brookings Institute (February 12), online: www.brookings.edu/research/papers/2013/02/water-politics-china-moore.

Moran, Theodore H. 2010. *China's Strategy to Secure Natural Resources: Risks, Dangers, and Opportunities*. Washington, DC: Peterson Institute for International Economics.

Moran, Theodore H., Barbara Kotschwar, and Julia Muir. 2012. "Resource Procurement: Not Just a Zero-Sum Game." *East Asia Forum Quarterly* (April–June): 28–30.

Morrison, Wayne M. 2009. "China and the Global Financial Crisis: Implications for the United States." Congressional Research Service: CRS Report for Congress.

Nanping Shi. 2004. *Nanping jiao yu ju dui fa zhan jiao shi dang yuan de diao cha yu si kao (Nanping City Education Bureau's Survey and Rethinking on the Prospect of Recruiting Teachers into the Party)* (June 28) (no longer online).

National Bureau of Statistics. 2014a. "Zhongguo dui shijie zhijie touzi (Stock of Overseas Direct Investment by China)," online: http://data.stats.gov.cn/workspace/index?m=hgnd.

National Bureau of Statistics. 2014b. "Table 4.2 Number of Employed Persons at Year-End in Urban and Rural Areas," "Table 12.1: Number of Cities at Prefecture Level and Above," and "Table 16.3: Length of Transportation Routes." *China Statistical Yearbook*, online: www.stats.gov.cn/tjsj/ndsj/2013/indexeh.htm.

Naughton, Barry. 1991. "The Pattern and Legacy of Economic Growth in the Mao Era." Pp. 226–54 in *Perspectives on Modern China*, edited by Kenneth Lieberthal, Joyce Kallgren, Roderick MacFarquhar, and Frederic Wakeman. Armonk, NY: M. E. Sharpe.

Naughton, Barry. 1994. "What Is Distinctive about China's Economic Transition? State Enterprise Reform and Overall System Transformation." *Journal of Comparative Economics* 18(3): 470–90.

Nee, Victor. 1992. "Organizational Dynamics of Market Transition: Hybrid Forms, Property Rights, and Mixed Economy in China." *Administrative Science Quarterly* 37: 1–27.

Nee, Victor and Sonja Opper. 2012. *Capitalism from Below: Markets and Institutional Change in China*. Cambridge, MA: Harvard University Press.

New York Times. 2013. "India in Reverse." *New York Times* (September 8), online: www.nytimes.com/2013/09/09/opinion/india-in-reverse.html.

Nolan, Peter and Robert F. Ash 1995. "China's Economy on the Eve of Reform." *The China Quarterly* 144: 980–98.

Nolan, Peter. 2004. *China at the Crossroads*. Cambridge: Polity.

Nye, Joseph S., Jr. 2011. *The Future of Power*. New York: Public Affairs.

O'Brien, Kevin J. 2004. "Neither Transgressive Nor Contained: Boundary Spanning Contention in China." Pp. 105–22 in *State and Society in 21st Century China*, edited by Peter H. Gries and Stanley Rosen. New York: RoutledgeCurzon.

O'Brien, Kevin J. 2009. "Rural Protest." *Journal of Democracy* 20(3): 25–8.

O'Brien, Kevin J. and Lianjiang Li. 2006. *Rightful Resistance in Rural China*. Cambridge: Cambridge University Press.

Oi, Jean C. 1989. *State and Peasant in Contemporary China: The Political Economy of Village Government*. Berkeley: University of California Press.

Oi, Jean C. 1992. "Fiscal Reform and the Economic Foundations of Local State Corporatism in China." *World Politics* 45: 99–126.

Oi, Jean C. 1995. "The Role of the Local State in China's Transitional Economy." *The China Quarterly* 144: 1132–49.

Oi, Jean and Zhukai Zhao. 2007. "Fiscal Crisis in China's Townships: Causes and Consequences." Pp. 75–96 in *Grassroots Political Reform in Contemporary China*, edited by Elizabeth J. Perry and Merle Goldman. Cambridge, MA: Harvard University Press.

Onis, Ziya. 1991. "Review Article: The Logic of the Developmental State." *Comparative Politics* 24(1): 109–26.

Oster, Shai, Norihiko Shirouzu, and Paul Glader. 2010. "Chinese Squeezes Foreigners for Share of Global Riches." *The Wall Street Journal: Asia Business* (December 28), online: http://online.wsj.com/article/SB100014240529702 03731004576045684068308042.html.

Page, Jeremy. 2011. "Wave of Unrest Rocks China." *Wall Street Journal* (June 14), online: http://online.wsj.com/article/SB100014240527023046659045763 83142907232726.html.

Palat, Ravi. 2010. "Outsourcing and Currency Wars," online: https://rpalat. wordpress.com/author/rpalat/page/6/.

Parker, James. 2013. "Is the World Ready for a Great Rebalancing?" *The Diplomat* (February 14).

Pei, Minxin. 2008. *China's Trapped Transition: The Limits of Developmental Autocracy*. Cambridge, MA: Harvard University Press.

Pei, Minxin. 2013. "China on Verge of Worst Economic Crisis in Decades." *CNN World* (September 4), online: http://globalpublicsquare.blogs.cnn. com/2013/09/04/china-on-verge-of-worst-economic-crisis-in-decades.

Peng, Xizhe. 1987. "Demographic Consequences of the Great Leap Forward in China's Provinces." *Population and Development Review* 13(4/December): 639–70.

Perry, Elizabeth. 2007. "Studying Chinese Politics: Farewell to Revolution?" *The China Journal* 57: 1–22.

Petras, James. 2006. "Past, Present, and Future of China: From Semi-colony to World Power?" *Journal of Contemporary Asia* 36(4): 423–41.

Pettis, Michael. 2010. "China's Financial Evolution Will Take the Slow Road." *Financial Times* (January 22), online: http://blogs.ft.com/economistsforum/2010/01/chinas-financial-evolution-will-take-the-slow-road.

Pettis, Michael. 2013. "The Changing Debate over China's Economy." *Credit Expansion, Predictions* (August 7), online: http://carnegieendowment. org/2013/08/07/changing-debate-over-china-s-economy.

Polanyi, Karl. 1944. *The Great Transformation*. Boston: Beacon Press.

Pomfret, John. 2009. "Unwrapping the Enigmatic Chinese Riddle (Book Review of *Postcards from Tomorrow Square; Reports from China*)." *Washington Post* (March 31), online: www.washingtonpost.com/wp-dyn/content/article/2009/03/30/AR2009033002964.html.

Pringle, Tim. 2002. "Industrial Unrest in China – A Labour Movement in the Making?" *China Labour Bulletin* (January 31), online: www.hartford-hwp.com/archives/55/294.html.

Puckett, Jim and Ted Smith (eds). 2002. *Exporting Harm: The High-Tech Trashing of Asia*. The Basel Action Network and Silicon Valley Toxics Coalition (February 25), online: www.svtc.org/cleancc/pubs/tech-notrash.pdf.

Pun, Ngai. 1999. "Becoming Dagongmei: The Politics of Identity and Difference in Reform China." *The China Journal* 42: 1–19.

Pun, Ngai. 2008. "'Reorganizing Moralism': The Politics of Transnational Labor Codes." In *Privatizing China*, edited by Zheng Li and Aihwa Ong. Ithaca, NY: Cornell University Press.

Pye, Lucian W. 1986. "Reassessing the Cultural Revolution." *The China Quarterly* 108: 597–612.

Qu, Geping. 2005. "China's Environmental Protection and the World: Replies to Questions Raised by the CCTV" (March 7), online: www.oei.bj.cn/report/1.doc.

Quinn, Andrew. 2011. "Clinton Warns Against 'New Colonialism' in Africa." *Reuters* (June 11), online: http://reuters.com/article/2011/06/11/us-clinton-africa-idUSTRE75A0RI20110611.

Ramo, Joshua Cooper. 2004. "The Beijing Consensus." *The Foreign Policy Center*, online: fpc.org.uk/fsblob/244.pdf.

Reiitsu, Kojima. 1982. "Accumulation, Technology, and China's Economic Development." Pp. 238–65 in *The Transition to Socialism in China*, edited by Mark Selden and Victor D. Lippit. Armonk, NY: M. E. Sharpe.

Roberts, Dexter and Jasmine Zhao. 2011. "China's Super-Rich Buy a Better Life Abroad." *Bloomberg Business Week* (November 22), online: www.businessweek.com/magazine/chinas-superrich-buy-a-better-life-abroad-11222011.html.

Rodrik, Dami. 2006. "Goodbye Washington Consensus, Hello Washington Confusion? A Review of the World Bank's Economic Growth in the 1990s: Learning from a Decade of Reform." *Journal of Economic Literature* XLIV(December): 973–87.

Rosen, Daniel H. and Thilo Hanemann. 2012. "The Rise in Chinese Overseas Investment and What It Means for American Businesses." *China Business Review* (July–September), online: www.chinabusinessreview.com/the-rise-in-chinese-overseas-investment-and-what-it-means-for-american-businesses/.

Roubini, Nouriel. 2008. "The Rising Risk of a Hard Landing in China: The Two Engines of Economic Growth – US and China – are Stalling." *Japan Focus* (November 4), online: www.japanfocus.org/-Nouriel-Roubini/2940.

Sachs, Jeffrey D. and Wing Thye Woo. 1994. "Structural Factors in the Economic Reforms of China, Eastern Europe, and the Former Soviet Union." *Economic Policy* 18(1): 102–45.

Sachs, Jeffrey D. and Wing Thye Woo. 2000. "The Debate on Understanding China's Economic Growth." Pp. 385–406 in *Planning, Shortage, and Transformation: Essays in Honor of Janos Kornai*, edited by Eric Maskin and Andras Simonovits. Cambridge, MA: MIT Press.

Saich, Tony. 2007. "Focus on Social Development." *Asian Survey* 47: 32–43.

Sanger, David E. 2013. "US Blames China's Military Directly for Cyberattacks." *New York Times* (May 6), online: www.nytimes.com/2013/05/07/world/asia/us-accuses-chinas-military-in-cyberattacks.html?pagewanted=all.

Sanusi, Lamido. 2013. "Africa Must Get Real About Chinese Ties." *Financial Times* (March 12), online: www.ft.com/intl/cms/s/0/562692b0-898c-11e2-ad3f-00144feabdc0.html#axzz3BqPtfthl.

Scheltema, Chet, Frank Yang, and David Chan. 2012. "Chinese Outbound Foreign Direct Investment Faces Rigorous Scrutiny." *China Briefing* (December 31), online: www.china-briefing.com/news/2012/12/31/chinese-outbound-foreign-direct-investment-faces-rigorous-scrutiny-2.html.

Schuman, Michael. 2013. "The Real Reason to Worry About China." *Time* (September 28), online: http://business.time.com/2013/04/28/the-real-reason-to-worry-about-china.

Schwartz, Jonathan. 2004. "Environmental NGOs in China: Roles and Limits." *Pacific Affairs* 77(1): 28–49.

Schwartz, Nelson. 2009. "Asia's Recovery Highlights China's Ascendance." *New York Times* (August 23), online: www.nytimes.com/2009/08/24/business/global/24global.html.

Scissors, Derek. 2012. "Chinese Outward Investment: Acceleration features the US." *The Heritage Foundation Issue Brief* 3656(July 9), online: www.heritage.org/research/reports/2012/07/chinese-foreign-investment-outward-investment-acceleration-features-the-us.

Segal, Adam. 2010. "China's Innovation Wall." *Foreign Affairs* (September 28), online: www.foreignaffairs.com/articles/asia/2010-09-28/chinas-innovation-wall.

Selden, Mark. 1982. "Cooperation and Conflict: Cooperative and Collective Formation in China's Countryside." Pp. 32–97 in *The Transition to Socialism in China*, edited by Mark Selden and Victor D. Lippit. Armonk, NY: M. E. Sharpe.

Selden, Mark. 1993. *The Political Economy of Chinese Development.* Armonk, NY: M. E. Sharpe.

Selden, Mark and Victor D. Lippit 1982. "The Transition to Socialism in China." Pp. 3–31 in *The Transition to Socialism in China*, edited by Mark Selden and Victor D. Lippit. Armonk, NY: M. E. Sharpe.

Shambaugh, David. 2009. "Is China Ready to be a Global Power?" *Global Times* (November 11), online: www.brookings.edu/research/opinions /2009/11/10-china-global-shambaugh.

Shambaugh, David. 2011. "Coping with a Conflicted China." *The Washington Quarterly* 34(1): 7–27.

Shapiro, Judith. 2012. *China's Environmental Challenges.* Cambridge: Polity.

Shen, Chunli, Jing Jin, and Heng-fu Zou. 2012. "Fiscal Decentralization in China: History, Impact, Challenges and Next Steps." *Annals of Economics and Finance* 13(1): 1–51.

Shi, Yigong and Yi Rao. 2010. "China's Research Culture." *Science* 329(5996): 1128.

Shirk, Susan L. 1984. "The Decline of Virtuocracy in China." Pp. 56–83 in *Class and Social Stratification in Post-Revolution China*, edited by James L. Watson. New York: Cambridge University Press.

Shirk, Susan L. 1993. *The Political Logic of Economic Reform in China.* Berkeley: University of California Press.

Shu, Xiao. 2013. "Dim Hopes for a Free Press in China." *New York Times* (January 14), online: www.nytimes.com/2013/01/15/opinion/dim-hopes-for-a-free-press-in-china.html.

Shue, Vivienne. 1980. *Peasant China in Transition.* Berkeley: University of California Press.

Silver, Beverly J. and Giovanni Arrighi 2000. "Workers North and South." Pp. 53–76 in *2001 Socialist Register: Working Classes, Global Realities*, edited by Leo Panitch and Colin Leys. New York: Monthly Review Press.

Simon, Denis Fred and Cong Cao. 2010. *China's Emerging Technological Edge: Assessing the Role of High-End Talent.* Cambridge: Cambridge University Press.

Skocpol, Theda. 1979. *States and Social Revolutions.* Cambridge: Cambridge University Press.

Smart, Josephine and Alan Smart. 1991. "Personal Relations and Divergent Economies: A Case Study of Hong Kong Investment in South China." *International Journal of Urban and Regional Research* 15(2): 216–33.

Smil, Vaclav. 2004. *China's Past, China's Future: Energy, Food, Environment.* New York: RoutledgeCurzon.

So, Alvin Y. 2001. "Introduction: The Origins and Transformation of the Chinese Triangle." Pp. 1–22 in *The Chinese Triangle of Mainland–Taiwan–Hong Kong*, edited by Alvin Y. So, Nan Lin, and Dudley Poston. Westport, CT: Greenwood Press.

So, Alvin Y. 2003. "The Making of a Cadre-Capitalist Class in China." Pp. 473–501 in *China Challenges in the Twenty-First Century*, edited by Joseph Y. S. Cheng. Hong Kong: City University of Hong Kong Press.

So, Alvin Y. 2007a. "Peasant Conflict and the Local Predatory State in the Chinese Countryside." *The Journal of Peasant Studies* 34(3/4): 560–81.

So, Alvin Y. 2007b. "The State and Labor Insurgency in Post-Socialist China: Implication for development." Pp. 133–51 in *Challenges and Policy Programmes of China's New Leadership*, edited by Joseph Y. S. Cheng. Hong Kong: City University of Hong Kong Press.

So, Alvin Y. 2010a. "Post-Socialist State, Transnational Corporations, and the Battle for Labor Rights in China at the Turn of the 21st Century." *Development and Society* 39: 97–118.

So, Alvin Y. 2010b. "Globalization and China: From Neoliberal Capitalism to State Developmentalism in East Asia." Pp. 133–54 in *Globalization in the 21st Century: Labor, Capital, and the State on a World Scale*, edited by Berch Berberoglu. New York: Palgrave Macmillan.

So, Alvin Y. 2012. "The Global Capitalist Crisis and the Rise of China to the World Scene." Pp. 123–44 in *Beyond the Global Capitalist Crisis: The World Economy in Transition*, edited by Berch Berberoglu. Farnham, Surrey: Ashgate.

So, Alvin Y. 2013. "The Post-Socialist Path of the Developmental State in China." Paper presented to the International Conference on "The Asian Developmental State: Reexamination and New Departures" at Hong Kong Baptist University, December 16–17.

So, Alvin Y. and Shiping Hua. 1992. "Democracy as an Antisystemic Movement in Taiwan, Hong Kong and China." *Sociological Perspectives* 35: 385–404.

So, Alvin Y. and Xianjia Su. 2011. "New Middle Class Politics in China: The Making of a Quiet Democratization?" Pp. 135–49 in *Whither China's Democracy? Democratization in China since the Tiananmen Incident*, edited by Joseph Y. S. Cheng. Hong Kong: City University of Hong Kong Press.

Solinger, Dorothy J. 1993. *China's Transition from Socialism: Statist Legacies and Market Reforms 1980–1990*. Armonk, NY: M. E. Sharpe.

Song, Xiaojun, Xiaodong Wang, Jisu Huwang, Qiang Song, and Yang Liu. 2009. *Zhongguo bu Gaoxing: Da shidai, da mubiao ji women de neiyou waihuan (Unhappy China: The Great Time, Grand Vision and Our Challenges)*. Nanjing: Jiangsu People's Press.

State Council. Central People's Government of the People's Republic of China. 2007. "Zhonghua renmin gongheguo laodong hetong fa (Labor Contract Law of the People's Republic of China)," online: big5.gov.cn/gate/big5/www.gov. cn/flfg/2007-06/29/content_669394.htm.

State Council. Central People's Government of the People's Republic of China. 2011. "Zhongguo de heping fazhan baipishu (White Paper on China's Peaceful Development)," online: news.xinhuanet.com/politics/2011-09/06/c _121982103.htm.

Steinfeld, Edward S. 2010. *Playing Our Game: Why China's Economic Rise Doesn't Threaten the West*. Hong Kong: Oxford University Press.

Strauss, Julia C. and Martha Saavedra. 2009. "Introduction: China, Africa and Internationalization." *The China Quarterly* 199: 551–62.

Summers, Tim. 2013. "China's New Leadership: Approaches to International Affairs." Chatham House Briefing Paper (1 April), online: www.chatham house.org/publications/papers/view/191079.

Sun, Liping. 2011. "Shehui Shi Xu Shi Dangxia de Yanjun (Social Disorder is a Present and Serious Challenge)." *Economic Observer* (February 28), online: www.eeo.com.cn/2011/0228/194539.shtml.

Suttmeier, Richard P. 2008. "The Discourse on China as Science and Technology Superpower: Assessing the Arguments." Paper presented at the International Symposium on China as a Science and Technology Superpower, China Research Center of the Japan Science and Technology Center, Tokyo (December 9–10).

Tabassum, Names and Mohammed Tangier Dubai Ahmed. 2014. "The Long Reign of the United States is Over; the 21st Century Belongs to China." *International Affairs and Global Strategy* 21: 57–61.

Tanner, Murray Scot. 2005. *Chinese Government Responses to Rising Social Unrest*. Testimony presented to the US–China Economic and Security Review Commission (April 14). Santa Monica: RAND Corporation, online: www.rand.org/content/dam/rand/pubs/testimonies/2005/RAND_ CT240.pdf.

Taubmann, Wolfgang. 2000. "Urban Administration, Urban Development, and Migrant Enclaves." Paper presented to the "International Workshop on Resource Management, Urbanization, and Governance in Hong Kong and the Zhujiang Delta," Chinese University of Hong Kong (May 23–4).

Taylor, Bill and Qi Li. 2007. "Is the ACFTU a Union and Does It Matter?" *Journal of Industrial Relations* 49: 701–15.

Thornton, Patricia. 2004. "Comrades and Collectives in Arms: Tax Resistance, Evasion, and Avoidance Strategies in Post-Mao China." Pp. 87–105 in *State and Society in 21st-Century China*, edited by Peter H. Gries and Stanley Rosen. New York: RoutledgeCurzon.

Tomba, Luigi. 2010a. "Communist Party in China." Pp. 155–60 in *A Dictionary of 20th-Century Communism*, edited by Robert Service and Silvio Pons, Princeton, NJ: Princeton University Press.

Tomba, Luigi. 2010b. "The Housing Effect: The Making of China's Social Distinctions." Pp. 193–216 in *China's Emerging Middle Class*, edited by Cheng Li. Washington, DC: Brookings Institution Press.

Trac, Christine Jane, Stevan Harrell, Thomas M. Hinckley, and Amanda C. Henck. 2007. "Reforestation Programs in Southwest China: Reported Success, Observed Failure, and the Reasons Why." *Journal of Mountain Science* 4(4): 275–92.

Tsou, Tang, Marc Blecher, and Mitch Meisner. 1982. "National Agricultural Policy: The Dazhai Model and Local Change in the Post-Mao Era." Pp. 266–99 in *The Transition to Socialism in China*, edited by Mark Selden and Victor D. Lippit. Armonk, NY: M. E. Sharpe.

Tu, Kevin Jianjun and David Livingston. 2013. "United States Should Welcome Chinese Energy Investment." *Energy Tribune* (January 28), online: www.energytribune.com/71732/us-should-welcome-chinese-energy -investment.

UNFAO [Food and Agriculture Organization of the United Nations]. 1999. "Poverty Alleviation and Food Security in Asia: Lessons and Challenges." RAP Publication 1999/1, online: www.fao.org/docrep/004/ab981e/ ab981e00.HTM.

UNFAO [United Nations, Food and Agriculture Organization]. 2010. "AQUASTAT Online Database: Total Renewable Water Resources," online: www. fao.org/nr/water/aquastat/data/query/results.html.

Unger, Jonathan. 2006. "China's Conservative Middle Class." *Far Eastern Economic Review* (April): 27–31.

UNOHCHR [United Nations Office of the Higher Commissioner for Human Rights]. 2010. "Preliminary Observations and Conclusions, Mandate of the Special Rapporteur on the Right to Food, Mission to the PRC from 15–23 December," online: www2.ohchr.org/english/issues/food/docs/ CHINA_food_preliminary_conclusions.doc.

Valigra, Lori. 2009. "The Innovation Economy: China Aims to Spark Indigenous Innovation." *Science Business* (August 27), online: www.science-business.net/news/69021/The-Innovation-Economy-China-aims-to-spark -indigenous-innovation.

Walder, Andrew G. 1982. "Some Ironies of the Maoist Legacy in Industry." Pp. 215–37 in *The Transition to Socialism in China*, edited by Mark Selden and Victor D. Lippit. Armonk, NY: M. E. Sharpe.

Walder, Andrew G. 1986. *Communist Neo-Traditionalism: Work and Authority in Chinese Industry*. Berkeley: University of California Press.

Walder, Andrew G. 1994. "The Decline of Communist Power: Elements of a Theory of Institutional Change." *Theory and Society* 23: 297–323.

Walder, Andrew G. 1995. "China's Transitional Economy: Interpreting Its Significance." *The China Quarterly* 144: 963–79.

Walder, Andrew G. 1996. *China's Transitional Economy: Interpreting Its Significance*. Oxford: Oxford University Press.

Walder, Andrew G. 2014. "Spontaneous Capitalism: An Entrepreneur-Centered Analysis of Market Transition." *Contemporary Sociology* 43(1): 40–4.

Wallerstein, Immanuel. 2010. "How to Think about China." *Commentary* 273(January 15), online: www.binghamton.edu/fbc/archive/273en.htm.

Wang, Feng. 2008. *Boundaries and Categories: Rising Inequality in Post-socialist Urban China*. Stanford: Stanford University Press.

Wang, Feng, Ruediger Kuehr, Daniel Ahlquist, and Jinhui Li. 2013. *E-waste in China: A Country Report*, online: isp.unu.edu/publications/scycle/files/ewaste-in-china.pdf.

Wang, Shaoguang. 1997. "China's 1994 Fiscal Reform: An Initial Assessment." *Asian Survey* 37(9): 801–17.

Wang, Shaoguang, Angang Hu, and Yuanchu Ding. 2002. "Jing ji fan grong beihou de shehui bu wending (Social Instability behind Economic Prosperity)." *Zhanluue yu Guanli* 3(May/June): 26–33.

Wank, David L. 1996. "The Institutional Process of Market Clientelism: *Guanxi* and Private Business in a South China City." *The China Quarterly* 147: 820–38.

Wassener, Bettina. 2013. "China's Trade Data Is Significantly Weaker Than Forecast." *New York Times* (July 10), online: www.nytimes.com/2013/07/11/business/global/chinas-trade-data-is-significantly-weaker-than-forecast.html?_r=0.

Wasserstrom, Joseph. 2010a. "Once a Winner, China Sees Globalization's Downsize – Part II," *Yale Global Online* (October 11), online: http://yaleglobal.yale.edu/content/china-sees-globalizations-downside-part-ii.

Wasserstrom, Jeffrey. 2010b. "Power in a Symbol: Commentary on China's Unwanted Nobel Prize." *New York Times* (October 9), online: www.nytimes.com/roomfordebate/2010/10/08/when-dissidents-win-the-nobel-peace-prize/power-in-a-symbol.

Wei, Shang-jin. 1995. "The Open Door Policy and China's Rapid Growth: Evidence from City-Level Data." Pp. 73–104 in *Growth Theories in Light of the East Asian Experience*, edited by Takatoshi Ito and Anne O. Krueger. Chicago: University of Chicago Press.

Wells-Dang, Andrew. 2012. "The China Rivers Network." Pp. 136–68 in *Civil Society Networks in China and Vietnam: Informal Pathbreakers in Health and the Environment.* New York: Palgrave Macmillan.

Wen Jiabao. 2013. *Nian zhengfu gongzuo baogao (Government Work Report 2013),* online: www.eeo.com.cn/2013/0305/240751.shtml.

Wen, Tiejun. 2001. "Centenary Reflections on the 'Three Dimensional Problem' of Rural China." *Inter-Asia Cultural Studies* 2(2): 287–95.

Whiting, Susan. 2001. *Power and Wealth in Rural China: The Political Economy of Institutional Change.* Cambridge: Cambridge University Press.

Whyte, Martin King. 1995. "The Social Roots of China's Economic Development." *The China Quarterly* 144: 999–1019.

Whyte, Martin King. 1996. "The Chinese Family and Economic Development: Obstacle or Engine?" *Economic Development and Cultural Change* 45(1): 1–30.

Whyte, Martin King. 2009. "Paradoxes of China's Economic Boom." *Annual Review of Sociology* 35: 371–92.

Whyte, Martin King and William L. Parish. 1984. *Urban Life in Contemporary China.* Chicago: University of Chicago Press.

Wines, Michael. 2009. "China Warms to New Credo: Business First." *New York Times* (August 14), online: www.nytimes.com/2009/08/14/world/asia/14china.html?gwh=DAA92B144398FDC748A861024AF892BF&gwt=pay.

Wines, Michael. 2010a. "As China Rises, Fear Grow on Whether Boom Can Endure." *New York Times* (January 12), online: www.nytimes.com/2010/01/12/world/asia/12china.html?_r=0.

Wines, Michael. 2010b. "China Fortifies State Businesses to Fuel Growth." *New York Times* (August 29), online: www.nytimes.com/2010/08/30/world/asia/30china.html?pagewanted=all&_r=0 29.

Wines, Michael. 2012. "A Populist's Downfall Exposes Ideological Divisions in China's Ruling Party." *New York Times* (April 6), online: www.nytimes.com/2012/04/07/world/asia/bo-xilais-ouster-exposes-chinese-fault-lines.html?pagewanted=all.

Wong, Edward. 2013. "In China, Widening Discontent among the Communist Party Faithful." *New York Times* (January 19), online: www.nytimes.com/2013/01/20/world/asia/in-china-discontent-among-the-normally-faithful.html?pagewanted=all.

Wong, Edward and Didi Kirsten Tatlow. 2013. "China Seen in Push to Gain Technology Insights." *New York Times* (June 6), online: www.nytimes.com/2013/06/06/world/asia/wide-china-push-is-seen-to-obtain-industry-secrets.html?pagewanted=all&_r=0.

Wong, Siu-lun. 1988. *Emigrant Entrepreneurs: Shanghai Industrialists in Hong Kong.* Hong Kong: Oxford University Press.

Wong, Sue-lin. 2013. "China Court Ruling Could Threaten Foreign Investment in Country." *International Herald Tribune* (June 17), online: http://rendez-vous.blogs.nytimes.com/2013/06/17/china-court-ruling-could-threaten-some-foreign-invested-companies/.

World Bank. 2009. *Addressing China's Water Scarcity*: www-wds.worldbank.org/external/default/WDSContentServer/WDSP/IB/2009/01/14/000333037_20090114011126/Rendered/PDF/471110PUB0CHA0101OFFICIAL0USE0ONLY1.pdf.

Wu, Xiaogang, 2009. "Income Inequality and Distributive Justice: A Comparative Analysis of Mainland China and Hong Kong." *The China Quarterly* 200: 1033–52.

Xia, Guang, Xiaofe Pei, and Xiaoming Yang. 2010. "Economic Growth and Environmental Protection in the People's Republic of China." Pp. 35–65 in *Economic Growth and Environmental Regulation*, edited by Tun Lin and Timothy Swanson. New York: Routledge in association with the Asian Development Bank.

Xiang, Da (ed.). 1961. *Liang zhong hai dao zhen jing (Two Books of Nautical Charts).* Beijing: Zhonghua Book Publishers.

Xing, Yuqing and Neal Detert. 2010. "How the iPhone Widens the United States Trade Deficit with the People's Republic of China." Asian Development Bank Institute, Working Paper Series No. 257.

Xinhua News. 2002. "Zhongguo Gongchandang di shiliuci qunguodaibiu dahui mishuchu jiu shiliuda tongguo de zhongguo gongchandang zhangcheng xiuzhengan da xinhuashe jice wen (The Secretariat of the Sixteenth National Party Congress of the Chinese Communist Party Replies to Xinhua News Reporters Concerning the 'Amendments to the Constitution of the Chinese Communist Party')," online: news.xinhuanet.com/newscenter/2002-11/18/content_632966.htm.

Xu, Baoguang. 2011 [d.1723]. *Zhongshan chuan xin lu (Records of messages from Chong-shan).* Beijing: Zhi shi chan quan chu ban she.

Xu, Zhun. 2013. "The Political Economy of Decollectivization in China." *Monthly Review* 65(1): 17–36.

Yan, Xuetong. 2013. "Strategic Cooperation without Mutual Trust: A Path Forward for China and the United States." *Asia Policy* 15: 4–6.

Yang, Guobin. 2004. "Is there an Environmental Movement in China? Beware of the 'River of Anger.'" Active Society in Formation: Environmentalism, Labor, and the Underworld in China. Washington, DC: Woodrow Wilson Center International Center for Scholars, Asia Program Special Report no. 124 (September).

Yang, Guobin. 2009. *The Power of the Internet in China: Citizen Activism Online*. New York: Columbia University Press.

Yang, Guobin and Craig Calhoun. 2008. "Media, Civil Society, and the Rise of a Green Public Sphere in China." Pp. 69–88 in *China's Embedded Activism*, edited by Peter Ho and R. L. Edmonds. London: Routledge.

Yang, Ruilong and Yongsheng Zhang. 2003. "Globalization and China's SOEs Reform." Paper presented at the International Conference on "Sharing the Prosperity of Globalization," organized by WIDER/UNU, Finland (September 6–7).

Yao, Shujie. 2009. "China Emerges as a Global Power on 60th Birthday." The University of Nottingham China Policy Institute Briefing Series no. 55.

Yu, Jianrong. 2008. "Emerging Trends in Violent Riots." *China Security* (Summer): 75–6.

Yu, Jianrong. 2010. "Yu Jianrong on Maintaining a Baseline of Social Stability." *China Studies Group* (April 3).

Yu, Yongding. 2009. "China Policy Responses to the Global Financial Crisis." Richard Snape Lecture, November 25, Productivity Commission, Melbourne.

Zakaria, Fareed. 2013. "China at a Crossroads." *Washington Post* (July 18), online: www.washingtonpost.com/opinions/fareed-zakaria-china-at-a-crossroads /2013/07/17/211799e0-ef01-11e2-bed3-b9b6fe264871_story.html.

Zhang, Gary. 2009. "Patent Revolution." *Forbes* (September 28), online: www. forbes.com/2009/09/25/patents-china-counterfeit-china-leadership-zhang. html.

Zhang, Weiwei. 2006. "The Allure of the Chinese Model." *International Herald Tribune* (November 2), online: www.nytimes.com/2006/11/01/ opinion/01iht-edafrica.3357752.html.

Zhao, Shelly. 2011. "China's Territorial Disputes in the South China Sea and East China Sea." *China Briefing*, online: www.china-briefing.com/ news/2011/05/31/chinas-territorial-disputes-in-the-south-china-sea-and-east-china-sea.html.

Zhao, Shukai. 2004. "Lishixing tiaozhan: Zhongguo nongcun de chongtu yu zhili (A Historical Challenge: Conflict and Governance in China's Villages)." Pp. 212–23 in *2004 Nian: Zhongguo shehui xingshi fenxi yu yuce (Analysis and Forecast of China's Social Situation, 2004)*, edited by Xin Ru, Xueyi Lu, and Peilin Li. Beijing: Shehui Kexue Wenxian Chubanshe.

Zhao, Yuezhi. 2012. "The Struggle for Socialism in China: The Bo Xilai Saga and Beyond." *Monthly Review* 64(5): 1–17.

Zheng, Bijian. 2005. "China's 'Peaceful Rise' to Great-Power Status." *Foreign Affairs* 84(5/September–October): 18.

Zheng, Yisheng and Yihong Qian. 1998. *Shendu youhuan: Dangdai zhongguo de kechixu fazaban wenti (Grave Concerns – Problems of Sustainable Development in China)*. Beijing: Jinri Zhongguo Chubanshe.

Zheng, Yongnian. 2004. *Globalization and State Transformation in China*. New York: Cambridge University Press.

Zheng, Yongnian and Minjia Chen. 2006. "China Plans to Build an Innovative State." The University of Nottingham, China Policy Institute Briefing Series no. 9.

Zhou, Liqun and Siquan Xie. 2008. "Jiben guoce de queli (The Establishment of Basic National Policies." Pp. 7–28 in *Zhongguo jingji gaige 30 nian: Minying jingji juan (Thirty Years of Economic Reform in China: Volume on the Private Economy)*, edited by Liqun Zhou and Siquan Xie. Chongqing City: Chongqing University Press.

Zhou, Qiong and Aili Yang. 2010. "The Fabricated High-Tech Boom." *Caixin Online* (August 10), online: english.caixin.com/2010-08-10/100168670. html.

Zhu, Tianbiao. 2003. "Building Institutional Capacity for China's New Economic Opening." Pp. 142–60 in *States in Global Economy: Bringing Domestic Institutions Back In*, edited by Linda Weiss. Cambridge: Cambridge University Press.

Zhuang, Pinghui. 2013. "Xi Jinping Calls for Curbs on Lavish Official Bbanquets." *South China Morning Post* (January 30), online: www.scmp.com/news/ china/article/1138864/xi-jinping-calls-curbs-lavish-official-banquets.

Zweig, David. 1989. *Agrarian Radicalism in China, 1968–1981*. Cambridge: Cambridge University Press.

Zweig, David and Huiyao Wang. 2013. "Can China Bring Back the Best? The Communist Party Organizes China Search for Talent." *The China Quarterly* 215: 590–615.

ZZDYY [Zhonggong Zhongyang Dangshi Yangjiushi Di San Yangjiubu] (Chinese Communist Party, Central Party Historical Research Section, Third Research Division) 2002. *Zhongguo gaige kaifang shi (History of China's Reform and Opening Up)*. Liaoning: Liaoning People's Press.

Index